THE HEIGHTS OF RIDICULOUSNESS

THE HEIGHTS OF RIDICULOUSNESS

The Feats of Baseball's Merrymakers

Jack Kavanagh

DIAMOND COMMUNICATIONS, INC.
SOUTH BEND, INDIANA

THE HEIGHTS OF RIDICULOUSNESS
The Feats of Baseball's Merrymakers

10 9 8 7 6 5 4 3 2 1

Manufactured in the United States of America

Diamond Communications, Inc.
Post Office Box 88
South Bend, Indiana 46624-0088
Editorial – (219) 299-9278
Orders Only – 1(800) 480-3717
Fax – (219) 299-9296
Website – http://www.diamondbooks.com

Library of Congress Cataloging-in-Publication Data

Kavanagh, Jack
The heights of ridiculousness : the feats of baseball's merrymakers / Jack Kavanagh
p. cm.
Includes index.
ISBN 1-888698-22-5
1. Baseball—United States—Anecdotes. 2. Baseball—United States—Humor. 3. Baseball players—United States—Anecdotes. 4. Baseball players—United States—Humor. I. Title.
GV873.K38 1998
796.357'0973—dc21 98–47745
CIP

Contents

* *Previously appeared in a SABR publication.*

Dedication

To Jim Kavanagh, my grandfather. Thanks for the wonderful book, "Athletes in America, Great Britain and Australia," you gave me from your own library when I was 17. The account of the 1888–89 World Tour which traveled around the globe and played its final game in Dublin, first awoke me to the intriguing past and persons of baseball. Thanks, Grandpa. We could have done a wonderful book together.

Batter Up!

The introduction to a book can do several things: most importantly, it gives a potential reader a way to learn what's coming. Sometimes a foreword is written by a better-known author. My books have had forewords by Bob Broeg and Jim Murray, both are members of the Writer's Wing of the Baseball Hall of Fame. This time I'll do it myself.

Take my word for it, then, these are the best stories I can write about baseball and the wonderful characters it has produced. I've spent an author's lifetime learning the craft of telling a story. Mostly, these stories are about people around whom curious events swirled. Some have appeared elsewhere but bear repeating. I've taken chapters from three of my baseball biographies which deal with the most exciting of all championship games. The 1920, 1924, and 1926 World Series are wonderful to revisit.

The content of these stories was gathered over a long time from many sources. Origins are fuzzy to recall. I have benefited tremendously from colleagueship within The Society for American Baseball Research (SABR). To name a few would be to leave out many. Let me ask Mark Alvarez, Publications Director for SABR, to extend my thanks to all SABR colleagues.

Jim Charlton, a book packager and editor, has been a fine friend and editor. Jill and Jim Langsford are particularly to be thanked. Their company, Diamond Communications, Inc., South Bend, Indiana, published four of my books with never a bruised feeling on either side.

I have been blessed to meet so many great people, mostly as colleagues in the best kept secret in baseball, SABR.

Have a good read.

Jack Kavanagh

Greenville, R.I. 1998

1

The Heights of Ridiculousness

Towering mountains are climbed "because they are there." People jump off high bridges to measure the margin between a stunt and a suicide. Others cascade over waterfalls inside barrels. Parachutists drop in free fall, testing their nerve as well as their equipment. These are adult versions of boyhood challenges. The mountaineer may have started as a boy by skinning up the tallest tree to carve his initials in the topmost boughs. The bravest, or most foolhardy, lad in the pack dared others to "follow the leader" when he jumped into the old swimming hole from the highest rocky point above it.

Among the reckless acts that mark the rites of passage for maturing youth can be included catching baseballs dropping from heights great enough to challenge the imagination as well as the skill of those who try to catch them. At first the ball may have been dropped from a church steeple or simply thrown as high as the strongest boy could hurl it over a barn. Later the ante was raised when buildings became skyscrapers and when man learned to fly high above the earth. It was inevitable that no matter from where a baseball began its downward plunge, someone willing to risk injury in exchange for a dubious fame would be waiting below.

The development of baseball as America's National Game and the erecting of the Washington Monument coincided to create a new challenge. The simultaneous rise of both the sport and the memorial obelisk made it possible to catch a baseball dropped from a height that was both daunting and measurable. Baseball had begun to be played in 1846 according to rules close to those still recognizable today. Two years later, On July 4, 1848, the cornerstone for the Washington Monument was laid. Of the two, baseball grew much more rapidly. The Washington Monument was much slower to get off the ground. The concept of a giant obelisk built of stones contributed by the nations of the world encountered more stumbling blocks than building blocks. The anti-Catholic "Know Nothings" had political clout that rejected a building block from the Vatican. The Civil War was fought and the Reconstruction Era came before construction of the monument began again in 1880.

By the time the Washington Monument was dedicated on February 21, 1885, baseball had developed into a professional sport which was outgrowing the era of bare-handed play. Early ballplayers had thought it unmanly to cushion the impact of a baseball by protecting their hands. However, by the late nineteenth century the game had become an entertainment venture with paid admissions. The spectators preferred to watch professionals at work rather than amateurs at play. Team sponsors believed it was good business to protect their investments by safeguarding the hands of the players. That a padded glove would also cushion the impact of a baseball dropped from a height came as an afterthought.

The first gloves were skin tight and flesh colored to sustain an illusion of barehanded masculinity. Then one of the first openly professional players, Bill McGunnigle, catching for the independent Fall River, Massachusetts, team in 1875, wore gloves in a game against Harvard. They were bricklayer's gloves with thick leather tips and provided a modicum of protection. Others began to insert padding inside all types of gloves, and ultimately—by 1890—catchers accepted the inevitable. Instead of continuing to throw caution to the wind, they made a virtue of it and the Decker Glove was manufactured. It was brought to the attention of the Reach Sporting Goods Company in Philadelphia by an obscure catcher, Harry Decker, who played for Philadelphia. Pillow-like, the glove cushioned the impact of balls hurled by such nineteenth century fastball pitchers as Amos Rusie—called "The Hoosier Thunderbolt"—who so overpowered batters that the distance to home plate had to be stretched in 1893 from 50 feet to the present-day 60 feet, 6 inches.

Decker did not invent the catcher's mitt. He appropriated the design from an equally obscure catcher, Joe Gunson It is Gunson's original glove—first used in Kansas City in 1888—which has been on display at the Baseball Hall of Fame Museum since it was dedicated at Cooperstown, New York, in 1939. Decker is mistakenly given credit for "inventing" the catcher's mitt. Gunson had entered into a loose arrangement with a teammate, Jimmy Manning, who lived in Philadelphia between seasons, to get the design patented and to approach the Reach Company. Manning went on the world tour arranged by A. G. Spalding. By the time he got back, Decker had claimed a patent and Spalding's budding sporting goods company was beaten to the marketplace by A. J. Reach's enterprise.

Regardless of the tainted pedigree, The Decker Glove made catching a baseball dropped from the Washington Monument possible. Earlier, several famous nineteenth century baseball players are reported to have tried. Baseballs were dropped from the observation deck 504 feet above the ground. The players, Paul Hines and Buck Ewing, eyed them with suspicion. Balls landing on turf buried themselves deep into the ground and those hitting pavement bounded high in the air. Hines, baseball's first triple crown winner in 1877 (if you believe in restructuring baseball records to identify runs batted in, a stat unknown to scorekeepers of Hines' era), was an outfielder of the barehanded variety. Ewing, one of the first players selected for the Baseball Hall of Fame, was a catcher and battery mate of Amos Rusie of the Giants. He had added padding to his glove even before the opportunistic Harry Decker's patented mitt had been marketed. However, he was not prepared to break the fall of a baseball dropping at an estimated rate of 125 miles per hour with the same fearlessness as he grasped Rusie's "thunderbolts."

Catchers were the most vulnerable of a team's nine players, and even before Joe Gunson had stuffed a sufficient amount of sheepskin inside two wire frames to create the first adequately padded mitt, protective paraphernalia began to be worn. A mask designed by Fred Thayer, Harvard baseball coach, was first worn by one of his players, James Tyng, in 1877. Charlie Bennett, a catcher for Detroit, benefited from his wife's skill as a seamstress when she made him a chest protector to wear in the mid-1880s. Shin guards did not appear until Roger Bresnahan of the New York Giants first wore them in 1907. However, these 'tools of ignorance," as a catcher's equipment came to be called, were immaterial as protection for anyone foolhardy enough to risk catching a baseball dropped from the

Washington Monument. Only the glove was of critical importance.

The best-known player of the nineteenth century was Adrian "Cap" Anson, who also managed the Chicago team of the National League. Each time the schedule brought Anson's Colts to Washington, D. C., he resumed an ongoing dispute with H. P. Burney, the head desk clerk at the Arlington Hotel, where the Chicago team stayed. Burney claimed a baseball dropped from the top of the Monument could not be caught by anyone foolish enough to try. Anson insisted his veteran catcher, Bill "Pop" Schriver, could do it. The matter was settled on a Saturday morning, August 25, 1894.

A dubious Schriver took his place at the base of the towering obelisk. His teammates, Pitchers Clark Griffith, later known as "The Old Fox" as manager and owner of the Washington Senators, and "Wild Bill" Hutchinson climbed to the top of the monument with a bag of baseballs. They were a good choice. Hutchinson, who led the National League in wins three years in a row, and in strikeouts—with 316—in 1892, could hurl the ball far enough so it would clear the gradually widening obelisk on the way down. If accuracy became the primary concern, Griffith was a crafty curveballer who could be counted on to drop the ball where Pop Schriver was standing 504 feet below.

Strangely missing from the group gathered at the foot of the monument was the event's instigator, Cap Anson. Pop Schriver stood alone, mostly surrounded by hostile witnesses betting against him. They insisted he would be badly damaged if he attempted to catch a ball. He might not even be able to see it clearly because it would come from a height much greater than a big league pop up. An experimental drop was ordered. Griffith tossed down a ball and Schriver eyed it all the way. He had been warned it would bury itself ten feet into the ground, shattering the pavement with its force. Instead, it bounded high into the air, but no higher than the equivalent distance a fast ball would bounce before it reached a backstop built at the customary distance behind home plate. At the time, catchers only crouched close behind the batter when there were runners on base. Schriver shrugged that if that was as fast as a dropped ball was going to plummet toward him, it was not that much different than catching "Wild Bill" Hutchinson's fast ball. He said he was ready.

The next ball came down and Doc Schriver caught it easily to the applause of the spectators who had gathered to watch the exhibition. At this point a policeman hurried to the scene to issue a cop's timeless injunction to "break it up." The group disbanded. Schriver went ahead to the ball park where he caught the afternoon's game. Although Washington beat Chicago, 9 to 4, Schriver not only caught flawlessly, but had two hits in two times at bat. However, his feat of catching a baseball dropped from the top of the Washington Monument went largely unappreciated during the years that followed. It had been reported in the feature section, August 26, 1894, issue of the *Washington Post,* but faded from memory. Other papers, having been scooped by an eyewitness reporter, did not comment on the event.

In 1908, Washington's manager, Joe Cantillion, had a new pitching phenomenon, 19-year old Walter Johnson whose fast ball was overpowering batters. Not knowing of the Schriver feat in 1894, he proposed comparing the speed of a Johnson pitch with the velocity of a baseball dropped from the top of the Washington Monument. On August 21, 1908, Johnson's catcher, Charles "Gabby"

Street, took immortality into his own hands. Once again the attempt was triggered by a wager. Two Washington sportsmen, John Biddle and Preston Gibson, obviously unaware of Pop Schriver's catch in 1894, got into a friendly dispute whether a ball dropped from the top of the Washington Monument could be caught. Biddle thought it could, and recruited Gabby to make the catch. Perhaps, as Street later claimed, it was because the attempt was made on a windy day that the first dozen balls fell out of his reach. Or, did it take that long for him to get up the nerve to actually risk getting his glove under the ball? At any rate, the thirteenth ball turned out to be the lucky one. It landed in Gabby's glove with an explosive sound, and, although he staggered wildly, he held his feet and, more importantly, the ball. Despite later fame as manager of two pennant winning St. Louis Cardinal teams, in 1930 and 1931, Gabby Street has remained a baseball legend as the man who caught a baseball dropped from the Washington Monument.

When Billy Sullivan, a catcher for the Chicago White Sox, and a far better receiver than Street, duplicated the feat two years later, on August 24, 1910, it was barely noted. The stunt had become singularly identified with Gabby Street. His catch became the model against which all future attempts were compared.

By another coincidence of timing, publicity stemming from the Gabby Street catch in 1908 coincided with the development of the airplane. Wilbur and Orville Wright had made the first flight at Kitty Hawk, North Carolina, in 1903. Just as the simultaneous rise of baseball and the Washington Monument had offered an opportunity for a ball to be caught from a significant height, aircraft provided a new challenge. On the eve of the First World War, planes were a novelty that drew crowds to watch flying exhibitions. Dare-devil pilots visited county fairgrounds with their newfangled machines. Baseballs began to rain down on any local ball players who could be persuaded to try to catch them.

One of the most popular legends associated with Wilbert Robinson, the Falstaffian manager of the Brooklyn ball club during the years they were justifiably called "The Daffy Dodgers," was his attempt to catch a baseball dropped from an airplane in 1915. Like all good stories, time has embellished it. During spring training at Daytona Beach, Florida, a rag-tag Brooklyn team was about to begin its second season with Uncle Robbie as its manager. Goaded by the ineptness of his squad, the rotund ex-catcher insisted that the players of "his day" were far more skilled than those who now played the game. In Cooperstown, the plaques of Uncle Robbie and his teammates require considerable wall space at the Baseball Hall of Fame. He is joined there by Old Oriole teammates, John McGraw, Hughie Jennings, Joe Kelley, Wee Willie Keeler and Big Dan Brouthers, as well as manager, Ned Hanlon.

Uncle Robbie scoffed at the challenge of catching a baseball dropped from a height, and when told Gabby Street had set the record at 504 feet and bragged about it ever since, The Old Oriole said he could do better.

As there was a lack of tall buildings in Florida, it was decided to use an aeroplane which would fly higher than the Washington Monument. The aviatrix, Ruth Law, was appearing in Daytona Beach, and she agreed to drop the baseball. Uncle Robbie agreed to catch it. And, at this point, the legend began to collect its embellishments.

Casey Stengel, to become famous in later life as manager of ten pennant-winning New York Yankee teams, was a young and brash outfielder with the Dodgers. His later stunts would include doffing his hat to jeering fans and having a bird fly out from under it. Although he never took credit or, perhaps, the blame for participating in the hoax played on his manager, it made retelling a good story even better to involve Casey. The tale was enhanced by supposedly having Stengel slip the team's trainer, Frank Kelly, a grapefruit to substitute for the baseball Uncle Robbie expected to come plummeting down. Kelly was to ride in the passenger's seat and make the drop.

In all truth, it was a grapefruit that landed in Uncle Robbie's upturned glove and then exploded. Sportwriters and players witnessed what happened, and the account became standard fare in the humor of baseball. Wilbert Robinson was knocked sprawling by the impact and, feeling warm juice trickling down his face and soaking into his uniform, believed it was blood.

"Help me, boys," the prostrate manager pleaded, "I'm covered with my own blood and killed entirely." The roars of laughter brought a quick recovery and Uncle Robbie toweled himself off and gruffly ordered the players to resume practice.

In 1957 a New York baseball writer, Harold Rosenthal, with a delayed interest in debunking at least one legend of Casey Stengel, learned that Ruth Law, the celebrated aviatrix of 1914, was alive and well and living in San Francisco. Now married, Mrs. Ruth Law Oliver put the story straight when visiting New York City.

Explaining that her mission that day was to draw attention for the local Daytona merchants who had booked her to fly over their city, she said: "A messenger was sent to me with a request that I drop a baseball from my aeroplane, at a little over 500 feet altitude. One of the Dodgers would attempt to catch it with the hope of establishing a new record. Time arrived for the demonstration, my plane was rolled out on the beach, and I was ready to fly. But alas, I had forgotten to bring along the ball from the Clarendon Hotel several miles down the beach. What to do? Time was running out; no time to send anyone for the ball.

"While I was considering the dilemma, a young man working in my outfit brought me a small grapefruit that he had intended to have with his lunch and suggested that I drop that. It looked about the size of a baseball and I thought what difference would it make if I dropped the pretty yellow fruit? Dummy that I was, I hadn't thought of its juicy inside.

"I took off, flying to about 525 feet altitude over the park and zip went the fruit to the fellow who was standing in the middle of the field waiting to make the catch. I didn't stay to see what the result of my first and only pitch of a "baseball" would be. I was busy with my flying activities the remainder of the afternoon."

Ruth Law Oliver said the next day she learned the event had been viewed as a deliberate practical joke which nearly killed the team's manager, Wilbert Robinson, and that for the rest of the winter season she carefully avoided flying over the Daytona ball park.

And so rests a legend. Casey Stengel did not conceive a plot against Uncle Robbie. He might have helped towel off his grapefruit-soaked manager but was not a conspirator. As no baseball had been dropped by Ruth Law, let alone caught, Gabby Street's record, although shared with Pop Schriver and Billy Sullivan, remained safe. It would stand until someone built a suitable structure taller than the Washington Monument or made a successful catch from an aircraft flying even higher than the Washington Monument.

There is a strong thread of a Chicago-bred determination to catch baseballs from heights running through the history of the feat. Pop Schriver, the original player to perform the stunt, and Billy Sullivan, who, like Street, duplicated it, played for Chicago teams. A White Sox catcher, Ray Schalk, came as close to matching the 504-foot Washington drop as the 460-foot tower of the Chicago Tribune building allowed. He made his catch on May 11, 1925, but it could only be regarded as a record set locally in the Windy City.

The next year Babe Ruth himself was enticed out to Mitchell Field, Long Island, on the morning of July 22, 1926, and asked to catch a ball dropped from a biplane circling the field. In 1990 a scratchy newsreel film clip of the event was included in a televised sports segment about Ruth. It shows the actual catch with the Babe snaring it with his fielder's glove. Ruth is wearing knickers as though dressed for a round of jazz-age golf.

The plane had begun dropping baseballs from 1000 feet and descended lower each time it passed over the field. Many of the balls fell far beyond the Babe's reach but finally, from 250 feet overhead, a ball came near enough for him to make a running catch and then trot smilingly toward the camera. Later that day at Yankee Stadium he had two hits, one a triple, and he also stole a base. To sustain "the Chicago connection," the Yankees' opponents were the White Sox, and Ray Schalk, who had caught the ball from atop the Chicago Tribune Tower, was behind the bat.

The ultimate airborne assault on the record was made, appropriately enough, on April Fool's Day in 1930. Once again it involved a Chicago player, Gabby Hartnett. To stretch credulity Hartnett was, as the Washington Senators' Gabby had been, a talkative catcher. Along with Ray Schalk and Uncle Robbie, Hartnett too would eventually be elected to the Baseball Hall of Fame. His record-setting accomplishment for catching a baseball dropped from the skies is not mentioned on his plaque and, perhaps, it should be. It still stands as the caught ball which fell the farthest. And Gabby did it twice, on the first day of April, 1930, in Los Angeles. The Chicago Cubs, who trained at nearby Catalina Island, were there to play an exhibition game against their farm team, the Los Angeles Angels of the Pacific Coast League. Before the game a blimp appeared above the diamond. It cruised at 800 feet.

Two catchers took positions in the middle of the diamond; the forty-year-old ex-Yankee, Frank Hannah, and cherubic, ruddy-faced Hartnett. Gabby snared the first ball to come down without apparent difficulty. He grabbed another before turning the job over to Truck Hannah. Some balls missed the target and some bounced off Hannah's glove. The blimp was lowered to 650 feet before a ball stuck in Truck's mitt. Still, that was good enough to be the second highest catch of all time, far exceeding any catches made from the Washington Monument.

The 1930s were a decade made giddy with players challenging records for balls caught from high altitudes. The feat was divided into two categories: balls dropped from buildings or from aircraft. There is a faint suspicion about the trustworthiness of altimeter readings. Although planes and blimps can ascend higher than man can build, there is more certainty about a height when a building, which can be resurveyed to settle disputed claims, is used.

In the category of catches from man-made structures, a 1938 venture was aimed at breaking Gabby Street's still legendary catch at the Washington Monument. A new railroad station was built in downtown Cleveland, Ohio. Rising high above it was the Terminal Tower. It was said to be 708 feet tall. Cleveland's civic pride demanded the new tower be used to eclipse Street's thirty-year-old record. Street's catch had been tied to the celebrity of pitcher Walter Johnson. In 1938 there was a new teenage strikeout phenom, Bob Feller. Johnson had been nineteen in 1908 and Feller was the same age when the Terminal Tower was proposed for an attempt to break Street's old record. Gabby Hartnett's 800-footer from a blimp above Los Angeles in 1930 was ignored, either forgotten or dismissed as unverifiable.

The Cleveland Indians were asked to provide someone to catch a baseball to be dropped from the highest ledge of the Terminal Tower. They sent all the catchers they had. Frank Pytlak and Rollie Helmsley, the regular catchers, arrived with their mitts, as did the rookie backstop, Hank Helf. Two coaches, Wally Schang and Johnny Bassler, both former big-league catchers, also were stationed below the tower. When the baseballs began to drop, claims on immortality for catching them would depend largely on where each catcher was standing. Twelve balls were dropped, and most fell too far from the quintet of catchers for anyone to catch. The first ball to come within anyone's reach was snared by Bob Feller's regular catcher, Frank Pytlak, and the next one caught was held by the infrequently used Hank Helf. It was a Mutt and Jeff demonstration. Pytlak was small, particularly for a catcher—5' 7 1/2", and 160 pounds—and Helf was a formidable 200 pounds and stood 6' 1". The "catch" gave both an immortality that followed them to the grave. When Pytlak died in 1977 it was mentioned in his obituary and, in 1984, stories of Hank Helf's passing had little else to recall from a brief big-league career.

The catch was listed as made from 708 feet, the height of the topmost ledge of a building that is a surveyed 758 feet, 8 1/2 inches to the tip of the flagpole which rises above the tower.

By 1970, doubts as to whether the catch had actually been made from the height claimed were expressed. A reader of the *Cleveland Plain Dealer* contended that the 1938 stunt had involved balls dropped only from the Terminal Tower's public observation platform many levels below the uppermost ledge. Although even this would make the drop 548 feet, a greater distance than the 504-foot catch from the Washington Monument by Gabby Street, Cleveland scoffers might next hint the balls had only descended from a furtively opened window even closer to the ground. Hal Lebovitz, the sports editor of the *Plain Dealer*, reopened the case. The first witness called was Ken Keltner, who is mentioned most often in historic dispatches about Joe DiMaggio's 56-consecutive-game hitting streak which he helped end with several spectacular plays. The Indians' third baseman had been recruited in 1938 to throw the baseballs wide enough of the tower so they would clear the sides of the building as they fell.

Keltner explained that he and Cleveland manager Ossie Vitt had taken an elevator as high as it went, forty-two floors, and climbed eight flights of narrow, winding iron stairs to reach the topmost part of the building. It was far above the public observation platform.

Although later-day doubting Thomases might suspect the balls had been dropped from a lower point, Keltner was a credible witness, but lacked corroboration from Ossie Vitt. Acrophobia had caused the Cleveland manager to retreat from the dizzying height, leaving Keltner and a building supervisor behind a low railing on a perilously narrow ledge. As Keltner was handed each ball he drew back his arm and flung it into space. Those that landed uncaught bounded eighty to ninety feet in the air, and it was later estimated they were traveling 138 miles per hour when they hit the pavement

As a result of Lebovitz' investigation, the height of the 1938 catches was changed. A careful re-measurement in 1970 set the height of the platform on which Keltner had stood at 674 feet, 8 1/2 inches. Add five feet for Keltner's shoulder height and the balls were thrown from just about 680 feet. That was, and remains, the record for a baseball caught from a building.

The craze for catching baseballs from high buildings continued the next year in Philadelphia even though it lacked anything quite as tall as Cleveland's Terminal Tower. The City of Brotherly Love was proud of its new city hall, a tall building made even higher by being atop steep stone steps. Later these were featured in the training regime of Rocky Balboa, a.k.a Sylvester Stallone, as he prepared for his championship title shot in the movie, *Rocky*. The Philadelphia Newspaper Guild organized the City Hall exhibition, and with thousands of spectators expected to gather for the noontime event, was cautious enough to obtain liability insurance. On May 10, 1939, four players of the Phillies, wearing their home uniforms and rubber soled beach slippers, agreed to try to catch baseballs thrown from atop the City Hall. Gibby Brack, an outfielder, and infielder Del

Young took places, but it was expected one of the catchers, Dave Coble and Walter Millies, would have the best chance. They had the biggest gloves and the most experience at catching high pop fouls. The regular catcher, Spud Davis, declined the challenge and, instead, went to the top of City Hall with the Phillies' manager, Doc Prothro. Davis was both playing it safe and contributing a strong throwing arm. Because of the slope of the City Hall and its position atop gradually rising steps, the balls would have to travel 230 feel horizontally before beginning to drop. This degree of difficulty was the basis for Philadelphia's claim that any catch under these circumstances was more spectacular then the ones made from the Terminal Tower in Cleveland, or at the ancient site for such stunts, the Washington Monument.

Seven tosses fell into the street and bounced three stories in the air. Dave Coble just missed catching the next two balls to come down, but on the ninth toss he circled under the descending ball, took two steps forward and, almost falling to his knees from the impact, clutched the ball in his glove. Gerald P. Nugent, president of the Philadelphia club, was the first spectator to reach Coble and congratulate him. He did not, however, sign him to a long-term contract. Coble's major league career lasted only for the thirteen big-league games he played in 1939. He made only 27 putouts. Or 28, if you count the catch from the top of Philadelphia's City Hall.

Despite forebodings and warnings, no one had ever been injured attempting to catch a baseball dropped from a height. This might have given Joe Sprinz, a forty-year-old veteran minor league catcher a false sense of security when he agreed to help a former Pacific Coast League teammate with his new job. Walter "Duster"

Mails, whose sense of self-worth also earned him the nickname "The Great," had been hired to promote the San Francisco Golden Gate Exposition. It was the West Coast's equivalent of the 1939 New York City World's Fair. It rose in hastily built splendor on man-made Treasure Island, a landfill addition in the bay between Oakland and San Francisco. Inevitably, Mails' baseball background prompted another version of the dropped ball stunt on August 3, 1939. The event, which would challenge the record book, had been preceded in May by catches made from atop the Tower of the Sun, a 400-foot spire which was as high as anything that rose above the Exposition site. In what was a warmup for the ultimate effort, Frank "Lefty" O'Doul, manager of the San Francisco Seals, had tossed balls down to Sprinz and two other Seals catchers, Larry Woodall and Bill Leonard, who had held them without difficulty. However, four hundred feet was far below the records set from structures in Washington, Cleveland and Philadelphia. Mails decided to double the height the only way he could. He ordered a blimp. He might not have known about Gabby Hartnett's 1930 catch in Los Angeles from a blimp at 800 feet. If he had, doubtlessly the rivalry between the two cities would have urged Mails to set his blimp higher than 800 feet. His announced goal was to outdo the 1938 catches in Cleveland. On what was to be a fateful day, Walter Mails stationed Joe Sprinz below a blimp floating 800 feet above an athletic field on Treasure Island. The first four balls fell near Sprinz, but it was the fifth one that hit the target. The ball struck Sprinz' glove with a terrible impact and drove it into the player's face. The old catcher was knocked to the ground and the ball rolled away. He received a broken cheekbone and a bloody mouth. In future years, recollections of the number of teeth Sprinz had spit out increased, as did the height of the blimp. The 1939 newspaper accounts said the damage was mostly to his bridgework and cost him the two teeth to which it was anchored. All subsequent claims of dental destruction were as false as Joe's teeth. However, not to make light of the damage, four physicists at the University of California at Berkeley estimated the ball was traveling at the rate of 217 feet per second—approximately 145 miles an hour—and had an impact of 8,030 foot pounds. This stopped such stunts temporarily.

However, bad news doesn't travel as fast as a baseball plummeting down from a great height. Despite the lesson to be learned from the Joe Sprinz fiasco, the stunt was revived to relieve boredom on the home front during World War II. In 1944, when the travel restraints imposed by the war required that major league teams do their spring training in the north, the New York Giants set up camp at Lakehurst, New Jersey, where the German dirigible, the Hindenburg, had crashed and burned on May 6, 1937. The site was now a facility for training crews of our own World War II blimps. The mix of airborne opportunity and a baseball team in spring training, no matter how unlike Florida, stirred atavistic impulses. Shades of Uncle Robbie and the grapefruit. Possibly because of wartime shortages of fresh produce, no one was tempted to substitute citrus products for the wartime baseballs. On April 6, 1944, a group of baseball players waited while a U.S. Navy blimp soared overhead. The height was only half of what it had been when the ball from a blimp felled Joe Sprinz five years earlier. At 400 feet it was a piece of cake, and even wartime players, Danny Gardella and Phil Weintraub, caught balls dropped from the blimp's gondola.

It was another ten years before the stunt was repeated, in separate events resulting in successful catches at impressive, but not record, heights. Another big-league catcher was lured onto a major league diamond on a dog day afternoon in August of 1954. Dutch Dotterer of the Cincinnati Reds snared a ball dropped 575 feet from a helicopter above Crosley Field. It does count in the narrow field of balls dropped from heights. It is, of course, the highest catch from a whirlybird.

Two months later, on October 17, 1954, a record was set in the sub-category of airplanes. The only thing that was shattered was Babe Ruth's old record of 250 feet. Perhaps made bolder by the protection of a thick beard, Bobo Nickerson of the barnstorming hirsute House of David baseball team caught a ball dropped 650 feet from a plane soaring above the State Line Airport in Kansas City, Missouri.

Catching baseballs dropped from heights became a lost art for the next several decades. The 1960s and 1970s were the dark ages for the feat. They had tossed frisbees at Woodstock, although some of the celebrants might have been high enough to set a record for dropping acid. The dissenting scoffers of establishment standards ignored the old marks originally set at the Washington Monument. They preferred to assemble at the foot of the monument for protest demonstrations.

Then in 1980 came the reenactment of the Pytlak and Helf catches of 1938. The Terminal Tower and the downtown Lakefront Area of Cleveland were undergoing a renaissance. The Tower, built in 1930 during the Great Depression, was also celebrating a fiftieth anniversary, and an encore performance of the great catches of 1938 was arranged by a local advertising agency. Ad men Don FitzSimons and John LeGrand contacted the Cleveland Indians but were rebuffed. Times had changed in baseball. No longer were major league teams willing to sacrifice players on the altars of commerce. The players, secure in their unionized ranks, did not even bother to have their agents attempt to negotiate a performance fee. Back in 1938, during the Depression, the Cleveland Indians probably made Frank Pytlak and Hank Helf give back the base balls they caught.

The entrepreneurs turned to Ted Stepien, the owner of another Cleveland sports franchise, the NBA Cleveland Cavaliers. It would have been better, as things turned out, had the basketball team been used and been asked to catch inflated basketballs. However, on June 24 the Cavaliers, even with the interminable NBA schedule finally over, were not available. Instead, Stepien turned to a professional softball team, the Cleveland Competitors, which he also owned and which was in need of some promotional publicity. They did require that the standard Dudley softball be used. It was firm but not so lethal seeming as a regulation baseball. The ten-inch diameter would also make it easier to see the ball.

As a promotion the event was a success. It drew five thousand people and was reported on network television by Dan Rather on the CBS News. Unfortunately, the stunt backfired, and the fiasco all but brought to an end the catching of balls descending from newsworthy heights. Stepien had placed six of his players in Public Square to catch the missiles. A noontime crowd ringed the area, hands upraised to shield their eyes from a bright sun. There was no barrier behind which the crowd could stand in assumed safety. The spectators gave the players enough room and expected the balls would land among the men with gloves. The crowd was wrong. One ball eventually did come close enough to the players to be caught, but the first four balls that were dropped by Stepien fell like mortar shells zeroing in on an enemy target. One ball hit the pavement and bounded into the air. Another hit a parked car on Superior Avenue, and two hit spectators, sending them to the hospital.

The most severely wounded was a young woman, Mrs. Gayle Falinski, an auditor with the accounting firm of Coopers & Lybrand. Her wrist was broken and she was treated at Lutheran Medical Center. Another innocent bystander, Russell Murphy, a sixty-six-year-old retired Ford foundry worker, was carted off to Deaconess Hospital with a badly bruised left shoulder. The victims did not even get to see the successful catch of the fifth ball dropped.

Fate had directed the ball to the glove of Mike Zarefoss, a reserve outfielder with the Cleveland softball team, who made a running over-the-shoulder catch. He now holds the record for catching a softball as well as equaling the old Pytlak and Helf mark for a ball of any kind which has dropped 680 feet from a building. The promoters, with the inclination toward exaggeration of the advertising trade, claimed a 700 foot catch, which had been the 1938 mismeasurement. They probably did not know of the reexamination of the feat by the *Cleveland Plain Dealer* in 1970, and Gabby Harnett's 800 foot catches seem to have slipped into a limbo of forgotten and neglected feats.

The challenge is still there. In 1982 Kurt Bevacqua, a more contemporary flake and then a San Diego Padre, who in a separate stunt won a bubble gum blowing contest, soon afterward accepted it. He caught five baseballs dropped from the roof of the newly built Imperial Bank Building in San Diego. The distance was a mere 390 feet, and the speed of the balls was estimated at only 110 miles per hour, about the speed of a Nolan Ryan fastball. That would not impress Joe Sprinz of the shattered jaw, or Mrs. Falinski and Mr. Murphy, felled with softballs in the 1980 Cleveland fiasco.

Incidentally, in 1939 Joe Sprinz simply gritted what was left of his teeth and shrugged off any thought of legal action against his old pal, Duster Mails. In the litigious eighties, Mrs. Falinski declined an invitation to a conciliatory luncheon by Ted Stepien and withered the flowers he sent to the hospital with a look. Her law suit was settled privately for an undisclosed amount. In a 1990 phone interview, she complained that her arm still hurt and that she had accepted too small a settlement.

The Guiness Book of World Records, which keeps track of bizarre and unusual stunts, discontinued the category of baseballs plummeting from heights after its 1990 edition. After reporting only the failed attempt by Joe Sprinz for thirty years, the Guiness editors, who had constantly dropped the ball in this matter, have now also dropped the subject. While still careful to tell us how many goldfish have been swallowed or students crammed into a telephone booth, in this instance they have shied away from giving credit where it is due.

It seems less than forthright for a publication which searches the world so it can record examples of fortitude, daring and ingenuity to default in the matter of catching baseballs dropped from challenging heights. Perhaps too many readers had questioned the credibility of the famous record book's integrity in this category. The Joe Sprinz attempt was reported in all the 1939 San Francisco newspapers as taking place at 800 feet, with the ball dropped from a blimp. It was reported in the fifteenth anniversary edition of the

Guinness record book in 1977 as "about 1,000 feet at a cost of four front teeth." The original newspaper accounts had Sprinz losing just two incisors. By 1989 *The Guiness Book of World Records* had elevated the feat to having been attempted from a *dirigible* 1,200 feet in the air at a cost to Sprinz of five teeth. One shudders at the post-event carnage that waited for poor Joe Sprinz had the category continued to be listed and rewritten by editors not yet born when the event was first performed.

Perhaps the editors at Guinness simply felt that, wrong as their description of the record might be, the fifty-year lapse since the Sprinz attempt placed a statute of limitations on the feat. That might be their reason for not retaining it. However, it cannot be long until some baseball promoter, perhaps eyeing the Gateway Arch in St. Louis, will hustle up another version of the feat. The arch looms just outside Busch Stadium, home of the St. Louis Cardinals, and is billed as "the tallest man-made monument in the nation." It is 630 feet at its highest point. It would not be a record, except for monuments, but might start balls dropping again.

We doubt that anyone, whether or not they have heard of the fates which befell Joe Sprinz and the two victims in Cleveland, will challenge the Canadian National Tower in Toronto. It, too, rises just outside a baseball stadium where the Toronto Blue Jays now play. The domed stadium's roof can be retracted to clear the way should the feat be attempted again. The CN Tower, which looms 1,815 feet and 5 inches above the city, can offer its Skypod, two-thirds up the tower. At 1,465 feet it is the world's highest public observation gallery and contains a revolving restaurant and viewing deck. Too high, surely. However, perhaps an olive dropped for a waiter to catch in a martini glass would be in keeping with the spirit of the stunt.

Probably it is a wise decision by the publishers of *The Guiness Book of World Records* to let the feat of catching baseballs dropped from on high simply lapse. The records they do list constantly attract newcomers who try to outdo old standards. Nothing succeeds like excess in these matters. In various feats of gluttony, there is probably no serious danger in overeating goldfish. However, for catching baseballs dropped great distances it is safest to accept that man has already answered the challenge at a satisfactory level.

2

A Dodger Boyhood

The longest journey of my life began with a single, tentative step out of my Brooklyn neighborhood in 1930. Another 10-year-old boy and I, restless on a sunny Saturday morning, began walking toward Grand Army Plaza. We lived on 12th Street, just off Prospect Park. We had invaded the park many times but had never tried to cross the three miles to its other side. Small boys test the limits of parental tolerance by pushing toward increasingly distant goals. I am sure we followed the outer perimeter of Prospect Park because it seemed safer. I don't believe we had a particular destination that day, just a sort of "I dare you" challenge to range beyond the familiar nearby streets. So, we began a journey, which, for me, still goes on although it has doubled back on itself and is traveled only in memory. It is the trail worn by Brooklyn Dodger fans who, since 1958, have no direction to move except backward in time. The traces of my own footsteps grow fainter as more recent travelers scuff away signs of my passage. Mine was a time when "Wait till next year" meant another try for first division, not a repeat meeting with the Yankees in the World Series.

Two small, knicker-clad boys walked along the Park Slope side of Prospect Park and, a mile later, circled Grand Army Plaza with its huge memorial arch. We were asked by a young man if we would pass out handbills to people entering the plaza from Eastern Parkway. He would give us each 50 cents. In advance. Being paid first offered an early temptation to cheat and challenged our budding integrity. We could have pocketed our half dollars and dumped the handbills down a sewer or into a trash basket. We didn't. We disposed of them all the way we had agreed to do. Then, instead of turning back, we pushed on along Eastern Parkway going past the Brooklyn Museum looking for a candy store where we could spend some of the money we had just earned. When we reached Bedford Avenue we followed it and saw Ebbets Field for the first time. In memory it still looms as Camelot.

If an event was needed to fix the moment in my mind, it happened as we walked behind the cement right field wall. Suddenly, the street swarmed with other boys running toward us. A baseball, having cleared the screen atop the wall, came bounding toward me. I like to think I fielded it with the grace of Glenn Wright, the Dodgers' star shortstop. Probably I clutched it with suddenly sweaty palms. But it was mine! In a few days the ball disappeared into pickup games played with other small boys on diamonds we improvised on the meadows of Prospect Park. It probably ended its usefulness wrapped in black friction tape. Small boys don't become collectors of baseball artifacts until they grow up and can buy back the talismans of their youth.

With each year my identification with Ebbets Field grew, as did my personal confidence. I would now cross Prospect Park on a time-saving diagonal just to hang around outside Ebbets Field. I began collecting autographs, cutting pictures from newspapers and pasting them in copy books whose unused pages should have been covered with school work. We lived in a 32-family apartment house and the superintendent stacked newspapers in the basement. He sold them, I'm sure, to a junk man, but first he let me cut out the photos.

I went to Alexander Hamilton High School. This pleased my parents because it had a good reputation as a college preparatory school and I was happy because the school was only several miles beyond Ebbets Field from where I lived. If I walked home from school, I would reach the ballpark, where games then began at 3:15, by the second or third inning. There was a place where a game-starved fan could obtain a limited view. A commercial garage provided an accessible rooftop behind the left field grandstand. It could be reached by climbing a ladder inside the garage.

From the edge of the roof you could look into Ebbets Field. You couldn't see the whole diamond but, between the upper and lower tiers of the stands, there was a view of the core area of the game. Home plate, with the batter, catcher, and umpire could be seen: the pitcher was visible, as was the first baseman. No other players were in sight. Fly balls disappeared from view but the crowd's reaction would tell whether they had been caught or fallen safely. On a single, the batter became a visible runner on first base. On the occasional homerun, we would see a hitter run toward first base and then slow down as he rounded the bag and left our view. Moments later the player would reappear as he trotted back into sight and crossed homeplate. We could keep track of the game from the right field scoreboard. It informed us of the score, the batter's number, and the outs. There were no radio accounts of the games. The broadcast era would arrive in Brooklyn, with Red Barber, in 1939.

When night baseball came to Brooklyn on June 15, 1938, I was up on the garage roof. Now a high school senior, I had gone home first and then walked back across Prospect Park to Ebbets Field. I was intent on seeing as much as I could of the event. Even though the Cincinnati pitcher, Johnny Vander Meer, had pitched a no-hitter in his previous start, it had been in Boston against the Braves. We had a higher opinion of the hitting ability of our Dodgers. Larry MacPhail, the new general manager, had been providing us with new heroes. Dolph Camilli, Leo Durocher, and Freddie Fitzsimmons had come from other teams to join such sturdy standbys as Babe Phelps and Buddy Hassett. However, Van Mungo had lapsed from being a pitcher we could insist was the equal of Dizzy Dean and Carl Hubbell. We had read that inept front office work had let Vander Meer himself get away after the New Jersey youth had tried out with the Dodgers.

As the game went on, the right field score board registered only zeroes for Brooklyn inning after inning. Not only were the Dodgers scoreless, they were also without a hit. Dodger players appeared on first base, but only after we saw them first drop the bat and trot there. Vander Meer was characteristically wild. Our Dodgers fell behind, trailing 6-0 with only one more inning left to win the game. They say that inside the ballpark the fans were rooting for Vander Meer to complete a no-hit game. I doubt it. Most of them probably didn't know the Reds pitcher was on the verge of making history with a second consecutive no-hitter. There were no ubiquitous transistor radios, a future plague of ballparks, to tell a dimly comprehending spectator, and people for rows around, what was happening. Even if the game had been broadcast, the superstition that it was a jinx to acknowledge a no-hitter in progress would have stifled any comment that an attempt to pitch a second no-hitter in a row was under way.

To the dozen or so of us on the garage roof, the game was not yet lost. We would have traded our roles as witnesses to baseball history for a winning Dodger rally in the ninth. When Vander Meer loaded the bases with walks, after two were out, we hoped the pesky shortstop, Leo Durocher, would keep the inning alive. When he sent a fly ball into the night, on a flight invisible from where we watched, a dozen breaths were held. We exhaled in common despair and, strangers again, but forever bonded by the inevitability of Dodger defeats, climbed down the ladder from the roof of the garage and passed into the dark night. The tiers of lights which had illuminated Ebbets Field for the first time were turned off and only the regular street lamps lit the outside of the ballpark. A block away I walked down Franklin Avenue, passing those coming from Ebbets Field. The shared attitude was not one of universal approval for Vander Meer's feat but of disappointment that the Dodgers had lost another game.

It was the last game I ever watched from the limited view on top of the garage behind left field. When the next season arrived I had graduated from high school and was in need of a summer job.

Maybe it wasn't what my mother had wanted me to be when I grew up, but becoming an usher at Ebbets Field was the perfect summer job, one I held for three years from 1939 through 1941.

After a boyhood spent outside the ballpark, the opportunity to be inside was a golden one. Word came from an older cousin that I should show up at Ebbets Field a week before the season began and apply for an usher's job. My name would be on a list. Jack Collins, the business manager of the Brooklyn Dodgers, had cleared me at the request of his nephew. The nephew was my cousin's best buddy.

Larry MacPhail was about to begin his second year as general manager of the Dodgers. He had spent 1938 sizing up the team's needs. Now he was ready to act. Leo Durocher became the new manager; the team was in the market for better players and better ushers. This last news was hardly earthshaking, but MacPhail had been appalled by the ushers who had menaced patrons in the past. Bully boys from political clubhouses, they had bulged in ill-fitting, sweat-stained red uniforms left over from years of second-division squalor.

Larry MacPhail had admired the ushering crews in the Chicago ballparks. At Wrigley Field and Comiskey Park, they were trained and directed by Andy Frain. His ushers were college types: young, lean, clean-cut. Of course they could be corrupted just as easily with a couple of bucks from a fan in need of a seat on an S.R.O. day, but they were impressive in their uniforms. MacPhail had hired a Frain assistant, a peppery man named Jack Haines, to recruit and train a new corps of Ebbets Field ushers.

A long line of applicants stretched through the rotunda entrance to Ebbets Field. When you reached a certain gate you gave your name. The fellows just ahead of me were turned away. My name got me inside. I joined a growing group sitting in the lower grandstand behind first base. When about 100 of us were in place, Jack Haines addressed us. We were hired, he told us, to be ushers. Not everybody would work every game; it would depend on the size of the crowd. For next week's opening day, we would all be used. Come back wearing a white shirt with a detachable collar. A green tie was required and black shoes. New kelly green uniforms would be provided.

The detachable collar was already passé, but maybe not in Chicago. The idea was to save on laundry bills. A man's collar got dirtier faster than the rest of his shirt. Cuffs, too, could be detachable, but the changeable soft collar for shirts was basic. The scorned ex-President Herbert Hoover had favored stiff collars, but only he and altar boys wore them. I still had front and back collar buttons from my own recent years as an altar boy. So, with three detachable collars and two collarless white shirts, and a Chinese laundry around the corner from where we lived, I was set. The green necktie was easily come by in an Irish family. It was standard neckwear for St. Patrick's Day.

I needed one more item. There was a new federal requirement. I had to have a Social Security card. Then, newly identified as 067-12-5890, wearing a white shirt, attached collar and green necktie, and (at my mother's insistence) a raincoat and rubbers over my black shoes, I reported at Ebbets Field at 10:00 a.m. on a rainy Tuesday, April 18. It was to be Opening Day and the New York Giants would be the opponents. If it stopped raining.

I was not one of the ushers issued a uniform. I was given a green visored cap and a badge to pin to my coat. Mr. Haines gathered us behind homeplate and read off our assignments. Mine was somewhere upstairs, far out along the left field foul line. We were to be in place when the gates opened and the crowds flooded in. At the moment, the only floods we anticipated were from the rain which pelted down on the infield tarp.

But the rain slowed to a drizzle. The ballpark opened as we ushers scurried to our posts. The players filed into the dugouts and one of them, a new pitcher, Red Evans, began to warm up. The game was played, the Dodgers lost, and Evans began a slow exit to anonymity. It was the first of his eight losses, measured against only one victory, before he went back to the minors. It seemed a dismal way to start a season. We had a new manager and 100 newly minted ushers. Maybe it was the overcast day, but it looked as though we would eventually heave the inevitable Brooklyn sigh, "Wait'll next year."

However, the team improved. And people heard about it because broadcasting the games on radio was part of the new era. MacPhail had imported Red Barber, with an improbable Southern accent, to report the games. Now I could simply walk in with the other ushers and see games. I cut as many classes as I could in April and May to be at Ebbets Field when the team was at home. Sometimes I worked, most times I didn't. The ranks of ushers multiplied. Every day new candidates would present letters of introduction from politicians. Borough President Robert Cashmore must have sent several dozen nephews himself. Finally, one day, after the number required to work the game had entered Ebbets Field, the rest of us were stopped at the gate.

My first concern was just to get inside and see the game. I hadn't objected to democratically rotating the assignments. Until summer arrrived, I had the alternate choice of going to my classes. Actually, I wasn't as upset about possibly losing my usher's job as I was about being denied entry to Ebbets Field on days when it wouldn't be my turn to work. I went to a nearby drugstore and called Jack Collins, the general manager. I reminded him whose cousin of his nephew's best friend I was and he instructed me to meet him at the rotunda gate. He said "follow me" and led me at a brisk pace to Jack Haines' office. "The kid works. Every game." A man of few words and decisive action, Collins pointed at me, Haines blanched, and after that I found myself outfitted with a full uniform, no longer being issued only the cap of an extra, and working every game. It was my first experience in the use of influence for advancement.

There really wasn't all that much to know about ushering. The work was crowded into a busy half-hour just before game time. Ushers stationed themselves where ramps led ticket holders into the reserved and box seat sections. You had to find those with tickets in your section quickly and size them up for tip possibilities. The experienced usher ignored customers wearing loud sports shirts, particularly if they were with a date and paired with other couples. They would try to maneuver someone else into tipping the usher. At best, one would slip you a dime after you had led the way to a row of seats, lowered them, removed imaginary dust with a cloth carried in the hip pocket and returned the tickets with the hand held palm up.

The patron you were happy to spot was middle-aged, wearing a hard straw hat and a dark suit. Usually alone, he would put a quarter in your hand. The worst was the out-of-towner. We were never sure whether his effusive thanks, instead of a tip, was an act or naivete. Apart from tips, we were paid $3.00 a game and $5.00 for double-headers. On a good day, tips would average about $6.00. Standing room crowds gave us an opportunity to make extra money. Working with the special cops, you could get a buck to allow someone to sit on one side of the aisle steps. A small trade could also be conducted by letting people take still empty seats after the game began. A full-time usher made about $80 a week when the team was home.

About half of us were saving most of what we earned for school expenses. Before a game, until the gates to Ebbets Field opened, ushers would sit in two groups. On one side, the students would have opened their books. They were offset by those just as diligently studying the *Daily Racing Form.*

As the season went along and the Dodgers rose in the standings, interest in the team grew. The crowds reached such numbers that, when the final day of the season arrived on October 1, Brooklyn's attendance had neared one million. The Yankees, winning a fourth straight pennant, and the Giants, playing in the bigger Polo Grounds, didn't reach that mark.

The season which had begun in a drizzle ended in one. On Sunday, October 1, the tail-end Phillies came to play a closing doubleheader. The Dodgers, who hadn't finished in first division since 1932, were in third place, a half game ahead of the Chicago Cubs. A rainout would insure that they would end there, but Larry MacPhail wanted to play the game and bring the attendance over a million. A brand new car would be given to the one-millionth customer. How they figured out who, among the 17, 152 who splashed into Ebbets Field, was Mr. Million, I don't know. The final total was 1,007, 762, and after the game, some happy fan climbed into the car that was driven, with its windshield wipers going, through the center field gate.

The 1940 season started with the Dodgers winning nine straight, climaxed by Tex Carleton's no-hitter in Cincinnati. There were new faces, one young enough to pass into the park with the college-type ushers. Twenty-year-old Pee Wee Reese became the new shortstop and was joined during the season by another boy wonder, Pete Reiser. Joe Medwick, a surly slugger from the St. Louis Cardinals "Gas House Gang," was added after the season began. He was beaned six days after joining the Dodgers by a former teammate, Bob Bowman. Larry MacPhail, who had been upstairs in the pressroom, raced down ramps and dashed out on the field. He raged in front of the Cardinal dugout, challenging their players to come out and fight. A later version had him vaulting over the railing of his field box. Wrong. I was ushering the section behind the Dodger dugout that day. When you drew that assignment you were particularly aware of where MacPhail was and who his guests might be. The Dodger G.M. rarely sat in his box, to the homeplate side of the Dodgers bench. He preferred the pressroom and its bar. But, he was always likely to turn up during the game, and it would cost the usher his job if someone not invited by MacPhail was sitting in his box.

The ushering staff was generally the same as had been assembled the year before. We wore the same green uniforms. Jack Haines had gone back to Chicago, we understood. A younger man, blond and handsome as a matinee idol, Jack Jordan, had replaced him. The theatrical good looks were a family trait: he was the brother of the stage and screen actress, Helen Twelvetrees. Unlike Haines, who rarely donned the gold-braided white jacket of the chief usher, Jordan preened in his. Four others wore white jackets to indicate they had the rank of captain. Oddly, there was little envy among the green-uniformed ushers. A white jacket denied its wearer the opportunity to pick up tips by dusting off seats, and the position was too important to risk by hustling standees for a buck.

There was one other who wore an usher's white coat. As good looking as Jordan in a darker way, Johnny Freund's voice earned him the role of announcing the lineup over the P.A. system MacPhail has installed. Other than irritating umpire Larry Goetz one day by identifying him as "Goats," Freund did his job effectively. One day we ushers were asked to audition to replace him for the summer months, as Johnny would be acting in summer stock somewhere. During that theatrical engagment he changed his name. He left as Johnny Freund but came back in September as John Forsythe.

The Dodgers had been feisty in 1939. In 1940, Leo Durocher turned them nasty. His constant braying, "stick it in his ear," made Brooklyn everyone's enemy. It was "us against the world."Apart from the new young shortstop, Pee Wee Reese, and the player the Dodgers had to call up during the season, Pete Reiser, the team's character changed by acquiring older, hard-nosed players. Joe Medwick was foremost among these. One story that circulated among the ushers involved Reese and Medwick.

There was nothing in the press about the incident and it might have been quietly ignored by the writers covering the Dodgers. More likely, it was hushed up among the players. Forty years after the alleged event, I wrote to Pee Wee Reese asking for confirmation. He didn't deny it outright, only asked that it be left unexplained. I had reminded him of a fight that was supposed to have taken place in the clubhouse.

We had noticed something unusual during a game and Danny Comeford Jr., an assistant to his father as a clubhouse attendant, explained it to us. We had seen Reese dash out to left field and do something that required Medwick to bring his glove back to the bench. In those days gloves were left behind when players changed sides each inning. The story we heard was that Medwick, a notorious hazer of rookies, had first spit tobacco juice into Pee Wee's glove when going out to his left field position. Some of the older players urged Reese to retaliate, insisting that he take his own first chew of tobacco and work up an appropriate amount of spit. The next inning, the egged-on Reese raced to left field and unloaded into Medwick's glove.

After the game Medwick, an angry bully who wanted to settle things with the slender youngster, charged Reese. At this point the team captain, Dolph Camilli intervened. He had boxed professionally until his older brother, fighting as Frankie Campbell, had died after a bout with Max Baer in California. Baer became the heavyweight champion and Dolph Camilli an MVP for the Dodgers. The way we heard it, Camilli dropped Medwick with one punch.

Being an usher provided an insider's view of events that sometimes were inadvertently misrepresented in newspaper accounts. Often an usher literally had another point of view than the reporters in the press box behind homeplate. For example, Brooklyn's nemesis in 1940 was the Cincinnati Reds. They had won the 1939 pennant with a team largely put together by Larry MacPhail when he had been their general manager. In 1940 they would repeat, mostly because of quirky games they won at Ebbets Field. The one which seemed to settle the pennant race early came in the opening game of a doubleheader on Sunday, June 16. The Dodgers were in first place and had beaten the Reds on Friday and Saturday. The team's emerging ace, Whit Wyatt, and Paul Derringer, one of the best right-handers in the league, pitched the first game. They matched zeroes until two were out in the top of the ninth inning. Then Lonnie Frey, a former Dodger, lined a drive to right field. It hit the foot of the screen above scoreboard and caromed high into the air. It came straight down, but not where rightfielder Joe Vosmik expectantly waited. Frey zoomed around the bases. It was a sure double, but when Frey saw Vosmik still pounding his glove in frustration he kept going. The third base coach waved him on and Frey scored standing up. He could have circled the bases all afternoon. The ball never came down.

The newspaper writers decided the ball had remained on a shelf formed by a wing of the scoreboard. The press box consenus was that the ball became stuck at the foot of the screen. No so. My view was from Section 1 of the upper grandstand, next to the right field wall. I was looking down at the small, triangular platform toward which the ball had dropped. The ball didn't become stuck, it disappeared.

Before the game a workman had climbed up to replace some rotted boards. As the game was about to begin, he was nailing new two by fours into place on the shelf when the umpires spotted him. Beans Reardon trotted out and ordered him down off the scoreboard. Apparently intending to go back and finish after the game, the carpenter left his toolbox behind. He also left the space for one board uncovered. That's where Frey's ball went, plummeting cleanly through the narrow opening. The next day the carpenter went back and rebuilt the platform so that it sloped, but it had been the missing board that gave Frey his homerun and the Reds a 1–0 win.

Both at home and away the Dodgers were embattled. At Ebbets Field they were viewed as playing aggressive baseball. On the road they were villified as dirty players with head-hunting pitchers and a manager without a conscience. Like hockey players whose brawls contagiously spread to the stands, the Durocher style of play drew people who not only wanted to be where the action was, they also wanted to be part of it.

Fighting among the spectators grew in direct ratio to the battles which broke out on the diamond. Somehow, Larry MacPhail expected his ushers to pacify the beer-swilling hooligans. He again turned to Andy Frain in Chicago, and the Ziegfeld of ushers rushed to Ebbets Field, accompanied by four assistants. We were to get a crash course in mob control. Better we should have been taught how to escape. After a lecture explaining how to identify the leaders who were stirring up trouble and how to talk them out of their intended mayhem, it occurred to the Dodger managment they already had special policemen to deal with roughneck patrons. Our problem as ushers was that, like in other situations in life, you couldn't find a cop when you needed one. By common consent we adopted the safest rule possible. When trouble loomed, we ran.

The ultimate in inciting the rougher elements in the stands came on September 16 when the Cincinnati Reds were visiting Ebbets Field. The game went into extra innings before the Reds scored a tie-breaking run on an umpire's questionable decision. If anything was arguable, Durocher would storm after the umpires.

On a force play at second, Pete Coscarart had juggled the throw. Larry Goetz hesitated, then called the runner out. No, overruled George Magerkurth from third base. He had a clearer view and told Goetz the Reds runner was safe. The run which scored on the play counted, and won the game.

When the game ended several fans stalked the 6' 3" Magerkurth, a hefty giant at over 200 pounds, and one tripped him. The umpire was flat on his back and his assailant, a stubby slugger, was astride him and viciously pummeled him. This was unseen by the ushers ringing the diamond. The fight took place behind them while they faced the stands. It was another technique imported from Chicago. It didn't make much sense to prohibit people in street shoes from crossing the diamond on the way to the center field exit gate after the players had been ripping it up with their spikes all afternoon. But it looked nice.

My own assignment when the game ended was to open a gate in the low fence that separated the downstairs reserved seat section from the rows of general admission seats farther back from the field. While I was doing this I heard noises that usually meant the blood lust of the crowd had been aroused. Whenever a fight breaks out in the stands at a ball game, people who have paid good money to see professionals compete climb on seats to watch a couple of amateurs maul each other. When I looked around I could see two men wrestling on the ground. One was an umpire. While I was sizing up this unlikely scene, I heard a deep-throated growl. A Neanderthal type was lumbering over rows of seats in my direction, grunting and shaking a ham-sized fist at me. I sensed that my green uniform identified me as "authority" and by some twist of a primitive intellect, this correlated with umpires and Magerkurth's decision. The beady eyes of the approaching beast glowed with hate. I did what any red-blooded usher would have done. I hurdled the rows of seats between me and the playing field.

Later I pretended I had been rushing to the rescue of umpire Magerkurth. Not so. He just happened to be where I was headed. My idea was to join the other ushers. They already formed two sides of a defensive square, although most of them were still blithely unaware that behind them an umpire was in a losing battle. A full-page picture of the huge Magerkurth being pummeled by a stumpy assailant sitting astride his stomach ran on the front page of the New York Daily News the next day. Behind them, an ushering colleague of mine, George Phillips, appeared to be gazing bemusedly at the fight scene.

Larry MacPhail was outraged. It was bad enough that his ushers hadn't intervened, the one whose picture was in the paper actually seemed to be enjoying the fight. When he arrived at the ball park, Phillips was told not to bother putting on his uniform. Instead he was to report directly to Larry MacPhail so that the general manager could fire him personally. If we'd worn epaulets, MacPhail would have snipped them off Phillip's uniform and handed him a white feather for cowardice.

Soon Phillips was back and putting on his uniform. We crowded around as he buttoned the coat and straightened his hat. Then we saw his swollen and blackened eye. No, MacPhail hadn't done it. In fact, it saved Phillip's job. MacPhail, having been told the picture had been snapped just as the usher had turned to investigate what was happening behind him, assumed Phillips had been slugged in the following melee. Actually, Phillips had gotten the shiner hours after the game was over. He had been the second choice of a young lady he had offered to escort home from a bar. In stepping outside to settle the issue with his rival, Phillips had caught a roundhouse thrown by a different antagonist for a different purpose. However, he accepted MacPhail's interpretation and the assurance of future assingments of choice ushering locations that went with it.

Magerkurth's assailant was a parolee, upset about a lost wager on the game and not a vindictive Dodger fan at all. Still, the hoodlum was portrayed sympathetically in the press. The era of "The Bums" had begun.

There was little concern expressed among the ushers for what was happening in Europe or Asia in 1941. We had our own wars. The Dodgers fought their way through another season. Strengthened by Kirby Higbe on the mound and catcher Mickey Owen, with Pete Reiser available from opening day and Billy Herman coming from the Cubs early in the season, Brooklyn seemed certain to make 1941 the "next year" we had been waiting for. The last time Brooklyn had won a pennant was the year I was born, 1920. Then, it seemed a longer time than looking back across the past years does now.

There were frequent changes in the ushering ranks during the season. A peacetime military draft was under way. A few ball players went into the army: Hank Greenberg from the American League and Hugh Mulcahy, of the Phillies, from ours. Ebbets Field ushers seemed to be very attractive to draft boards. Every home series ended with a collection being taken up for some one of us who was being inducted. I had been classified 1A and told not to bother to return to school in the fall. The draft board predicted I would be called in October. I was as concerned that I would miss seeing the Dodgers in the World Series as I was about going into the service.

Everyone has a favorite year of his life. Mine is 1941. There was no point in saving money for another school year. Even clothes were a waste of money as I would be trading in my green Brooklyn usher's uniform for a khaki one. One of the summer's activities when the Dodgers were away on a road trip was to use the vacant Ebbets Field to play ballgames in a four-team league. The ushers had two teams, one from the ranks of the regular staff and the other from the part-timers who worked when the crowds were large. The field maintenance people made up another team, and the league was rounded off by a team from the vendors. Thanks to a fat peanut seller who played right field for the vendors, I hit a ball off the Abe Stark sign at the bottom of the scoreboard. The sign, unmarked by a baseball since Woody English was reported to have done it during the 1930s, promised a suit of clothes if a batted ball hit it. Because of the angle, and with a major league outfielder always playing immediately in front of his sign, Mr. Stark had gotten great publicity without having to give away so much as a vest. It's just as well that Uncle Sam was already pledged to give me my next outfit as Abe Stark did not return my phone calls.

I was still available for ushering duties when the Dodgers cinched the pennant in Boston and bunting was hung at Ebbets Field in anticipation of a World Series victory over the New York Yankees. As a Dodger fan I was ecstatic. As an usher I was sanguine. The regular crowds would mostly be replaced by the kind of people who get the tickets that are denied to the fans who have supported the team all season. The World Series crowd would be "out of towners" who never seemed to know they were expected to tip the usher who showed them to their seats. Worse, there would be no standing room crowds to squeeze into places on the steps. Although we did get to work the three games scheduled for Brooklyn, they were emotional disasters as well as meager paydays.

The first game played at Ebbets Field, after the two games at Yankee Stadium had been split, was on October 4. Freddie Fitzsimmons was knuckleballing the Yankees to impotency until his rival pitcher, Marius Russo, also pitching shutout ball, lined a drive off Fitz's knee. The ball bounced as high as the light towers, finally came down like a pop fly, and was caught by Pee Wee Reese to end the seventh inning. Fitz was on the ground, his knee broken. Hugh Casey couldn't keep New York from scoring twice in the eighth and we lost 2–1.

October 5 is another one of those dates bitterly fixed in tribal Brooklyn memory. Yet it gave me one of my most unique experiences as an Ebbets Field usher. My assignment was the field boxes between the Dodger dugout and the home plate screen. It was fine for collecting autographs, but not tips. Randolph Scott and Groucho Marx led large parties, effusively greeting everyone but ignoring the usher trying to get one last tip with his soon to be retired seat-dusting rag.

Then Casey Stengel arrived. He was the manager of Boston that season. I remembered him as the Dodgers manager when I had been a kid getting autographs. His was the hardest to get. Then one day, while the others were chasing someone coming down McKeever Place, I saw Casey walking alone along Sullivan Street. I waited with my back to him, then wheeled around and held out my book. "Sign for me, Casey, before the others see you." He did.

Now I was too mature to ask another grown man to write his name for me. But I was happy with the opportunity the seating arrangments gave me. Apparently his wife, Edna, had found something to do other than come to Ebbets Field. There was an empty seat beside Casey. At a regular season game I might have hustled a fan without a box seat ticket for a couple bucks to sit there. This time I took it myself.

Casey accepted me and, with no one else to talk to, the loquacious Stengel carried on a nonstop analysis of the game. He managed for both teams. Like all Brooklyn fans, I had thought I knew everything there was to know about baseball strategy. Casey dazzled me with his anticipation of coming circumstances. He didn't second-guess Leo Durocher or Joe McCarthy, he was two and three innings ahead of the action as he outlined all pending strategy moves.

It looked good for the Dodgers. They overcame a 3-run Yankee lead and went into the ninth inning leading 4 to 3. Hugh Casey retired the first two batters and, as every mournful Dodger fan knows, struck out Tommy Henrich and that should have ended the game. Instead, the ball spun into the dirt and bounced away from catcher Mickey Owen. Henrich ran for first base and the ball rolled all the way to where Casey and I were sitting. It stopped in front of us.

What followed was a nightmare. The savvy Leo Durocher and his brainy assistants, Chuck Dressen and Red Corridon, let a red-faced Hugh Casey go on uninterruptedly trying to overpower the

Yankee batters. As base hits rained all over the park, the Dodgers choked. Owen the catcher, in shock himself for the passed ball, didn't go to the mound to confer with Casey. No one called time. The carnage went on.

Casey Stengel was nearly out of his mind with frustration as Durocher remained, out of sight, on the bench. At one point, Casey had his leg over the low railing. I thought he was going to go out and stop the action himself. Actually, he was trying to get the attention of the Dodger bench. The side of the dugout blocked him from the view of the players like blinders on a horse. When the Yankees finally were retired, they had a 7 to 4 lead. The Dodgers batted listlessly in the bottom of the ninth. I guess I said goodbye to Casey Stengel as I went off to my postgame assignment. The loss had left me numb. I don't recall leaving Ebbets Field.

I walked back across Prospect Park to my home neighborhood and instinctively headed for McCauley's Bar & Grill. The bar was lined with silent men. Steins of beer and shot glasses of whiskey were in front of each mourner. I found a vacant stool and Tom McCauley, grief on his face, set up my boilermaker. There were no postmortems, just quiet despair. When a man emptied his glass, a raised finger brought the refill.

Hours later I was shaken from my morbid stupor by the arrival of Jim McDonald, another Ebbets Field usher. He angrily reminded me we had arranged a double date for that evening. He was to pick up the girls and we would meet in the lobby of the Empire Theater on Broadway. "Life with Father" was enjoying a popular run. We had been lucky enough to get tickets—the very ones which I still had in my wallet. Jim and our dates had waited for me in vain.

In the aftermath of the game, stunned by the misfortune which always seemed to plague the Dodgers, I had blanked out all social responsibility.

The World Series ended the next day and so did my career as an Ebbets Field usher. Actually, my draft board didn't send me off to the military until January. Between the disasterous World Series loss to the Yankees and the start of my military service, the country had gone to war. A real one, not the skirmishes of the Dodgers on baseball diamonds. We were assured we would always "Remember Pearl Harbor" and the sneak Japanese attack of December 7, 1941. Today's peace-oriented society chooses to focus sympathy on the holocaust of Hiroshima that ended it. I remember both. I remember being in the Phillipine Islands and expecting to be part of the blood bath that would accompany an invasion of Japan. The night we heard about the atomic bomb it meant, to some of us, that we would be able to return home and see Ebbets Field and the Dodgers.

I never went back to ushering at Ebbets Field. I had married, was working, and going to school at night. The G.I. Bill would cover the expenses of my education better than hustling tips at the ballpark.

I rarely go to major league games anymore. I lost much of my interest when the Dodgers moved to Los Angeles. When I do go to a game, I tip the usher. At times he seems surprised. I understand they belong to a union now and work steady. I had three wonderful seasons as an usher at Ebbets Field. Everything considered, and I never told Sally, the lady I married in 1943, this, it was the best job I ever had.

This memoir first appeared in Baseball History: Volume 3, 1990

3

An Appreciation of Uncle Robbie

The rough and tumble time of "baseball's lost era," the nineteenth century, is being phased out by "modern historians." The icons of the receding past and their deeds fade as we approach another millennium. As fast as you can say "Jackie Robinson," the memory of Wilbert Robinson disappears.

Wilbert Robinson was the hard-nosed team captain of the Baltimore Orioles of the 1890s. The team and its manager, Ned Hanlon, invented or polished much of the strategy still used by modern clubs. Later, Robinson was a convivial, jovial coach for rancorous John McGraw's New York Giants from 1911 to 1913. Next he became an easy-going manager, winning pennants with cast-offs and pitchers he rescued from the discard heap. Uncle Robbie was a dominant figure in baseball when games were played in sunlight and on grass.

Wilbert Robinson might be famous today for pennants won by the New York Yankees. One Yankee owner, Colonel T. L. Huston, wanted to hire him to manage the team. But the bankroll and ego of his partner, Jacob Ruppert, was bigger. He bought out Huston, and Miller Huggins got to win pennants with Babe Ruth and Lou

Gehrig leading the way. Uncle Robbie was better suited, actually, to managing the ragtag teams of Brooklyn.

The baseball career of Uncle Robbie, a rotund man with a sunny disposition, spanned more than fifty years, during which professional baseball grew from a shaky proposition to a national institution. He came up in 1886, and was one of the best players of the 1890s. He once went seven for seven, a record which is still unmatched in a nine-inning game. Robbie began catching when cannon ball pitchers were only 50 feet away. When they were moved back to the present 60' 6", he caught the first no-hitter at that distance, pitched by William Hawke on August 16, 1893.

In the rapidly changing game of the nineteenth century, Robbie was one of the first catchers to dare to crouch directly behind the batter on every pitch. As a boy learning the receiver's trade, young Billy Rob, as the town of Hudson, Massachusetts, knew him, taught himself to deal with foul tips. Years later he reminisced, "Funny how I learned to catch behind the bat. I rigged up a clothesline in our back yard and fixed it just as high as my face when I leaned over. Then I would have a boy throw a ball to me." When the ball hit the line it would be deflected. Bare hands would adjust to the change in trajectory. Black eyes and swollen features were the price young Robbie paid to learn how to catch foul tips.

As the field leader of the Orioles, Wilbert Robinson was the team's "salver," pouring the balm of blarney on waters roiled by his tempestuous teammates. But he was tough, and he personified the spirit of "the old Orioles." When one of his fingernails was ripped off by a sliding base runner, he ground the bleeding digit into the dirt and roared, "Let's play ball." The tip of the bleeding finger was later amputated.

This and other injuries lent truth to the jest that shaking hands with an old catcher is like grabbing a bag of peanuts. But it was always known that the main characteristic of a Wilbert Robinson handshake was not the broken digits it may have revealed, but the fact that it was his bond in any agreement. His hands might have been gnarled, but his handshake was firm and more sincere than the manicured offering of a bank president.

A wonder at salvaging or reinventing the careers of pitchers, Robinson gave up a comfortable Baltimore merchant's life in 1911 when his friend John McGraw persuaded him to come to the Giants spring training camp to coach the pitchers, especially the failed prospect, Rube Marquard. With Marquard finally living up to his potential, the Giants won pennants in 1911, with Robbie as a part-time coach, and with him on the coaching lines full time in 1912 and 1913. Each season he added another pitching star to McGraw's staff. Jeff Tesreau in 1912 and Al Demaree in 1913.

But the Giants couldn't win the World Series, and the genial but secure and self-confident Robinson could not accept McGraw's blame-shifting tirades. He left the Giants. The Dodgers, floundering and broke, hired him for 1914 and he crossed the bridge to Brooklyn. Two years later he brought the team a pennant, and repeated as National League champion four years after that.

Robinson was beloved by Brooklyn's fans, who renamed their team, "the Robins" in his honor. His genial good humor brought him the fond designation of "Uncle Robbie" after his friend and nationally read newspaperman Damon Runyon wrote about everyone's "Uncle Wilbert." It was said that he knew the game the way an old hound dog knows quail hunting, "by instinct and experience."

Uncle Robbie, regretfully, is remembered more for the foibles of the Daffy Dodgers in the late years of his career. Eccentric players gravitated to his roster and he patiently endured them even when three arrived at third base together. He couldn't cure the most colorful of them all, Babe Herman, from turning a fence clearing home run into a single by watching the batter race past him while he stopped and admired the blow. Herman did it twice in one season.

Brooklyn beat writers of the 1920s did not have to invent incidents to amuse their readers. They just observed and wrote about what actually happened. The Robins manager was like a fun-loving uncle romping with his favorite nephews. He made fun of his own ample girth. The rotund Robbie laughed at the idea that being late to arrive for spring training would delay Babe Herman's readiness. "He can just take a couple of laps around me and he'll be in shape," Uncle Robbie said.

Wilbert Robinson's image was shaped by a prank played on him in spring training in 1915. He accepted a challenge by reporters to catch a baseball dropped from an airplane. The old warrior lined up the plummeting pellet and grabbed it with his catcher's mitt. To everyone's merriment, and his own—eventually—it turned out to be a grapefruit which exploded on contact.

However, the bizarre incidents and the "Daffy Dodgers" of his later seasons fall far short of defining a career that began when organized baseball was only in its tenth season. Cap Anson and others who had played even before the National League was formed in 1876 were still major leaguers when Robbie debuted in 1886. When he retired after the 1931 season—against his will and the better judgment of the Brooklyn fans—he left a personal imprint on generations of players. His last big league pitching discovery, Van Lingle Mungo, who, until his arm went bad, was regarded as the peer of Carl Hubbell and Dizzy Dean, pitched into World Was II baseball, ending in 1945, the year Jackie Robinson signed his Dodger contract.

After Uncle Robbie went to Atlanta for his twilight years, another big, hard throwing youngster impressed him. Hugh Casey, an Atlanta native, became a premier reliever and, with that other Robinson, brought Brooklyn a pennant in 1947. That was also the final playing season for Al Lopez, a Hall of Famer who broke in as a teenager under Uncle Robbie. Some of Robinson's managerial magic rubbed off on his players. Lopez won two pennants to interrupt runs of New York Yankee championships by Casey Stengel, who won ten. Stengel had played for Uncle Robbie's pennant winner in 1916, and his antics helped set the eccentric style expected of Brooklyn players.

Robinson's career extended through generations of baseball's development and improvement. He left the arena before artificial turf, domed stadiums, luxury boxes, batting gloves, million-dollar salaried utility men, the designated hitter, and interleague play were grafted onto the declining national pastime.

Uncle Robbie surprised baseball with two pennants in eighteen seasons in Brooklyn, in 1916 and 1920. He challenged better teams with near-miss finishes in 1924 and 1930. Other managers won more pennants and a few managed for more years. Their records reflect superior, dynastic teams more than inspired leadership. Robinson had no superior in extracting better performances from players than anyone—themselves included—had reason to expect.

Few managers have been affectionately regarded for long, and none remained a beloved leader longer than Uncle Robbie. Even Connie Mack angered the fans by selling off his star players and endured fifty years mainly because he owned the team.

Uncle Robbie always did his best with what he had to work with. He won more often than he lost, though not by much. In nineteen managerial seasons, eighteen with Brooklyn, He won one more game than he lost, 1,399 to 1,398. But you can't quantify a man like Wilbert Robinson. He is beyond statistical measurement. How do you weigh affability, honor, decency? How do you measure a warm smile, a hearty clap on the back? When Wilbert Robinson was everyone's Uncle Robbie, fan appreciation did not have to be orchestrated. Balls hitting scoreboard signs won the batter a suit of clothes. Now million-dollar scoreboards tell people when to clap their hands and make noise. In Uncle Robbie's time they knew…and they also knew that he would remain true to the love they gave to him.

WILBERT ROBINSON
(UNCLE ROBBIE)
Born: June 29, 1863, Bolton, Mass.
Died, August 8, 1934, Atlanta, Ga.
BR TR 5-8 1/2, 215

Fondly remembered as a fun-loving manager when baseball was the people's sport and flourished with the greatest gusto in Brooklyn, a rotund icon in the twentieth century first had his spiked shoes firmly planted in the nineteenth. The fourth of five sons of Henry and Lucy Robinson, Wilbert was born in Bolton,

Massachusetts in 1863. The town later became part of Hudson. Henry Robinson was the town butcher, and his sons learned his trade. When the teenaged Wilbert began to turn up at the practices of the Haverhill team in the New England League, he was hailed as "the butcher boy," and his earliest nickname in baseball was "Pork Chop." Managed by Frank Selee, destined to be among baseball's greatest leaders, Haverhill had Robbie behind the plate and a lineup whose players all reached major league level. John Tener, who would become National League president as well as governor of Pennsylvania, was a battery mate.

In 1886 Robinson moved up to the major leagues with Philadelphia in the American Association. He was quickly recognized as a rising star, one of the first to move up close to the batter on all pitches. Not yet filled out to the XL uniform size of the future, he was lean enough to be a base running threat. He stole 33 bases his rookie season.

From the very first, young Wilbert was a good-natured keeper of the peace among his rancorous nineteenth century teammates. Walter Prince, one of his Haverhill teammates, recalled: "His good nature was a sure remedy to drive away all blues. No cliques could last while Robbie was around. He drew us together as a sociable, harmonious club."

Arlie Latham, the great base stealer and comic dynamo of the St. Louis Browns when they were winning American Association championships, later compared the styles of Uncle Robbie and John McGraw, his closest companion. Latham described the genial influence of Robinson on umpires when the duo was part of the dynastic Baltimore Orioles in the 1890s.

"Robbie and McGraw are working both ends against the middle," Latham complained, "When a poor, inoffensive and well-meaning umpire appears in Baltimore, Robinson meets him at the plate, shakes hands with him and remarks: 'They tell me you've been doing great work out west. The boys say you're the best in the business and between us, I'm glad you're here. These are pretty tough games, old man, and that other fellow we had here was a little to the bad. Of course, he's a good fellow, but I'm glad you're here now. You want to watch this pitcher we're trying today. Great lad. Keep your eye on the outside corner. He gets lots of them just on the edge and the other fellow missed a lot of them.' All of this time," Arlie continued, "McGraw is barking and snapping around the umpire's heels and threatening to bite him. If one system doesn't work the other usually does."

Robbie was the hub around which Ned Hanlon's demons whirled like dervishes. This was the band, with Robinson and McGraw joined by Willie Keeler, Joe Kelley, Hughie Jennings, and Dan Brouthers, that invented inside baseball. Ned Hanlon would propose the hit and run, squeeze play, double and triple steal, design cutoff plays and backing up other positions, and his stars would bring off these innovations. In three successive seasons, 1894–1896, Hanlon's team won championships and created a legend for brilliance and determination. Uncle Robbie contributed the prototype gesture. When a sliding runner ripped away a fingernail, he ground the damaged digit into the dirt and snarled, "Let's go."

The finger was later amputated at the first knuckle. It only impaired Robbie by curtailing his ability to signal for a curve ball.

Perhaps it explains his future managerial focus on big pitchers like Dazzy Vance, all of whom featured a great fast ball.

Stamina went with the butcher boy's physique. He once caught all games of a triple header and came back the next day to catch both ends of a double header. He hit NL pitching better than the pitching he faced in the AA, batting .301 in nine NL seasons, after averaging just .201 in six seasons in the AA.

Robbie enjoyed his greatest day soon after his Baltimore club moved from the defunct AA to the expanded NL in 1892. On June 10 the Orioles routed the hometown St. Louis Cardinals 26–4. St. Louis starter Pretzel Getzein, in the last season of a nine-year career during which he won 145 games, was driven to cover; J. B. Young, in his only major league appearance, relieved and gave up 13 runs; and Ted Breitenstein, a rookie headed for stardom, mopped up.) By the game's end, Robinson had hammered out seven hits, one of them a double, and driven in 11 runs (nearly 20 percent of his season total), plus scoring one himself. Sadie McMahon, the Baltimore ace, was Robbie's battery mate.

Just as Uncle Robbie's big league seasons, as player, coach and manager, are divided by the turn from the nineteenth century to the twentieth, the demographics of his life fall into two different centuries. He married the former Mary Spiegel, visiting here from Ireland. They raised four children.

While together in Baltimore, John McGraw and Wilbert Robinson formed a partnership off the field as well as on. They owned The Diamond, a hotel and café. McGraw and Robinson moved on to St. Louis for a year, then jumped to the new Baltimore American League club, managed by McGraw in 1901.

When McGraw left Baltimore in mid 1902 to take over the Giants, Robbie assumed the reins, and the Orioles dropped a notch from seventh place to the cellar. The Orioles moved to New York and became the Highlanders in 1903, but Robinson remained behind to manage the Eastern League Baltimore Orioles briefly, then served as an advisor to Hughie Jennings and Jack Dunn. In 1911 Robbie rejoined McGraw as a Giants coach. Then in 1914, he began 18 wonderful, daffy, sunny years managing the Brooklyn Dodgers—known as the Robins during much of his tenure—during which he won NL pennants in 1916 and 1920.

In 1945, nearly 11 years after his death, Uncle Robbie was elected to baseball's Hall of Fame.

In 1999 SABR will publish a full-length biography of Wilbert Robinson, co-authored by Norman Macht and Jack Kavanagh.

4

Turkey Mike Donlin and Mabel Hite's Ashes

Mike Donlin was a superstar early in the twentieth century. He averaged .333 in 12 seasons. At first glance his stats should send him to Cooperstown. Instead, he is in the limbo of "might have beens" although he was a full fledged superstar when it suited his diverse career interests. He was a close second to Honus Wagner as the National League's premier player, twice being runner up when The Flying Dutchman won batting titles.

Mike Donlin lead a double life. At the peak of his fame and popularity, Mike fell in love. He was the beau ideal of Gotham, the toast of the sporting crowd and a familiar face along the Great White Way. Then Mike saw Mabel Hite sing and dance on a Broadway stage and he was smitten.

Mabel fell just as much for Mike, an athlete who strutted across his domain, the outfield of the Polo Grounds. His walk earned him the nickname of "Turkey Mike." He didn't much care for it. He once charged the press box at the Polo Grounds and poked his finger through the chicken wire protection. "Don't you ever call me 'Turkey' in that paper of yours," he told a cowering scribe. Still, sandlot kids copied his strut. It exuded confidence and challenge.

At that, Donlin's strut was a more appropriate explanation of his nickname than being dubbed "Turkey" because of his elongated, sunburned neck. The Giants wore collarless uniforms and Mike's long neck, burnished to a turkey red, drew snickering remarks. Mike didn't like those either. Mike was a bit feisty, frequently losing arguments with umpires, but he got along well with other players. If a foe was too big to fight, Donlin would sweet talk him into becoming a buddy.

The 21-year-old Mabel was loved by her stage fans and Mike Donlin had to elbow his way past a platoon of stage door Johnnies when he came to take her to a late night supper. The courtship coincided with the New York Giants' early success under manager John J. McGraw. When the Giants won the pennant in 1905, Mike Donlin and Christy Mathewson were the team's most popular stars. Matty, with a 31–9 record, was the idol of those who appreciated great pitching, and Mike Donlin was the toast of those who delighted in slashing, speedy baseball. He batted .356, second highest in the league and led everyone in runs scored with 124.

The courtship of Mabel Hite had to be worked around their professional schedules. Mabel played as many Broadway show dates as she could, but had to tour at times. The Giants schedule had Mike on the road half the season. After the Giants defeated the Philadelphia A's in five games in the 1905 World Series, with Matty pitching three shutouts and Mike Donlin leading in runs scored, the courtship continued into baseball's offseason. Mike went trouping with Mabel as her escort, luggage handler and, one expects, discreet lover. Then, with the Giants about to open the 1906 season, Mabel and Mike married on April 12. Mike and

McGraw could not get together on a contract. Donlin wanted $8,000 and McGraw offered $6,500. Mabel's solution was to take Mike into her act and pay him more than McGraw. Donlin was a natural for the stage. He sang well and could deliver a song. When Mabel taught him a time step he became her partner in a song and dance act, Hite and Donlin. What with Mabel's established stardom and Mike's baseball fame, they were a headline act from the start. A broken leg suffered in a sandlot game played between theatrical engagements eliminated comeback thoughts for 1907. As soon as it healed, Mike rejoined Mabel and strutted his stuff on the boards for another missed baseball season.

We have a good idea of Hite and Donlin's vaudeville turn. She was the star. Mike was a competent stage companion. He held the stage while Mabel made quick costume changes. He delivered a humorous monologue, filled with baseball jokes. Then he shuffled off when Mabel returned to enthrall her audiences. She was a graceful dancer, a stage beauty whose luminous, waif-like personality was projected to the boys in the topmost balcony.

Somewhere there might yet exist a "talking film" of the Hite and Donlin act. Made in 1908, it played on Broadway at the Rivoli Theater 21 years later in 1929. An article in the *New York Evening World* explained that the film had been resurrected for showing with a current Mike Donlin film, "Thunderbolt." This was one of the early "talkies," as sound films were then called.

Back in 1908, when Hite and Donlin were Broadway headliners, a technique of combining sight and sound was developed by the Cameraphone Company. Most entertainers of the day shied away from putting their acts on film. They feared this would kill an audience's interest when the act came to town for a live stage appearance. Hite and Donlin changed their act each season, easier to do with a song and dance act than one with a set script and permanent dialogue.

The press agent who had dug up the old film had been there when it was made at the Bijou Theater, on 23rd Street between Sixth and Seventh Avenues in Manhattan. No cameras turned until the act had been recorded on a phonograph record, including the taps of the dance routines. Then, in separate stages, Mabel and Mike mouthed their lines and pantomimed songs, and synchronized them with the motion picture. When played together, the "talking movie" was an accepted novelty. Perhaps a print and disk still exist. Maybe they will turn up in a Christy's auction of sports memorabilia, or maybe, as a theatrical curiosity.

After a two year absence from baseball, John McGraw offered a contract that Mike Donlin would accept. The press and public wondered if the Giants were resurrecting an idol whose time away from the game, trotting the boards with Mabel, would have taken the jaunty stride from his legs and dimmed his batting eye. He showed an overflow crowd at the Polo Grounds on opening day, 1908, that he had lost none of his ability. Where once Donlin's fans had shouted, "Oh you, Mike," now they chanted their approval with cries of "Oh, you, Mabel's Mike." They gave Mrs. Donlin co-billing when they cheered their returning hero.

The game had reached the bottom of the ninth, with the Giants a run down, 2–1, to their rivals, the Brooklyn Dodgers. Two men were out and Fred Tenney was on second base when Mike Donlin strutted to the plate. He glared out at pitcher Harry McIntire and worked the count to three and two. A hush came over the Polo Grounds, only the murmuring of prayers could be heard. McIntire wound up: he threw his fast ball. Crack! When the ball landed in the right field bleachers the crowd went wild, jubilantly pouring from the stands. A thousand fans rushed to accompany Mike Donlin as he trotted around the bases.

Mike again had a career year in 1908. He hit .334, second again to Honus Wagner for the batting title. Mike never won one. Wagner took eight of them. Donlin batted in a career high of 106 runs. He played in every one of the team's 155 games. The final game, of course, was the pennant play off contest between the Giants and Cubs. It had been made necessary when Fred Merkle failed to touch second base and became a force out. (For details of the showdown at the end of the 1908 season, see "No Touch At Second" in this collection). Donlin had raced for the clubhouse, a few strides ahead of Merkle. When Johnny Evers got Umpire Hank O'Day to call Merkle out on a force play at second base, leaving the game still tied, players and fans roiled around in confusion. In the melee, Mike Donlin squared off against big Frank Chance, the Cubs "Peerless Leader." Heavyweight champ Jim Jeffries had called Chance "the best brawler outside the prize ring." Mike explained he risked a pummeling in hope of having Chance thrown out of the game. The Cubs leader didn't take the bait, saying he'd settle with Donlin in the future. That deferred encounter was a long way off. Having completed the 1908 season, a personal triumph that lacked a World Series share of the receipts, the act of Hite and Donlin went back to work. This time Donlin was gone for two more seasons. He was about finished as an everyday player when he came back to the Giants in mid-season, but he could still hit. John McGraw used him mostly as a pinch hitter, then gave him an unconditional release. This was done as a favor. To have traded him would have brought the Giants another player or two, or cash. By making him a free agent, McGraw put Mike in a position to negotiate a contract with another team which might use him as a regular. Mike signed with Boston and batted .316 for the combined season. During the winter, Mike Donlin was traded to the Pittsburgh Pirates. He would have a final season hitting over .300, compiling another .316 batting average in 77 games. Mike was a distracted player. Mabel's health was failing. She moved into her mother's apartment at 525 West 111th Street, Manhattan, so that Mrs. Hite could care for her. They had come from Louisville, Kentucky when Mabel was a child performer and the two were very close. When Mrs. Hite learned of Christian Science, using prayer as an alternative to accepted medical practice, she believed it would be the answer to Mabel's failing condition. For a brief time it was. Her pain stopped and she even began to plan to revive the act of Hite and Donlin. She was ready to go into rehearsal with her husband when she relapsed. She had cancer. Her mother may have had other hopes, but a physician pronounced it incurable. Mike, too, took up Christian Science. But his added prayers did not turn the tide. On October 27, 1912, Mabel died in her mother's apartment. She was 27 years old and Mike was 34. Mabel was buried from Campbell's Funeral Home, her wake attended by thousands of her admirers and her husband's baseball friends. Mike was a bereaved, confused man. Mabel's remains had been cremated but Mike was indecisive about what to do with the silver urn containing her ashes.

"Just leave it with us," the friendly undertakers told him. "We'll guarantee safekeeping until you decide how to dispose of them."

Mike vacillated. Whether he was forced to delay distributing the ashes somewhere Mabel had requested or just kept delaying a sad occasion, they remained in the safekeeping of Campbell's Funeral Home for several years. Meanwhile, Mike married again. He wed Rita Ross, a singer and actress, on October 20, 1914. It is doubtful that the second wife wished to have an urn with Mabel's ashes on her mantle piece. They remained in the keeping of Campbell's Funeral Home.

Then in 1915, Campbell's decided to relocate their undertaking business. This required the relocating of Mabel's ashes or, finally, a decision by Mike Donlin. Ray Frye, an undertaker's assistant, took a personal role in maintaining the pledge that Mabel's ashes would be kept safe. He placed the urn in a cardboard box to take to the Campbell's new location on West 23rd Street. On the way he stopped for dinner at White's Restaurant on West 42nd. Frye checked the box in the cloakroom, telling the attendant, "be extra careful, it might explode." Rye claimed later this was simply to insure careful handling, not to be taken as a bomb threat.

However, the attendant was cautious. The Bolsheviks had been exploding bombs in public places and blowing up government buildings, and concern was justified. The attendant carefully tore a hole in the paper wrapping of the box and saw a wire protruding from a metallic object. Quickly he took the box to the night manager who, just as quickly, called the local police station to send someone over from the bomb squad. A police sergeant responded and took the suspected box into the lavatory. He unscrewed the top and peered in. A powdery metallic substance could be seen. At this point, through many re-tellings, the story of Mabel Hite's ashes has changed endings. There are several variations, only one of them true. The one most often told by baseball story tellers has the police sergeant pouring Mabel's ashes into a urinal trough and letting the running water wash her remains down the drain. It did not happen quite that way. The real disposal of Mabel's ashes took place years later, although under somewhat similar circumstances.

Mike Donlin brought matters to litigation in 1915. He regarded Ray Frye's action as degrading to his late wife's remains, even though her ashes still remained intact in the urn. All that handling, including a rumored soaking in a pail of water when it was still thought to be a bomb, must have some standing in a court of law. Mike pleaded his case against Campbell's and lost. Nonetheless, the ashes still remained in the possession of Campbell's, still waiting for Mike's decision on their disposal.

A year went by and, with a new wife to support, Mabel and her ashes passed from Mike's immediate concern. Then Campbell's called and jogged his memory by insisting he claim the remains or they would be thrown away. Mike got the call at White's, where he was drinking with friends. They all piled into a taxi and went to pick up the box which contained the urn. Back to White's restaurant they went to resume their imbibing. When a woozy Donlin departed hours later, he forgot to take Mabel's ashes.

The place closed and the cleaners found the box. It was given to the bartender to hold until its owner came back to claim it. It was placed under the bar on a lower shelf. It went unclaimed. The box was pushed deeper on the shelf and other forgotten items placed in front of it. It had disappeared from sight and memory when Prohibition took effect in 1920. The police let it be known that all places that sold alcoholic drinks could stay open until supplies ran out. A final night was declared at White's Restaurant and patrons drank the place dry.

The owners and employees wanted to raise a final glass but could not find a full bottle among the empties that littered the place. Then a bartender dug out a dusty box from far under the bar. He unwrapped it and, at first, thought he had found a bottle of wine. However, when he rubbed the encrusted surface clean he read, "This urn contains the ashes of Mabel Hite." Disappointed, perhaps not even having heard of Mike Donlin's wife, the bartender unscrewed the top and peeked inside. Then he set it down on the duckboards behind the bar. Below them coursed flowing drain water. It was an accident, of course, but the urn was knocked over and the ashes spilled out. They went into the flowing water and Mabel made her final exit, going down the drain.

Mike Donlin became part of the booming movie industry in Hollywood and lived there with his second wife. They were as devoted to each other as Mabel and Mike had been. Relations with women, particularly actresses and chorus girls, had not always been peaceful for Mike Donlin. John McGraw and Wilbert Robinson, when they switched from the National League to join the just formed American League in 1901, recruited Mike Donlin. He arrived in Baltimore with his pockets full of money and wild oats yet to be sown. Mike cruised Baltimore's bars, hung around music halls and met show girls.

On March 12, 1901, the Orioles were about to leave by boat for Georgia and spring training. Mike Donlin gave himself a bon voyage party, but never sailed. After a day's drinking, Mike started his night shift. He was thrown out of a hotel for relieving himself into a potted plant and next was seen weaving his way along Howard Street, near the Diamond Café, the sporting man's hangout owned by McGraw and Robinson. Nearby was the Academy of Music where a musical comedy was playing. Two of the girls from the show crossed the street to their boarding house with Mike Donlin trailing them and whistling his approval. A friend of the young ladies criticized Donlin for his boorish behavior. Donlin hit him. The young lady, Mamie Fields, tried to reason with Donlin. So Mike hit her, too.

Mike Donlin fled, leaving the city, but he was arrested the next day in Washington, D.C. Brought back, he was taken before the Grand Jury and the Criminal Court. Judge Albert Ritchie fined him $250, even though Donlin was now out of a job with the Orioles, and sentenced him to six months in jail. Donlin served his time and missed all but 34 games of the 1901 season, playing them with Cincinnati.

Like the telling of the saga of Mabel Hite's ashes, this early escapade went through several embellishments. In one version, the chorus girl and Mike had been living together. Her defender was Mike's rival for the lady's affections. Mike was possessive, that version goes. "He hit her like he owned her," was the punch line.

Mike was jailed much later in his career in Albany, New York. However, his career had ended and he had been a rowdy train passenger with a handful of ball players on their way from New York City to play a game of indoor baseball, in Troy. Johnny Evers, a noted home town boy, gathered up a local team to put on the game. Mike and his several fellow hooligans got out of jail in time to play the game, despite Mike being charged with the possession of a hand gun.

Mike Donlin's years were lived at full tilt. His theatrical life was sporadically successful. After all, when Mabel died it broke up the act and Mike wasn't good enough to get steady bookings as a single. Still, he got parts in films, including the second lead to John Barrymore in the silent classic, "Raffles," filmed in Queens. He and Barrymore became great friends and drinking chums later in Hollywood. The life of Turkey Mike Donlin is a fascinating one and holds hundreds of anecdotes not touched upon in this piece. He died September 24, 1933, in Hollywood, California. He was making a film with Ed Wynn when he died in his sleep. His death at 55 was attributed to "an athletic heart." His candle, having burned furiously at both ends, sputtered out, leaving behind hosts of friends in baseball and movies and the stage.

Mike's second wife, Rita, who had moved with him to California, wanted no mistakes made with her husband's ashes. There weren't to be any. There was no cremation of Mike Donlin's remain. There had been too much confusion about Mabel Hite's urn and its contents. When Rita Ross had married Mike Donlin in 1914, she lived in Asbury Park, New Jersey. She had Mike's coffin shipped there for safekeeping with the burial in her family's cemetery plot.

5

Fate Deals Shufflin' Phil Douglas A Bad Hand

In the imaginative motion picture, "A Field of Dreams," baseball players wearing the 1919 style uniforms of the Chicago White Sox emerge from a corn field. They appear for modern scrutiny, perhaps to be forgiven for ancient offenses against baseball. Their shades linger in a limbo with other outcasts condemned by Judge Kenesaw Mountain Landis, purger of players with character defects that threatened the integrity of the game. Still waiting for redemption is Phil Douglas. While many present day baseball fans argue the case for several of the banished players, poor Phil lacks support for forgiveness. His credentials, unlike others, are not great enough to qualify him for election to the Baseball Hall of Fame. His career was cut short before he achieved totals worthy of enshrinement. Yet reinstatement to good standing in organized baseball would erase the stain on his record. It could not give him back his career or posthumously ease the hardscrabble life he and his family endured after Douglas was banished by Judge Landis. Douglas differs from other miscreants: *he never threw a game or bet on one.*

Whether Joe Jackson and Buck Weaver, of whom it is said they played honestly in a cause they knew was tainted, should be pardoned for concealing guilty knowledge, is not a factor in the Phil Douglas case. He had no accomplices, he was not offered a bribe nor did he accept one. Douglas, a proud man of singular ways, had a different concept which could change the outcome of a pennant race. The leading pitcher of the pennant-bound New York Giants proposed to derail them by jumping the team in mid-season. His 11–4 record as the 1922 season reached August would be hard to replace, he reckoned.

He wouldn't deliberately lose any games in vengeance for the brutal treatment he had received from the New York Giants and their tyrannical manager, John J. McGraw. His simple idea of justice and vengeance was to deny McGraw the victories he counted on from Phil to win a repeat championship. Douglas had been the Giants star in the 1921 World Series, beating the Yankees twice and losing narrowly in a third game.

Douglas suggested to a former teammate, but not a warm friend, Les Mann of the closely contending St. Louis Cardinals, that some money be raised for his personal needs while away from baseball. Unfortunately, he made his proposal in a letter. There are no minutes of the clandestine meetings Chuck Gandil might have chaired with Black Sox teammates who participated in rigging the 1919 World Series. A deranged Douglas, wobbling from an abusive detoxification program, put his offer in writing. Worse, he sent it to Mann, whose career in baseball, particularly his post-playing years, was that of a promoter and entrepreneur. Leslie Mann was a graduate of the YMCA's Springfield College, at a time when it was virtually a seminary for young men with high moral values. Leslie Mann was not so much devout as zealous. In later years he organized the first Olympic demonstration of baseball. The contest, between collegians recruited by Mann, drew 100,000 uncomprehending German spectators at the 1936 Olympics in Berlin. Always a person with his eye on his own main chance, Mann immediately turned the Douglas letter over to his manager, Branch Rickey.

Rickey was a tricky moralist. His deeds were often splendid examples of righteous behavior, such as signing Jackie Robinson as the first black player to reach the major leagues in the twentieth century. That would be a "golden entry" for perusal by St. Peter when Rickey reached the Pearly Gates. Of more immediate earthly benefit, Rickey got a Hall of Fame ballplayer and quick access to stars of the Negro Leagues. This meant pennants for Rickey's Brooklyn teams for years to come and bonus payments for achievement and attendance for Mr. Rickey.

Poor Phil Douglas had given Mr. Rickey an opportunity to indulge his moral outrage by referring the letter to Judge Landis, the despotic Commissioner of Baseball. Landis was entrenched as the guardian of baseball's integrity. Singlehandedly he protected the sport against the stain of rigged games. His brief from the owners who hired him included using the elastic accusation of "anything detrimental to the good of the game of baseball." The vigilant Commissioner could be counted on by Rickey to at least suspend Douglas. In this way he could remove the Giants best pitcher from the 1922 pennant race. It might have disturbed Rickey's Christian conscience that the action might also destroy the life of a poor sinner who was cursed by alcoholism. Douglas had stepped into a judgmental trap. Mann was a doubtful choice for a confidant; Rickey was dubious in the role of intermediary; and

Judge Landis was ruthless in punishing those who had sinned against baseball. Poor Phil Douglas, never had a chance.

Douglas was set up for disaster by his manager, John J. McGraw. He treated most of his players, Christy Mathewson an exception, with tyrannical disdain when they failed to follow his instructions or botched up a play he had called for. He had banished Bugs Raymond, whose thirst for alcohol was compared to the cravings of Douglas. McGraw had twice traded away the strong-willed Buck Herzog, expressing loathing for the player but admitting he couldn't win pennants without him. He had forced a breach with his closest friend, Wilbert Robinson, firing him as the coach of the New York Giants. The beloved "Uncle Robbie" was hired by the Brooklyn Dodgers for whom he managed 17 years as the object of everyone's affection. McGraw later forced his captain, Frank Frisch, with a fiery personality of his own, to pack his equipment bag and jump the team. This is what Phil Douglas had proposed to do. However, poor Phil had been lassoed by a hostile posse and handed over to a hanging judge.

Phillip Brooks Douglas was a product of his rural environment. He was born and lived in a succession of small towns and on farms in a triangle, bounded on the south by Atlanta and Mobile and by the Sequatchi Valley, just above Chattanooga to the north. It had never been an area of prosperity, yet folks remained there, imprisoned by their lifestyle. Men were content to hunt with a good hound dog and sip corn whiskey of their own making. When Phil Douglas emerged as a professional baseball player, he was a rare man who would leave home. Of course, after each baseball season he headed south like a hunting dog hearing its master's whistle.

Phil Douglas had an almost unhittable spitball and great control of all his pitches. At 6' 3" and 200 pounds, he could rear back and hum a fast ball past a batter. He learned the spitter while breaking into the major leagues with the Chicago White Sox in 1912. His mentor was Big Ed Walsh, owner of a devastating spitter. Learning how to throw the wet one was the only time a player ever showed Phil Douglas anything about baseball. He was both a natural star and a somewhat solitary teammate. After his brief time with the White Sox, he was sent to the Pacific Coast League to develop. He spent more time with his foot on the brass rails of Barbary Coast saloons than on the PCL pitching slabs. When the season ended the White Sox cut him loose.

Luckily for Phil Douglas, the Cincinnati Reds could not afford to be too choosy. Their last place team needed pitching in 1914 and Douglas gave it to them. Despite several absences for his self-designated "vacations," he won 11 while losing 18 games, impressive stats for a last place team. He was in 45 games, 25 as a starter and the rest in relief. Like many players of his time, who could not consistently resist the lure of whiskey, much as more recent players could not abstain from cocaine and other drugs, Douglas had good days and bad. He failed to reach the heights expected of him at Cincinnati. He won when he was half sober and lost when half drunk. He was never far from the dividing line. He was waived to the Brooklyn Dodgers after losing five of his first six decisions in 1915.

His brief stay with the Brooklyn Dodgers, under the benign management of Wilbert Robinson, illustrates how frustratingly inconsistent he could be. His drinking had put him in disfavor with the Reds. Uncle Robbie had rescued Rube Marquard from the lifestyle of a Broadway playboy when he got a Hall of Fame pitcher for the waiver price from the Giants. Kept on a loose rein between starts, Rube pledged to show up sober on days he was expected to pitch. Maybe Uncle Robbie hoped to arrive at a comparable agreement with Phil Douglas. For almost three mid-season months, Douglas, almost alternately, pitched sensationally and dismally. In all he won five games and lost five games. One of Phil Douglas' efforts was a 16 inning scoreless tie game against the Boston Braves. Douglas allowed only one hit over the first nine innings and gave up just four in all. Although Uncle Robbie and Brooklyn owner, Charley Ebbets, almost always agreed, they differed in their tolerance of Douglas' drinking absences. Without telling Uncle Robbie, Ebbets put the pitcher on waivers. Phil Douglas pitched a three hit shutout the same day the Chicago Cubs claimed him.

The Cubs had a taste of Douglas' behavior, as he ended with a 1–1 performance in the final weeks of the 1915 season. For 1916, while Wilbert Robinson, his staff led by Rube Marquard, won a surprise pennant, Phil Douglas pitched for St. Paul in the American Association. He pitched himself back to the major leagues and the Cubs recalled him for 1917. Douglas went 14–20 for a second division team and led the league in pitching appearances. He was in 51 games, starting 37 times and pitching 20 complete games. Five of these were shutouts.

1918 should have been a great season for Phil Douglas. However, he staggered through it with a break even mark of nine wins and nine losses. Grover Cleveland Alexander had been bought by Chicago, with his battery mate, Bill Killifer, for $50,000. However, Alex was drafted for military service after pitching only three games. He was shipped to France as an artillery gunner with the AEF. He spent seven weeks in the front lines of the western front and was permanently deafened in one ear. Worse, he developed epilepsy. To fight off the pain he began to rely on alcohol and became as addicted as Phil Douglas.

Back for a full season in 1919, Alexander and Douglas made a devastating pair. They were a strong pitching combo but manager Fred Mitchell, trying for a repeat pennant, found the stress of tracking both Ol' Pete, as Alexander was now called, and Shufflin' Phil, Douglas' new sobriquet, too great. He traded Shufflin' Phil to John McGraw and the New York Giants, despite his 10–6 record. Charlie Dryden, a witty columnist for the *Chicago Record*, had dubbed Douglas "Shufflin' Phil" for his shambling gait. He dragged his feet like a farm boy reluctant to carry out his chores. It is typical that a modern writer, doing a piece mostly about Douglas' statistics, credited the nickname to a case of boyhood polio. That is another fictional statement which will take on a life of its own as additional writers whose research consists of re-writing earlier works, wrongly explain the Douglas nickname.

In 1920, while Uncle Robbie pulled off another unexpected pennant in Brooklyn, Douglas and McGraw tried to master each other. Shufflin' Phil was over matched by a tyrannical boss who assigned detectives to trail him. McGraw, armed with reports of saloon visits, would then tongue lash his pitcher in front of the other players when, hung over, he returned from one of his "vacations."

In 1921 McGraw had assembled a team that would win the first of four consecutive pennants. Shufflin' Phil Douglas straightened himself out by mid-season and, by World Series time, was McGraw's best pitcher. The Giants manager opened the first subway World Series by sending him against the New York Yankees and a publicly unrepentant Carl Mays. The underhand thrower had fatally beaned Ray Chapman the year before, yet never expressed regret. He was not popular, even with Yankees fans. Phil Douglas was everyone's underdog.

Although he lost the opener, 3–0, to Mays, Phil Douglas won his next two starts, again meeting Carl Mays. In the second encounter, Babe Ruth hit his only home run of the Series. In the third game Douglas pitched, Ruth, suffering an infected elbow, did not appear as Shufflin' Phil pitched a shut out. The win made the Series four games to three in the Giants favor. However, it was a "best of nine" arrangement which the Giants finished off the next day as Art Nehf beat Waite Hoyt, 1–0.

After the World Series, some players went on barnstorming tours and some did vaudeville turns. Phil Douglas, with his wife and children, boarded a southbound train. The Douglases decided to invest his $5,265 World Series winner's share in a house in Birmingham, Alabama. An earlier announced intention to buy 50 acres of good farm land was put on hold. After the cheers he had heard in the World Series and his 15 wins during the season, he expected a substantial raise in salary. He was wrong.

The Giants sent Douglas a contract calling for a meager raise of several hundred dollars. Angrily, he sent it back and shuffled off to a favorite fishing hole to wait for a better offer. Finally, the Giants upped his increase by 25% of his last salary. It was still unfair but the easy going Douglas reported for the 1922 season, little expecting it would be his last in baseball.

McGraw began harassing Douglas from the start of the season. Instead of just having him followed, he paired him with a companion who went everywhere with him. Unhappy though he was, with only a few short excursions into oblivion to interrupt stretches of winning pitching, Shufflin' Phil had an 11–4 record and a league leading 2.63 ERA when his world collapsed.

Douglas slipped the vigil of his assigned dinner partner and went on another "vacation." He was missing for several days when McGraw learned he was sleeping off his jag at a friend's apartment. The politically connected McGraw used his contacts to have a squad of policemen break in on him. They hauled him, half dressed, to the police station to grill him. He was put through a third-degree as violently as though he was suspected of child molestation. The cops then loaded him into a squad car and drove him to a New York City sanitarium. Here he was turned over to a detoxification program called "The Keely Cure." It was a feared procedure, known for the violent way a "patient" was treated. The program, conducted over several days, called for purgatives, vomit-inducing liquids, boiling hot baths alternated with icy cold showers, and shouted verbal abuse. Not until he had been in the program several days were his frantic wife and children even told where he was. Even then, John McGraw glossed over the severity of the treatment. When he was finally brought back to his apartment, he was a shattered wreck. Douglas was befuddled, convinced McGraw had done this to him as punishment prior to firing him from the team.

In this condition he dragged himself to the Polo Grounds to pack his stuff and say goodbye to his teammates. After they had filed out to the ball field, leaving Douglas alone with his jumbled thoughts, he found some paper and wrote "the letter." Dated August 7, it read:

Dear Leslie,

I want to leave here but I want some inducement. I don't want this guy to win the pennant and I feel if I stay here I will win it for him. You know I can pitch and win. So you see the fellows, and if you want to, send a man over here with the goods, and I will leave for home on the next train. Send him to my house so nobody will know, and send him at night. I am living at 145 Wadsworth Avenue, Apartment 1R. Nobody will ever know. I will go down to fishing camp and stay there. I am asking you this so there won't be any trouble to anyone. Call me up if you all are sending a man. Wadsworth 3210. Do this right away. Let me know. Regards to all.

Phil Douglas

Later, Phil Douglas explained to a reporter that after sending the letter, he called Les Mann that night and asked him to tear it up. But, he said, Mann crossed him. On Rickey's advice, Mann forwarded the letter to Judge Landis.

A week went by. The Giants were playing at home but Phil Douglas stayed away from the ballpark. The team doctor came to see him several times and drugs were administered. Douglas was not told what they were. McGraw had Phil report to the Polo Grounds to have his arm tested. He worked out strongly and McGraw ordered him to join the team for their western swing. Douglas didn't know that McGraw and Landis had already agreed on a rendezvous in Pittsburgh where the road trip would begin. On August 15 all three checked into the Hotel Schenley. They all met the next morning when Phil was summoned to Landis' suite.

A grim faced Judge Landis stood beside John McGraw. In his hand Landis held "the letter." Asked it he had written it, Douglas admitted it, stammering an explanation about how a man needed to live. That he had figured he was out of a job and wanted to salvage something from the wreckage of his career. It was Douglas' chance to tell the commissioner how he had been treated by McGraw and the Giants, but he hung his head and waited for the ax to fall. It did.

Judge Landis pointed a bony finger and declared, "Douglas, you are out of organized baseball." Phil Douglas was stunned. He searched the faces of the two men who were condemning him to a bleak life without an ability to pitch baseball, the only way he knew how to make a living for his family. There was no pity or sympathy for him from Landis and McGraw. Phil Douglas shuffled out of the suite and out of baseball.

There was never a reprieve. Douglas went back to his roots, back to doing odd jobs, pitching now and then for a local team against barnstorming visitors. He reached the Depression years, lucky to find a job with the WPA when Franklin D. Roosevelt was elected in 1932. Twenty years of a hard life, the death of his first wife, Louise, and the raising of his daughters, Mary Louise and Eunice Lee, and knowing his grandchildren was ended by a series of strokes. He was left bedridden, cared for by his second wife, Jacqueline, in a shack on a back lot of a relative's property. He died in his sleep on July 31, 1952. There were 250 floral pieces crammed around his coffin at the small Sequatchie Valley Baptist Church where the services were held. Phil Douglas was still a popular hero to the country folks with whom he had lived out his years of banishment from baseball.

From time to time a newspaper writer has done a story about Shufflin' Phil Douglas and the injustice done to him. In 1979, a wonderfully researched book, *One Last Round for the Shuffler*, was published. It was written by Tom Clark. In soft cover the 160 page book, with many family photos as well as major league pictures, cost $4.95. Not many copies were printed and book is now a collector's item, bringing high prices for the few copies which turn up. Try your inter-library loan service. The book is well worth reading. Who knows? If enough people learn the sad story of Phil Douglas, a successful effort to have him restored to eligibility might be made. His case seems more worthy than those of confessed culprits and convicted felons. Unlike others who stir emotional pleas for clemency for past sins, poor Phil never committed any. He never threw a game, never bribed any one, never bet on a ballgame, his team or another, never did anything but drink too much too often, and write a letter.

6

"Roaring Bill" Kennedy: The First of the Daffy Dodgers

Bill Kennedy is listed in baseball encyclopedias as "Brickyard." He was better known to those within earshot as "Roaring Bill." Bill had a loud voice. His conversation was bellowed, as though he were across the room instead of the dining room table. When he asked someone to pass the potatoes, it sounded like a demand.

Bill, from the small Ohio city of Bellaire, was not prepared for the cosmopolitan life of a major league baseball player. Luckily, he joined Brooklyn when they were known as "the Bridegrooms." A flurry of marriages to Brooklyn girls had changed the rough-edged ballplayers into teammates who could enjoy Kennedy's eccentricities without putting him through the hazing usually given unsophisticated rookies. John Montgomery Ward, a gentlemanly graduate of Columbia University's law school, was the manager. He and the wealthy Charles Byrne, who owned the team, set the tone for expected behavior. They were put to the test the day Bill Kennedy burst into their office at Eastern Park to report for the 1892 season. Kennedy was late to check in, having been lost in transit from his home in Ohio.

Ward and Byrne were startled by the rookie's manner and appearance. His clothes were even louder than his voice. He was dressed in a fashion worn only by traveling salesmen and on vaudeville stages by "rube comics." His suit was a bilious yellow, with wide green checks. A pink shirt, a bright red bow tie, an out of season straw boater and highly polished "yaller shoes" completed the rookie's attire. He held a legal looking document in his hand.

"Brought my contract with me," he said.

"Anything wrong with it?" asked a puzzled manager. "We've been waiting to hear from you."

"Nah, nothing wrong. I had a lawyer friend back home check it over and he says its okay. It's already signed."

Looking back, Ward and Byrne might have guessed their loud voiced rookie was also illiterate. Kennedy's inability to read and write led to many hilarious misunderstandings.

After taking the new comer around and introducing him to his incredulous teammates, Monty Ward turned him over to one of the veterans to help him find a place to live. Although most of the regulars were qualified "bridegrooms," living with their wives, many unwed rookies and elusive bachelors lived in boarding houses near Eastern Park. Bill Kennedy was checked into one and was advised by his mentor that he replace his new outfit with more subdued duds. He learned the rules of the house. It was easy to handle meals. He'd just sit down at the communal dinner table and help himself as platters were passed around. It wouldn't be until the team went on the road and ate in hotel dining rooms that he would have to face a printed menu. For a time he avoided revealing that he couldn't read one. He would wait until a teammate ordered a dinner that he liked. He'd look brightly up from the menu he'd been pretending to study and say, "that sounds good. I'll have the same."

Then one evening Bill Kennedy was late getting to a hotel dining room. The other players had eaten and were filing out. Thinking quickly, he asked the last one out the door, "didja have a good meal?" When he was told the meal had been a good one, Bill told the waiter, "I'll have the same as he did."

Dinner ended with a dessert which Bill had never seen before. He was told it was a new confection called Charlotte Russe. It was sponge cake, served in a cardboard cone and topped with whipped cream.

The player who had guided Bill's dinner choice asked later if he had enjoyed dinner. "It was very good," Kennedy told him, "except for the dessert. I guess Amos Rusie has a sister and they named it for her. It tasted all right except for the crust. I could hardly chew it."

Brooklyn's schedule called for a game with the New York Giants at the Polo Grounds. Directions to New York City's uptown ballpark were written out and posted in the Brooklyn clubhouse. Kennedy stared at them uncomprehendingly. Saying something about needing his glasses, he asked that the message be read to him. He listened carefully. "Take the trolley marked for the Brooklyn Bridge and go over to the New York side. You take an uptown elevated train. Anyone can tell you when to get off for the Polo Grounds. If you have any trouble just ask a policeman," he was advised.

On the Manhattan side of the Brooklyn Bridge, Bill looked around and spotted one of "New York's finest." Kennedy approached him with a smile and outstretched hand. In an out-of-town twang he said, "Hi, I'm from out of town, come from Bellaire in Ohio. I'm a little turned around and I'd appreciate it if you'd help me find my way to where I'm going."

The policeman assumed Bill was on his way back to Ohio. He told him, "just take this cross town trolley to the Hudson River. The ferries there will take you over to the Jersey side. The trains going west leave from there."

Bill let himself be put aboard the cross town trolley and ended up on a train that would take him to Bellaire. Being a bit homesick, he simply went back home. After a few days, he had someone send a postal card to the ball club saying where he was and someone was sent to bring him back to Brooklyn. Soon he was off on an impressive major league career that falls just short of making him a candidate for the Baseball Hall of Fame in Cooperstown, New York.

For a number of years a group of sports-minded citizens in Bellaire conducted a campaign to have their home town hero posthumously honored. He never did receive substantial support and when a committee was appointed to thin out the ranks of the nineteenth century candidates, Bill Kennedy did not make the cut. His 12 year total of 187 victories, even with a .540 winning average, was not enough to impress the selection committee, none of whom had ever seen any of the candidates play. Despite four seasons when he won 20 or more games, Bill Kennedy's idiosyncrasies are more memorable than his pitching record.

In his second year, Bill Kennedy was the work horse of a team which lacked any other pitchers of note. He won 25 games, but also lost 20. His best career day on the mound came on Memorial Day, May 30, 1893. Kennedy pitched a double header, winning both games from Louisville, 3–0 and 6–2, giving up 8 hits in all. Two years later, on Labor Day, September 7, 1895, Roaring Bill came within a whisper of a no-hitter, marred by a lone Cincinnati single in a 6–1

Brooklyn win. Kennedy had a knack of winning news-making ballgames.

In 1897, when pennant bound Boston had won 17 in a row, Bill Kennedy stopped them. That night, in the Hub city, the visiting Bridegrooms celebrated by going to the theater. They went to see Edwin Booth in Shakespeare's Hamlet. They invited Bill, who was suspicious he wouldn't like it. The other players told him Hamlet was a comedy. "Biggest laughs you'll ever have," they assured him. Dubiously, Kennedy went along, falling into a trap. The players had bought a block of seats, three deep. Bill's ticket was for the center seat in the middle row. He was hemmed in by teammates.

Bill squirmed through the opening scenes. "When does it get funny?" he asked.

"In the next scene," they promised him, "Hamlet has a lot of good lines. You'll die laughing."

Soon Bill realized he had been duped by his buddies. He wanted out. He couldn't get past the knees of his companions in the dark and those in front and behind him couldn't be budged. Not until the intermission lights came up was Bill Kennedy able to vault over a couple of rows of seats and bolt for the exit.

Although Roaring Bill was good-natured about the tricks his friends played on him, he had a temper on the ballfield. Later in 1897 he ran into Hank O'Day, an umpire around whom controversy constantly swirled.

On July 31, after O'Day had made several decisions to which Kennedy took loud exception, the umpire stalked away. Roaring Bill hurled the ball after him. Pinpoint control had never been a Kennedy asset. Each season he walked more batters than he fanned. As usual, his control was off and the ball whizzed past O'Day's ear. While it was being chased down, George Davis scored the winning run for the Giants.

Through his years with Brooklyn, Bill Kennedy usually pitched the season opener. In 1899, on April 15, he hooked up in a duel with future H of F member, Kid Nichols of Boston. While 21,000 watched, the scoreless game reached the eleventh inning before Boston's Fred Tenney tripled home the winning run. Bill ended up 22–9 with pennant-winning Brooklyn and was 20–13 when they repeated in 1900, ending one century and starting a new one with pennants. Ned Hanlon was the new manager, adding the two Brooklyn pennants to the three he had won earlier in Baltimore. A popular vaudeville act of acrobats was billed as Hanlon's Flying Superbas. The team nickname was switched from the Bridegrooms to the Supurbas in Ned Hanlon's honor.

While they still qualified as the Bridegrooms, Roaring Bill Kennedy married a local lady about whom nothing is known except some old Bellaire gossip. Bill returned after one season with a bride who carried an infant in her arms. They climbed down from the train in Bellaire's dusty depot, facing on Main Street.

Mrs. Kennedy looked up and down the quiet center of her husband's home town. She compared it with the metropolitan life she had left behind and changed her mind about staying. She and Bill's daughter boarded a train headed back east and she was never seen again, either in Bellaire or by Bill. He lived out his years as a bachelor. Somewhere there may be descendants of Roaring Bill Kennedy, unaware of a major league ball playing ancestor.

A sore arm ended Bill Kennedy's career in Brooklyn in 1901.

After two 20 game winning seasons, he went 3 and 5. The Giants signed him but the newly arrived manager, John McGraw, sold Roaring Bill to Pittsburgh for the 1903 season. There was to be an innovation in post season play that year. An event called the World Series would be inaugurated. The newly established American League would send its champion to meet the National League's pennant winner in a best of nine series. It was an instant media success. Both the Boston Pilgrims, later the Red Sox, and the Pittsburgh Pirates were easy pennant winners and the first "fall classic" brought a new interest as the year moved into October.

Pittsburgh had only one top pitcher ready for the series, Deacon Phillippe. He was almost enough. Sam Leever, top man on the staff, had injured his shoulder in a trap shooting contest and pitched with an impaired shoulder. Ed Doheny, who had won 20 games, had a mental breakdown late in the season and was in an institution. Boston had the great Cy Young and, for the season, an equally great Bill Dinneen. What with travel time and rain cancellations, Young and Dinneen alternated the first four starts for Boston, losing three games to Phillippe. It looked bleak for Boston, but Pittsburgh had run out of starting pitchers and Cy Young would try to pull Boston back into contention.

The date was October 7. It was Roaring Bill Kennedy's 36th birthday. From 50 miles down the Ohio River, trainloads of Bill Kennedy's friends and neighbors traveled to Pittsburgh to see if Bill could take Cy Young. It was a meeting of two Ohio born pitchers, Cy coming from Peoli.

Kennedy had been a spot starter. He had started 15 games and won nine of them, one a shutout. Manager Fred Clarke had no one else to send to the mound. The game was a scoreless duel for the first five innings. Then, in the top of the sixth, Boston's leadoff man was safe when manager Fred Clarke, in left field, pulled up to avoid a collision with Honus Wagner, charging out from shortstop. Then a single, then a Wagner error when he dropped a force out throw covering third base.

Bill Kennedy's always uncertain control—he'd once walked six Phillies in a row in one inning—wavered and a base on balls forced in the first run. On a grounder to short stop, Wagner scooped up the ball and whipped it to second. No one had covered the base. The throwing error sent two more runners home. Both base runners moved up on a sacrifice bunt. Cy Young scored them both with a long triple. Dougherty also tripled, scoring Young for the sixth run of the inning. Kennedy was hit hard for four runs in the seventh inning. That was the end for Roaring Bill Kennedy. Wagner's errors alone had been enough to cost him the game. Time had tired his arm and he could not match Cy Young inning for shut out inning. After that game the tide of the World Series turned. Deacon Phillippe could not win again and the Young-Dinneen duo defeated Pittsburgh in eight games.

Disappointed that his friends had seen him lose his final major league game, Bill Kennedy went home to Bellaire. He was a popular man, organizing a strong independent baseball club, Kennedy's All Stars. They played all comers, eventually meeting the Honus Wagner All Stars after the Flying Dutchman retired to live in Pittsburgh. There was no love lost between the two men. Kennedy reminded Wagner of the game when he made two errors behind him. The 1903 World Series had not been a good one for Honus. He played on a bad leg, batting only .222 and making six errors.

Kennedy was a sometime bar owner and some time patron. He came to visit Brooklyn in 1914, while on a trip to Atlantic City with a group of Elks. He detoured just to see the modern Ebbets Field, opened two years earlier. He was welcomed in the press box by writers, some of whom had never seen him pitch, but had heard stories about Roaring Bill. Those who had been there in Kennedy's time had difficulty recognizing him. The once strapping six-footer showed signs of the cancer which ravaged him. It killed him the following year, back home in Bellaire on September 23, 1915. His grave is known, but it has no stone to mark it.

7

Bill Lange: San Fransisco's Other Great Center Fielder

Bill Lange and Joe DiMaggio have more in common than a San Francisco birthplace. Lange played in the 1890s, a time in baseball when power was reflected in doubles and triples, not home runs. Joe DiMaggio starred when power prevailed. Statistical comparisons of players from drastically different eras are specious. What can be judged more impartially is the status a player had among his contemporaries. How was he regarded among his peers when he played? Joe DiMaggio's admirers called him "The Yankee Clipper." He outranked all other center fielders during the first seven seasons he played for the New York Yankees. After time out for military service in World War II, he returned for six more seasons, not quite as stellar as his earlier career.

Joe DiMaggio's first seven years provide a perfect comparison with Bill Lange who only played seven seasons of major league ball. From 1893 through 1899, playing for Cap Anson's Chicago Cubs, Lange drew rave reviews for his dashing style of play. Unlike DiMaggio, whose feats were usually accomplished with the extra attention given to pennant winners, Lange's Cubs got out of second division only once, a distant fourth in a 12 team league in 1894. Otherwise, his star had to shine in the darkness of second division.

Over his first seven seasons, Joe DiMaggio's batting average was .337. When Bill Lange retired his mark was .336. Re-examination of box scores of the 1890s lowered this to .330, still a comparable figure. However, that is the only statistic that can be used for comparison. All others are the result of styles of play and length of seasons. These differences make statistic by statistic comparisons a matter of judgmental weighting.

Bill Lange's feats had to be spectacular to catch attention. They were not the kind that decided pennants. They were seen only be the spectators at the game. Reporters described them in words. The press also reported Bill Lange's antics off the field. On one occasion, Lange, the playboy and the player, were combined. Clark Griffith, a nineteenth century star pitcher and twentieth century manager and magnate would recall both Lange's behavior, which drew a stiff fine, and a game-saving catch which resulted in his manager rescinding it.

Lange's catch was the final out of an 11 inning pitching duel between Griffith and Win Mercer, an early Washington ace. The game was played in Washington and Bill Lange barely made it to the playing field. Known for spending late hours in saloons, Lange missed the team train to Washington. He overslept the next train as well. Finally, he climbed aboard a train to catch up with his team. The game was about to start when Lange sprinted past manager Cap Anson to take his position in the field. Between innings Lange was told, "Your lateness will cost you $100." When Lange smiled and shrugged his shoulders, Anson upped the fine to $200.

Chicago broke the tie by scoring in the top of the eleventh. Griffith's job was to hold the one run lead. He got the first two batters but the next batter walked. That brought Al Selbach to the plate. Even in a dead ball era, Washington's slugger was capable of clearing the fence. He tagged a pitch and drove it on a high arc to the deepest part of center field. Back, back, back raced Bill Lange as the tying and winning runs circled the bases. At the last second, Bill Lange made a turning leap and grabbed the ball in his tiny glove. His momentum carried him crashing into the board fence. The ball was not jarred loose. It was clutched in Bill's grip as he struck the fence. Boards flew and when the debris had settled, Bill Lange, covered with splinters, was holding the ball for the final out.

Bill Lange's nimble footedness earned him the nickname, "Lil' Eva." Harriet Beecher Stowe's heroine in *Uncle Tom's Cabin* was remembered for escaping across freezing waters by leaping from one ice floe to the next. By a journalistic stretch, this was compared to the way Bill Lange covered the expanses of nineteenth century outfields. His base stealing feats contributed to the metaphor, although Ms. Stowe's heroine never had to slide. When Bill led the league in stolen bases in 1897, different rules accounted for them. For many years he was thought to have broken the century mark. However, as later baseball statisticians applied revised scoring methods to games of the past, Lange's leading total shrank to 73. This is far more than Joe DiMaggio ever swiped, although the graceful Yankee was admired for his base running skills.

So, why did superstar Bill Lange only play seven seasons, quitting when only 28 years old? Love, or perhaps, a wish for security, ended his career. He told the Cubs on November 11, 1899, they would have to plan their team for the new century without him. He had courted one of San Francisco's daughters, both pretty and rich. Her father, a self-made magnate in real estate, considered a professional baseball player an unsuitable match for his daughter. He made Bill an offer he couldn't resist. Give up baseball and become a partner in his successful company. Lange accepted the offer. There was no Baseball Hall of Fame beckoning a future installation in Cooperstown, New York in 1899. It wasn't dedicated until forty years later. The idea of playing a minimum of ten seasons in order to be eligible for election would not have occurred to anyone in Lange's time.

Bill had the best of possible worlds. He was free to continue to play locally, particularly the classy winter league that existed in the Bay area. He had already recruited a strapping first baseman from the local scene for the Chicago Cubs. A teammate for Lange's final two season was Frank "Husk" Chance. Then Lange left and Chance stayed on to become "The Peerless Leader," winning three pennants for the Cubs and, himself, reaching the Hall of Fame. This honor was primarily the result of Franklin P. Adam's doggerel rhyme, "Tinker to Evers to Chance," which put all three into the Hall of Fame.

The San Francisco earthquake of 1908 crippled local baseball. It also had another impact on Bill Lange, the real estate operator. It demolished much of the city. Judging from Bill Lange's subsequent prosperity, he fared well in rebuilding San Francisco. However, despite its romantic start, the Lange marriage did not last. Much of Bill Lange's real estate profits went into a divorce settlement.

However, Bill Lange lived on to witness the arrival of Joe DiMaggio and to comment favorably on the next native son to achieve center field stardom. In 1941 when Joe DiMaggio's 56 consecutive game hitting streak was set, he broke Willie Keeler's record set back in 1894. Bill Lange gave interviews to the San Francisco papers, explaining how Wee Willie, his rival, had "hit 'em where they ain't."

Lange died in 1950, at age 79, in San Francisco. Joe DiMaggio was still playing but retired with his pride intact after 1951. Joe was elected to the Baseball Hall of Fame in 1955. Later, Bill Lange sent his nephew, "Long George" Kelly, another superstar born in San Francisco, to Cooperstown as his proxy. Also called "High Pockets," Kelly's full name was George Lange Kelly. Kelly's mother was Bill Lange's sister and young Kelly had adored his uncle. In accepting his plaque when he was inducted in 1973, Bill's nephew told the audience, "You should've seen my Uncle Bill play!"

8

Bugs Raymond: The Nickname Tells The Sad Story

There have always been baseball players of promise or prominence who have destroyed their own careers. Today's million-dollar stars most often do it with drugs. Alcohol was the demon of choice when Arthur Raymond set the pace for those who drink themselves into oblivion. Few players ever followed such a determined, if unsteady, path to disaster as "Bugs." His nickname is the tipoff. It was given him for his behavior, a shortened form of "bughouse," as insane asylums were called.

Raymond might have passed, like a hiccup in the night, had he remained in the last-place obscurity of the St. Louis Cardinals. However, he became a reclamation project for John J. McGraw, the martinet manager of the New York Giants. In 1908, the Giants lost the pennant to the Chicago Cubs in a playoff game caused by "Merkle's boner." The story of how rookie Fred Merkle failed to touch second when he saw "the winning run" score on a base hit has been told many times. And it is also well known that McGraw never turned his famous temper on the young first baseman. What did leave McGraw furious was the lack of another top flight pitcher to join 37-game winner Christy Mathewson. Between seasons he looked for a way to improve the team he considered the best in the league, no matter what tricky decisions umpires called against him.

He knew where a superstar pitcher was buried with a last-place team.

Bugs Raymond had already earned his nickname and a drinker's reputation. But in a rotation that only required he be reasonably sober every fourth day, he had won 15 games, nearly a third of the meager 49 the Cardinals won all the 1908 season. True, he had led the league in losses, with 25, but he had a 2.03 ERA and had been fourth in strikeouts with 145. Mathewson had led everyone with 259. Still, despite his renowned dissipation, Bugs Raymond was tied for second with 48 games pitched. In shape or not, he showed up when his turn came around. All he needed, McGraw reasoned, was a strong hand to steer him onto the right path and he would join Matty at the top of the staff. Connie Mack once had held the same expectation of Rube Waddell. Mack was a saintly man with enduring patience, but it had run out after six seasons of the Rube's antics. McGraw's temperament was the opposite of Mack's. However, McGraw knew he could not browbeat Bugs Raymond into becoming a reformed drunk. It would take strategy, John McGraw's strong suit.

First, he had to get the Cardinals to give up their one prize player. McGraw held an ace card. St. Louis, in the manner of managements of tailenders, believed a change of managers was necessary. John McCloskey, having suffered his second eighth-place finish, was perhaps too tolerant. The Cards coveted the Giants' great backstop, Roger Bresnahan, to run the team from behind the bat. McGraw made them pay a high price. In addition to Raymond, he took Red Murray, a hard-hitting outfielder, whose immediate payoff in 1909 was to lead the National League with a Dead Ball Era home run total of seven.

Needing a catcher to replace Bresnahan, McGraw persuaded St. Louis to get Admiral Schlei, nicknamed for a now forgotten naval hero, from the Cincinnati Reds and include him in the Bresnahan package. Schlei was a first-class catcher. To get him the Cards turned over two starting pitchers. One, Art Fromme, won 19 games for the Reds the next season.

Bresnahan failed to make a significant change in the Cardinals' future pennant races. After four second-division finishes, he was replaced by Miller Huggins, who began a Hall of Fame managerial career in St. Louis.

Bugs Raymond arrived penniless in Marlin, Texas, where McGraw's Giants assembled for spring training. Warned of Bug's insistence on spending all his money for booze, McGraw had drawn up a contract with Mrs. Raymond. She was an invalid and lived in Chicago, where Raymond had grown up. She was paid her husband's salary directly. This met her bills and enabled her to put away money for the times between seasons. She was forbidden to send Bugs any money. What pocket money he obtained he got directly from McGraw, one thin dime at a time. It would buy an ice-cream soda, nothing stronger.

This began a series of maneuvers between two adversaries, the tyrannical manager and the wily drunk. Bugs Raymond was a man of great charm when it suited his purpose. As his purpose was to drink himself insensible, Raymond spent his time trying to find ways to outwit McGraw's stratagems. McGraw learned not to give Bugs a pack of cigarettes, which he could sell. Bugs had to roll his own with Bull Durham. Other players were ordered to always open a pack Bugs might wheedle from them and take out several cigarettes to spoil the resale value.

McGraw was responsible for keeping his pitcher clothed, but when he bought him a suit, Bugs immediately returned it to the clothing store and persuaded the tailor to exchange it for a less expensive model. He came out seven dollars ahead and was off on a monumental drunk.

1909 was the only useful season McGraw got out of his wayward spitball pitcher. Bugs turned in an 18–12 record, behind Matty's 25–6 and leading 1.14 ERA. Even with Hooks Wiltse contributing 20 wins, the Giants were no match for Honus Wagner and the 1909 Pittsburgh Pirates. McGraw's team fell short and ended the season without the services of Raymond.

At one point the exasperated McGraw hired a former New York policeman, Dick Fuller, to keep track of the wandering pitcher and file a report. Raymond spotted the detective and decided to lead the flatfoot on a tiring trail. He strolled along, eyeing items in store windows, cutting across lots covered with broken bricks and shards of smashed glass. He walked miles and roundabout miles back to the hotel. It took hours and Fuller, his feet aching, trailed Bugs all the way. He wrote a report for McGraw and turned in a masterpiece of injured self-justification.

McGraw summoned Raymond to his dressing room office and closed the door. "Listen to this," he roared and read aloud from Fuller's account of trailing Raymond. "It says here, after leaving the ball park, instead of going directly to the hotel, you walked down Eighth Avenue and went to Tom Fannion's bar over on 145th Street. You went to the free lunch counter and helped yourself to a cheese and onion sandwich."

Raymond was outraged. "That's a dirty lie. I never ate an onion in my life!"

The stories of Bugs Raymond's determined efforts to evade McGraw's surveillance are part of baseball legend. The one which is told most often is of him trading a baseball for two shots of whiskey, but the swap involved a lot more. At the Polo Grounds, there was an exit from the clubhouse onto Eighth Avenue, which was lined with bars. Bugs was warming up in the bullpen late in a game when suddenly he was gone from McGraw's view. The manager sent one of his substitutes out to the center field warmup area to locate Raymond. Then, suddenly, Bugs was seen again, tossing his warmup pitches. Confronted by McGraw after the game, his nonchalant explanation was that he had gone into the clubhouse briefly to relieve himself.

Someone snitched and McGraw learned that Bugs Raymond had slipped out the back way to Eighth Avenue. Bugs had swapped his warmup ball to the first bartender he found for a drink. Fortified, he scrambled back into the Polo Grounds. McGraw tracked down the friendly bartender and told him, and every bartender along the street, that if Bugs Raymond ever tried that trick again, he'd have his friends at City Hall cancel the bar's liquor license.

The next time Raymond decided in the middle of his bull pen warmup that his thirst needed slaking, he took the ball, offering it in trade but with no takers. Finally, he entered a bar far enough uptown that McGraw's warning had not reached its owner. Here Bugs Raymond swapped the ball for a couple of shots of rye and washed them down with beer chasers. He got back to the ball park, but the game was over and the jig was up. Bugs Raymond never finished a season with the Giants. Even the year he won 18 games, he was suspended in the final weeks. Ironically, it was a breach of conduct while soberly having a glass of water with his dinner in a restaurant that caused his downfall.

The waiter, a baseball fan, kept pressing Bugs to reveal how he threw his spitball. The waiter pestered Bugs. How did he get the ball to break? Finally, Raymond drained his water glass and used it to demonstrate his spitter. He wet two of his fingers and wrapped them around the glass. Standing beside the table he took an elaborate windup and threw the glass across the room, shattering it against the wall.

"There," he said, resuming his dinner, "did you see it 'break'?"

Finally, Bugs Raymond disrupted McGraw's peace of mind a final, and for him, fatal time. He was banished. There was no place for him and his thirst in baseball. Instead of contributing to a string of Giant pennants, Bugs Raymond was doomed by his unquenchable thirst.

He went back to Chicago to pitch semipro ball. Then baseball fans read in the papers that Arthur "Bugs" Raymond was dead at age 30. He was found in a rooming house, and, at first, it was thought he had died of heat and suffocation on September 7, 1912. But an autopsy showed he had died of a cerebral hemorrhage and a fractured skull. Investigation turned up an assailant who admitted being with Bugs at a ball game at Lawrence and Elston Avenues. He admitted having coshed him with a brick in a fight. Bugs had made it back to his rooming house to die.

Mrs. Arthur L. Raymond appeared at the inquest and explained that they had been separated for several years. His drinking had become intolerable. Bugs Raymond's potential, perhaps nearly as good as Matty's, was never realized. Bugs is forever trapped in baseball's memory for his alcoholic sprees and not for the victories he might have won had he been able to win the critical one over himself.

9

The Brooklyn Bridegrooms First Widow

A century ago Brooklyn was a city made up of dozens of small communities. They were linked together in a spirit of neighborliness that was derided by the sophisticates of Manhattan. Each community had its churches, taverns, and ball fields. Houses were large not out of ostentation, but to provide bedrooms for large families. Brooklyn was a grand place to raise children. The romantic expectations of marriage were fulfilled amid friendly neighbors. The professional baseball players who wore Brooklyn on their uniforms shared the middle class values of the community so enthusiastically that many of them became newlyweds. They married local girls or brought a wife from back home when a baseball season began. Eventually, the team earned the nickname, "The Bridegrooms."

In 1892, Hub Collins, the latest player to marry, brought his bride from Louisville, Kentucky to set up housekeeping for the approaching baseball season. The married players mostly lived in rented houses near Eastern Park, where the team played its games. The few holdout bachelors lived in boardinghouses along what is now Pitkin Avenue. The manager, John Montgomery Ward, commuted from Manhattan across the Brooklyn Bridge. He was unmarried, having recently been divorced by the musical comedy headliner Helen Dauvray. However, this uncharacteristic circumstance was prudently overlooked by the populace. Monte Ward had more value to Brooklyn's baseball fans than simply being a good family man. Those they already had in abundance.

John Montgomery Ward was a rare educated man among the rough and ready players of the time. Between seasons, Ward studied law at Columbia University. The fans were duly impressed by Monte Ward's erudition, but they appreciated his ability on the ball field even more. After many seasons as one of baseball's best pitchers, Ward had switched to shortstop. He was paired with Hub Collins as a surehanded keystone combination.

There was a special bonding among professional ball players 100 years ago, not just the Brooklyn Bridegrooms. The players were even more in revolt against the owners of teams than they are today. They had no union and today's multi-million dollar contracts were beyond imagination. In 1890 Monte Ward had organized the Players League. For one season the ball players controlled their salaries.

However, the established National League outwaited the underfunded outlaws. When the Players League collapsed, the next year it was business as usual on the owner's penny-pinching terms.

The Brooklyn Bridegrooms had won the National League pennant in 1890 more by default than ability. While the stars of the other teams jumped to the new Players League, believing in Monte Ward's vision and promises, Brooklyn's players listened to their wives. A steady paycheck was too important in their households to risk in a dispute with management. The Bridegrooms, having benefited from weakened opposition in 1890, were content to be comfortably in the middle of the pack two years later.

Monte Ward, the leader of the aborted Players League, was now in exile as Brooklyn's playing manager. Hub Collins was his second baseman. A woodcut drawing shows Collins was a good looking 28-year-old man, modishly wearing a pompadour hairstyle and a handlebar mustache of modest dimensions. He threw and batted righthanded. He was 5'8" and weighed 160 pounds. Collins was a steady player, solid defensively, and he left a respectable .284 batting average behind in the record books. In 1892 he was beginning his seventh major league season.

Soon after Mr. and Mrs. George Hubert Collins had settled into their new home, the Bridegrooms traveled to New England to play Boston. Collins returned a sick man. Typhoid fever was a constant threat in the non-septic nineteenth century. Baseball players might have been at an even higher risk. The fever usually was traced to drinking water and the players shared a common pail and dipper on the bench.

Collins had played his final game on May 14. A week later he was dead of typhoid-pneumonia.

The sudden death of the popular player and the plight of his widow touched off a remarkable response. A benefit baseball game, to be played May 29, a Sunday, was proposed. Arcane, but rigorously imposed "blue laws" prohibited playing baseball professionally on the Sabbath. Yet even in "The City of Churches," as Brooklyn was then called, a charity game for a good cause would not only be allowed, but the power of many pulpits would add to the publicity. Monte Ward, who had never played baseball on Sunday out of principle, made the Hub Collins Benefit Game the only exception in his long career.

A well-known opponent to face the suddenly bereaved Bridegrooms was needed to draw a good crowd. Fate, unkind to Hub Collins, smiled on the promoters of the benefit for his widow. The best team of recent years had been the dynastic St. Louis Browns. They had won four straight pennants, 1885–1888, in the then major league American Association. In 1889, Brooklyn had ended the Browns string of pennants before moving into the National League. The elements of a rivalry remained and many of the former St. Louis Browns, now with new teams, were about to play in Memorial Day games in New York and Brooklyn.

Dave Foutz, who organized the game, was a former pitcher with the Browns. He was now an outfielder with Brooklyn and could be spared for the game. Charley Comiskey, for whom two Chicago ball parks have been named, currently played first base for Cincinnati. The Reds were in town for a Memorial Day game with the Bridegrooms.

In addition to ex-Brownie Comiskey, the Reds also had Tip O'Neil. In 1887 he had batted an incredible .492. Granted, in 1887 bases on balls were counted as base hits, but even after the stats are adjusted to modern rules, O'Neil's consequent .435 is the second highest average of all time.

Cincinnati also sent along three of the best players in the league, Bid McPhee, Arlie Latham, and Pete Browning. They were among the 19th century's greatest players. Browning was such a renowned batter that Hillerich and Bradsby, wood turners in Hub Collins's own home town, had fashioned the first Louisville Slugger for him.

Other ex-Browns were found across the Brooklyn Bridge. The present St. Louis team had Parisian Bob Caruthers, a star pitcher. They were to play the Giants at the Polo Grounds on Memorial Day. When the Giants contributed Shorty Fuller, former Browns shortstop, and their own catcher, Morgan Murphy, the team was set. Made up of some of the best players of the time and representing five different teams, it can be considered as baseball's first All Star team.

Notable among the Brooklyn players was Dan Brouthers, winner of four batting titles, who played first base and, of course, Monte Ward. He had moved from shortstop and taken Hub Collins's place at second base. Brouthers and Ward are honored with plaques in the Baseball Hall of Fame in Cooperstown, New York. Adonis Terry, one of the few remaining bachelors on the Bridegrooms, would be on the mound. His matinee idol good looks attracted ladies to games on the days he was scheduled to pitch.

The New York Times reported over 7,000 were present and gate receipts netted $2,804.90. Players and friends donated cash and a special program was sold. The paper predicted the purse for Mrs. Hub Collins would exceed $3,000. Played under sunny skies, with the outfield at Eastern Park ringed by horse drawn carriages, the reassembled Browns, with their superstar reinforcements, won 6–1. The receipts added up to far more than a widow's mite at a time when even the charity game's all-star caliber players did not make as much for a season's salary.

This article first appeared in Oldtyme Baseball News, *Volume 5, Issue 5.*

10

Baseball's Phony Anniversary Party

Even before the doors of the Baseball Hall of Fame swung open 50 years ago, there was a tinge of uneasiness to the local boast that a native son, Abner Doubleday, had invented the national pastime. There was no plaque for Doubleday, although one for Alexander Cartwright was fastened to the wall. Historians had identified Cartwright as the one who laid out a diamond, with bases 90 feet apart. His rules included the basics of nine players to a side and two teams changing places after three were out.

Doubleday was not without identification. Nearby, the Works Progress Administration had built a ballpark on the site of a Cooperstown pasture where Lil' Abner might have romped with other boys at games with sticks and balls early in the nineteenth century. They named it Doubleday Field and left it for those who love a good story to further the fable of Abner Doubleday.

The claim that Doubleday had invented baseball was a fortuitous outcome of a search made in 1907 to find baseball's origins. It did not sit well with the jingoistic Americans of the time that the country's favorite sport owed its ancestry to the British Isles. To true believers, it was heresy when Henry Chadwick, baseball's first newspaper reporter and inventor of the box score, attributed baseball's origins to the ancient English game of rounders. When Harry Wright (who had organized and led baseball's first professional team, the 1868 Cincinnati Red Stockings, on an unbeaten tour) pointed to the obvious kinship to cricket, this was dismissed because he, like Chadwick, had been born in England and both were prejudiced.

Opposed to Chadwick and Wright—both of whom have been enshrined in the Hall of Fame—was Albert G. Spalding. He had been baseball's first professional pitcher, but gave up active play to become a sporting-goods tycoon whose company is still a major supplier of athletic equipment. Above all else, as America marched into the twentieth century, Al Spalding was a patriot and believed, with a zealot's fervor, that baseball owed nothing to English forebears. He insisted the game was too good, and too symbolically superior, to have been invented by the British.

Determined to find the Holy Grail of his faith, Spalding assembled a committee impressive in its blue-ribbon make-up, but also inclined to cower before Spalding's thundering dictates that they locate baseball's progenitor—and that he had better be an American. The committee lacked scholarship and research techniques and it was Spalding himself who produced the witness on whose memory rests the contention that a Cooperstown youth, Abner Doubleday, had sprung the whole game on his playmates one summer day in 1839.

An octogenarian named Albert Graves had written a letter to Spalding and offered a 68-year-old recollection that more than fit the purpose. The Doubleday lad had grown up to be Major General Abner Doubleday, a Union officer present at Fort Sumter when the first shots of the Civil War were fired. What better way to meet Spalding's expectation of parenthood than have the game created by a genuine American war hero? Instead of relying on fiction to substitute for fact, General Doubleday provided a welcome fact to enhance the fiction.

Actually, to America's baseball fans early in the twentieth century, it mattered little who had created the game they adored. Every town had its team and the big leagues provided larger-than-life heroes for boys to worship and elders to admire. The fans didn't care about ancestry. It would eventually be a matter of great interest, of course, in Cooperstown, New York, which Spalding's committee had decreed was baseball's birthplace.

Cooperstown already had an identity. It had been founded by the father of James Fenimore Cooper, whose Leatherstocking Tales had been a reading staple for boys of Al Spalding's generation. It was an idyllic community on the shores of Lake Otsego. Cooper had called the long, narrow lake "Glimmerglass" in his stories of colonial pioneers and the Indians they dispossessed of their land.

The area had been turned largely into estates where wealthy owners kept cool in the summers and abandoned the town to jobless locals in the winter. In the mid nineteenth-century, Cooperstown was the summer home of Edward Clark, whose fortune came from a partnership with Isaac Singer, an undisputed American inventor. Singer had patented the sewing machine, America's favorite appliance. Edward Clark was a lawyer and, as is often the case with attorneys, benefited both from the genuine achievement of Singer and the spurious accomplishments claimed for Doubleday.

The Singer connection made Clark a man of great wealth and his family became patrons of Cooperstown's civic affairs. The Clark family also built (and continued to expand) a town gymnasium, and endowed a scholarship fund for local students that is the envy of admissions officers at universities everywhere. He founded a Farmers' Museum, and, with the New York State Historical Association, established a folk-art museum. Both provide alternate or additional places to visit in Cooperstown.

In 1935, Edward Clark's grandson, Stephen, was told an old baseball had turned up in a nearby community and he bought it for five dollars. He decided to display it in the village library and the Clarks began to round up other artifacts without yet realizing they had taken the first steps toward creating a national shrine. Mindful of the Doubleday legend, the approaching one hundredth anniversary took on importance. Spurious or not, a centennial celebration could be organized. Such activities were good for civic pride and provided jobs for local people. Even if only a once-in-a-century event, any boost to the economy was welcome in the 1930s, the grim decade of the Great Depression.

The driving force which focused national interest on the glimmering of a local enterprise was Ford Frick, president of the National League. He had been a sportswriter and broadcaster and jumped from league publicist to president. Eventually, he became a commissioner of baseball and was a sharp administrator and motivator. He wasn't about to quibble whether baseball had first been played in Cooperstown, New York, or who had laid out the diamond and made up the rules. He wanted the attention and excitement of a major baseball event. He ignored the debunkers and disbelievers. He knew people preferred a good fable to a dull fact. Cooperstown is not far from Cardiff, New York, where P.T. Barnum had exhumed the Cardiff Giant and displayed it as a prehistoric discovery until it was proved a hoax (whereupon people continued to pay to view the fake that had fooled others).

Ford Frick enlisted the help of his former colleagues, the baseball writers, and they named the first five players elected to the Hall of Fame: Ty Cobb, Babe Ruth, Honus Wagner, Christy Mathewson, and Walter Johnson. They were elected in 1936; subsequently, other baseball greats were named, including nineteenth century stars who might have been forgotten. As remodeling continued on one of Ed Clark's gymnasium buildings, people excited by the concept of a baseball museum emptied their attics of old uniforms, gloves, balls from famous games, and bats which had been used to achieve unforgotten feats.

Finally, on June 12, 1939, major league baseball set aside a day to gather in Cooperstown and formally dedicate the Baseball Hall of Fame and Museum. Judge Landis, baseball's first commissioner, had given his blessing and 11 of baseball's living greats were there to be inducted: Ty Cobb, Babe Ruth, Honus Wagner, Walter Johnson, Nap Lajoie, Tris Speaker, Eddie Collins, Connie Mack, Grover Alexander, Cy Young, and George Sisler. Over at Doubleday Field, two all-star teams from the National and American leagues, their lineups studded with future Hall of Fame members, played a game. The U.S. Postmaster General, James A. Farley, sold special commemorative stamps at the post office.

The citizens of Cooperstown kept a good thing going all summer. There were special events almost every week. Williams and

Amherst Colleges, which had played the first college game in 1859, met at Doubleday Field. Teams of minor league stars faced off, and the New York Yankees, headed on a western swing, stopped off on August 21 to play an exhibition game with their Newark farm team.

Memories are magnets that attract baseball fans to Cooperstown. Sentimental pilgrimages are made by parents who want their children to know of the continuity of baseball. Today's heroes become the venerated idols of those who cherish the past. Each generation adds to the ranks of immortals. On July 23, 1989, Johnny Bench and Carl Yastrzemski were inducted. They were elected as promptly as the rules (waived once for Lou Gehrig) permit, five years after their careers ended and are fresh in memory. With them was a star several generations removed from his prominence, Red Schoendienst, and former umpire Al Barlick. Some 5,000 people gathered to watch the ceremonies on the steps of the library. They are part of the 250,000 tourists who come each year, providing jobs and income to the local economy.

This article appeared in Delta Airline's SKY Magazine *in 1989.*

11

No Touch At Second

Runner Fred Merkle should have gone on to second base, was the final decree. The game would be a tie. For both Giants and Cubs, the season would now rest on a rare playoff.

Henry McBride missed the climactic game of the 1908 baseball season. But that was not all he missed. McBride, a New York City fireman, wanted to see the end-of-season playoff game between the Chicago Cubs and his Giants. Like 250,000 others swirling around New York's Polo Grounds, he couldn't get inside. Frantic fans, some with tickets, and yet unable to pass the police lines because the ball park was overflowing, clogged the streets and sidewalks.

McBride and others agile and eager enough clambered up the pillars that supported the elevated train tracks outside the outfield fence. Hundreds perched, like curious sparrows, on cross beams. McBride had climbed as high as he could. He perhaps had a tantalizing glimpse of the green outfield grass before he lost his hold and plunged to the pavement below.

Instantly killed, the newspapers said, and went on to report the police had to use their billy clubs to hammer the hands of other enthusiasts who, leaping past the fallen McBride, wanted to climb the stanchions from which he had fallen—frantic to see the ball game that was about to be played.

One last game would finally decide the year's National League pennant race and conclude the most dramatic, controversial season ever played in the major leagues. Curiously, in 1908 both leagues ended with three teams virtually tied for first place, but only the National League would require a post-season contest. It would settle a bitterly disputed tie game played a few weeks earlier. The American League had squeezed to a finish. Detroit edged out Cleveland by half a game.

The 1908 season was one to keep the nation's sports interest at a fever pitch. The three teams dominating the National League in the early years of the century were locked in the tightest triumvirate of all time. Pittsburgh, Chicago, or New York won every pennant from 1901 to 1913 and, in 1908, all three were in hot contention from opening day until the season ended.

In the American League race there had been other frontrunners during the season than the final three. However, National League fans could check the paper every day and find either the Pirates, Cubs, or Giants on top and, by mid-season, the other two right on the heels of the leader.

After the last scheduled game had been played on October 7, the Cubs and Giants had identical records, 98–55. The Pirates had finished 98–56, assured the small comfort of a tie for second with whichever team lost the final Cubs-Giants contest. This post-season playoff would replay a rabidly disputed game which had been called a 1–1 tie on September 23. It was a game which stirred emotions, launched arguments, and bestowed on a rookie ball player, Fred Merkle, the nickname which haunted him all his life, even beyond baseball, "Bonehead."

In professional baseball shortly after the turn of the century, it was customary to scoot for the clubhouse, and get to the showers first, as soon as the winning run crossed home plate in the bottom of the last inning. True, Rule 59 specified a forced runner from first must run down and claim second base, even if the batter had made a clean hit and the winning run was across home plate beyond dispute. That was the rule, but the practice was to ignore it.

When the Giants came to bat in the bottom of the ninth in that disputed game of September 23, the score was tied, 1–1, and the great Christy Matheweson was locked in yet another duel with his frequent adversary, Mordecai "Three Fingered" Brown. The Cubs' only run had been an inside-the-park home run by Joe Tinker that outfielder Mike Donlin tried to stop by sticking his foot in the way of the bounding ball. He made amends later by driving in the Giants' only run.

Matty had retired the Cubs in the top of the ninth, and now Brown would try to do the same to the Giants and send the game into extra innings. He got the first batter out, but then Art Devlin singled. When Moose McCormick forced Devlin at second base there were two out and the tie was standing on first base. The rookie Fred Merkle won temporary favor with a single that sent McCormick to third. Then Al Bridwell, a light-hitting shortstop, rifled a line-drive single to center field, and Moose lumbered in with what should have been the winning run.

The crowd erupted, pouring out on the field, and then all hell broke loose. Merkle, in his innocence—but also in keeping with the custom of the time—deserted the base path and raced through the engulfing crowds. He was jubilant, but his euphoria was to last only a short while.

Was the game over? Not according to the Cubs. On September 4, in Pittsburgh, playing against the other team of the top trio, another rookie, Warren Gill of the Pirates, had done what Merkle did. As the winning run scored in the bottom of the tenth inning, Gill darted from the baseline before reaching second base and sprinted for the locker room. The crafty Johnny Evers shouted for the ball and, when it was thrown to him, stepped on second base and asked umpire Hank O'Day to call Gill out. It was a force play argued Evers, his manager, Frank Chance, and other belligerent Cub players. The run from third didn't count, they insisted.

O'Day, the game's only umpire, said he had been watching the run score and the batter reach first base. He wouldn't rule on the appeal at second base, claiming he hadn't seen the play. He refused further pleas from the Cubs, but worried about it. He was a stickler for rules. They meant much more to an umpire than custom.

As it turned out, for the Cubs-Giants game on September 23, Hank O'Day was again umpiring, this time with a partner, Bob Emslie. O'Day, the chief umpire, was behind the plate and Emslie was the base umpire. This time, when the Cubs again clamored for a ruling, O'Day was predisposed to make a decision in keeping with the rules of the game, not its customary practice.

With a sense of deja vu, O'Day this time hurried toward the

middle of the infield to watch whether the runner from first, Fred Merkle, actually reached second base. It was his partner's call, but Emslie had fallen, getting out of the way of Bridwell's hit, and, anyway, he hadn't been involved in the hassle in Pittsburgh on the similar play. O'Day was sure the Cubs would try the same appeal if Merkle didn't reach second base. Sure enough, with a crowd of spectators surrounding him, there was Evers again brandishing a baseball and screaming for O'Day's decision.

Before we consider O'Day's options, however, to say nothing of the cauldron of confusion that boiled up in the aftermath of the game, a review of the top teams for the 1908 National League season is in order.

The Chicago Cubs, whose double-play trio was to be immortalized in 1910 by the Franklin P. Adams poem, Tinker To Evers To Chance, were the defending champions. They had won the National League pennants, easily, in 1906 and 1907.

This was one of the finest all-around teams ever assembled. Defense was the team's strong suit; it led the league in fielding each of its pennant winning seasons.

A great pitching staff, which had a league-leading ERA the last three seasons, was headed by Mordecai "Three Fingered" Brown, whose pitching hand had been mutilated in a boyhood farm accident. With the exception of the Giants' Christy Mathewson, Brown was the league's most-praised pitcher. And, although Matty's total record was superior, when they faced each other, as they frequently did, it was more often Brown who won. He had beaten Matty in seven of 11 games before the 1908 season and would continue his mastery in the crucial games coming up.

Also, in any conflict with New York, the Chicago Cubs could call on left-hander Jack Pfiester, whose effectiveness against this particular opponent had earned him the nickname "Giant Killer." The Cubs also had the huge Orvie Overall and Ed Reulbach, the league-leader in winning percentage each of the Cubs' three championship years. Catching for these stalwarts was Johnny Kling, a smart, steady-hitting backstop with a deadly throwing arm.

The Pittsburgh Pirates were, more than either of their rivals, dominated by a single superstar, Honus Wagner. In 1908 he would win another of his eight batting titles. He would capture his fifth stolen-base title and lead the league in hits, doubles, triples, finish second in home runs, and have the best slugging average and the top mark in runs batted in.

The bow-legged, scoop-handed Wagner was equally dominant in the field. He used his great speed to range farther than short-stops were humanly expected to travel in pursuit of balls, and he topped all fielders in put-outs. Such statistics were standard for Wagner, and, in 1908, he was at the peak of his career.

The Pirates had other stars, too. Playing manger Fred Clarke was an outfielder later elected to the Baseball Hall of Fame, and Tommy Leach, the team's peppery third- baseman, surely belongs there too. Had he played in the publicity spotlight of New York, and not in Wagner's shadow, his attainments would have had him elected.

These three, Wagner, Clarke, and Leach, were the strength of the team and supported a strong pitching staff. It was led, in 1908, by Vic Willis, who won 248 games in 13 seasons and has been shamefully neglected for post-career recognition by those who elect players to the Hall of Fame. (Note: Finally elected in 1997)

The New York Giants were John McGraw's team and, playing in the nation's largest and most exciting city, claimed the pre-season media spotlight. After winning in 1904 (and snubbing a World Series against the champions of the new American League) and in 1905 (when Mathewson pitched three shutouts against Connie Mack's Philadelphia Athletics), they had been badly eclipsed by the Cubs the past two seasons. McGraw prepared for 1908 by overhauling his team.

In a pre-season trade he brought Fred Tenney and Al Bridwell from Boston. Bridwell was a fine fielder and timely hitter. Tenney was considered the best defensive first-baseman in the league and was the prize acquisition by McGraw. He was a rarity in baseball, a college graduate. He had a degree from Brown University, whereas Bucknell's Christy Mathewson had not graduated before entering professional baseball. Tenney had been manager of the hapless Boston Doves (named for owner George Dovery, who voted on the September 23 disputed game as one of the neutral owners).

Tenney had been a left-handed catcher when he broke into the National League in 1894, but found his niche at first base. He developed a style ranging far off the base and consistently led the league in assists as well as topping .300 frequently as a batter. McGraw needed him and got almost a complete season from the veteran, who finished gamely although impaired by lumbago. Tenney missed only one game all year—rookie Fred Merkle was his substitute on that fateful September 23 when Tenney nursed his aching back.

McGraw had a pair of rookies new to the team. Larry Doyle became a regular at second base; a joyous, exuberant youth who declared, "Gee, it's great to be young and a Giant!" Buck Herzog made his first appearance with the Giants and began a love-hate relationship with McGraw. This resulted in the scrappy, hot-tempered Herzog being traded away and then reacquired by the Giants three times during his subsequent career. In 1908 he would hit .300 as a utility player.

The slow-footed Moose McCormick, like Matty a collegian from Bucknell, was picked up during the season as an outfield replacement and pinch-hitter. He became an early specialist in that role with the Giants.

The team had established stars in Roger Bresnahan, the sturdy catcher who would be elected to the Baseball Hall of Fame in 1945; Cy Seymour, who had won a batting title in 1905, and Art Devlin, a stellar third-baseman.

However, the superstar in the lineup in 1908 would be Mike Donlin. He had been a holdout and missed the 1907 season. In fact, 1908 would be the only season he would play between 1906 and 1912, choosing a stage career instead. McGraw named him captain for the 1908 season, and Donlin performed better than anyone in the league—except for Honus Wagner. Donlin finished second to Wagner in batting, after dueling for the lead all season. He also was runner-up to Wagner in slugging percentage, total bases, hits, and runs batted-in.

Donlin's nickname, "Turkey Mike," was due to his long, sunburned neck, which protruded from the collarless uniform worn by the Giants. He also strutted when he walked. He was a star player and off the field a bon vivant and humorous storyteller who was at home among the theatrical crowd that patronized the Polo

Grounds. He had a natural talent for the stage and, when he married Mabel Hite, a musical-comedy star, he chose a theatrical career during what would have been his prime baseball years. As it was, he played 12 seasons and had a .333 lifetime batting average. In 1908 he elected to play baseball, and Mabel Hite cheered from the stands.

Christy Mathewson, of course, was the kingpin of the pitching staff. He was clearly the best pitcher of his time and in 1908 would demonstrate this by winning 35 games, as well as leading the league in ERA, complete games, innings pitched, and strikeouts. He led in games pitched, starting 45 and saving five others in 12 relief appearances. He pitched 11 shutouts.

Another future Hall of Fame member, "Iron Man" Joe McGinnity, Matty's partner in earlier years, would be a spot starter in 1908, his final big-league season (although he continued to pitch in the minor leagues until 1925). The rugged McGinnity was no longer capable of pitching both ends of a double-header but was useful in selected situations, particularly after mid-season.

In 1908 Matty's chief support would come from the slender left-hander George Wiltze, who would win 23 games, and a rookie, Doc Crandall, a starter in 1908 who would become one of the first pitchers used extensively as a relief specialist on future Giant teams.

The rest of the eight-team National League began the season without serious expectation of contending for the pennant, although the Phillies and Reds made promising beginnings. When the season settled down in earnest, it was Pittsburgh, Chicago, and New York battling it out for supremacy, rotating the lead and maintaining a steady pace. None of these contenders had an exceptionally long winning or losing streak all season.

The Chicago Cubs immediately claimed first place in April and remained the front runners until mid-July against the persistent pressure of the Pittsburgh Pirates, who stayed right at their heels. The Giants, off a bit more slowly, moved up during June and, by July 4, traditionally the date which marked the mid-point of the season, had joined the Cubs and Pirates in a closely contested struggle among the three teams for the rest of the year.

The struggle for first place became the focus of sport interest, and much of America had little else in which to take a partisan position. The outcome of each day's games was the daily lead story in the nation's sports pages.

The play-by-play accounts of key games were telegraphed to newspapers, which posted inning-by-inning scores to keep fans, who often blocked the street, aware of how the teams were doing. Stockbrokers would find the scores and details of the games on their Wall Street ticker and call favored customers with the latest baseball news.

A new form of theatrical entertainment became popular, particularly as the games between the top contenders were sold out at the ticket windows of the ball parks. An electric baseball board, mounted on a theater's stage, tracked the progress of a game, as the details were telegraphed. The familiar names of players would be posted and replicas of the athletes in action would be moved around the base paths.

Baseball was indisputably the national pastime in 1908. Football was a sweaty struggle played by collegians and of no real account until after the World Series was over. Other sports which today compete for attention and overlap the baseball season were of interest to very few followers. Basketball and hockey were of minor interest; boxing could capture enthusiasm for the occasional heavyweight championship. Horse racing drew a gambling crowd, but bookies would take bets on baseball, too. Golf and tennis were the province of the elitist wealthy. It was baseball alone that occupied center stage from April into October.

American working men had little leisure time, but newspapers were plentiful and cheap. A man could form his opinions after dinner at the kitchen table, then share them at the corner saloon or at the cigar store and newsstand. Anyone could have a favorite team to root for and find statistics to support his arguments in its behalf. Fans who lived in cities with contending teams were strong supporters of their hometown team. Those who lived outside big-league metropolises rooted for any team they liked. No one liked the New York Giants and, unless you were a New Yorker, you hoped the cocky, belligerent John McGraw was about to take a tumble.

McGraw was a bantam fighting for every advantage. The crowds who went to the Polo Grounds helped him rattle opponents and intimidate umpires. He insisted his players perform in the same obnoxious way. Despite a shining example in the gentlemanly Christy Mathewson, an exception among the brawling, cursing players, the team would use every trick possible to win a ball game. The Giants were loved in New York but loathed everywhere else.

As the 1908 season rollicked along, certain omens of ill-fortune began to appear. Winning a no-hitter is not usually considered a dubious outcome. However, when George Wiltze reached his 27th consecutive batter one day without a runner reaching base, he believed he threw a third strike to retire the opposing pitcher, George

McQuillan. Not only Wiltze thought it was a strike. Newspapermen covering the game, perhaps prejudiced in favor of a big story, thought it was a strike. Umpire Charles Rigler decided otherwise. McQuillan was still at bat.

The next Wiltze pitch hit the batter and, although he retired the next man up to maintain a no-hitter, the rare "perfect game" had been lost on an umpire's call. Only Cy Young had pitched a perfect game, in 1904, in the American League. None had been pitched in the National League since 1880.

The Giants seemed to lose games they should have won. They made many base- running blunders while John McGraw was off the coaching lines during a suspension for behavior that the National League President Harry Pulliman decided not to tolerate. Still, the New York press almost gleefully anticipated a successful windup. The schedule favored the Giants, who played most of their final games at home and against inferior teams. One of these anticipated soft-touches was the Philadelphia Phillies.

The Phillies, however, brought in a strapping young Polish pitcher, Harry Coveleski, from the Tri City League, a semi-pro circuit, and he proceeded to beat the Giants three times in less than a week. This dropped the Giants into a position that required them to sweep Boston in their final three games. They did, a factor that made the tie game of September 23 even more galling. Had the Giants been credited with a win that day, instead of losing the winning run on a technicality, they would have won the pennant.

What had been a cloud no bigger than McGraw's fist, now loomed in importance. A playoff of that disputed game would now determine the winner of the 1908 National League pennant. The protests both teams made had run their course and the incident could be understood by any and all still capable of considering the circumstances dispassionately.

One who could not placidly contemplate the consequences of Merkle's blunder was, obviously, John McGraw, the Giant's vitriolic manager. He insisted forever after that his team had been robbed of the 1908 pennant on a technicality. He never criticized Fred Merkle for what others had called "a bonehead play." McGraw kept Merkle for seven more seasons as the Giants first-baseman, while winning pennants in 1911, '12, and '13.

McGraw would defend Merkle for having been smart enough to clear out of the way of trouble with the unruly crowd pouring onto the field. He castigated umpire Hank O'Day for imposing a technicality when, only a few weeks earlier, he had refused an identical appeal by the Cubs.

McGraw was even more vehement when he commented on the decision of League President Pulliman, who had denied the Cubs their claim against the Pirates, saying at that time, "Games should be won on the playing field, not in this office." McGraw insisted Pulliman was inconsistent and prejudiced against the Giants.

There is reason to believe the dislike which was directed against McGraw and his Giants influenced both O'Day and Pulliman. The decision to call the game a tie was delayed, not made on the spot, at the Polo Grounds, on September 23. O'Day left the ballpark to write his report, although it was hardly needed by the league president, who had been at the game. While O'Day was quoted by the press as having departed the Polo Grounds with the comment, "the run doesn't count, it's a tie game," the Giants left to celebrate a victory and the Cubs to plot their strategy for claiming a forfeit of the tie game when the teams met the next day in Chicago's last visit to New York. If the September 23 game were a tie, then a double-header had to be played the next afternoon.

The Cubs actually took the field for a phantom one o'clock game and, despite an absence of umpires, as well as opponents, contended victory was theirs. The League refused to countenance such trickery. The Cubs had also thickened the plot by filing a protest to claim victory by forfeit of the September 23 game. As President Pulliman pointed out, he was obliged to provide the Giants with five days in which to respond to the charge, making it impossible to play any kind of make-up game the next day. The five-day process had to be followed first.

In their protest, the Cubs claimed that the Giants had failed to clear the field after Merkle had been called out at second base. There was plenty of daylight left, the Cubs further insisted, to resume the game.

Throughout the process of getting O'Day's decision, and then, as League President, upholding it, Pulliman acted carefully. He might have loathed the spiteful McGraw, but he gave him every right to appeal. Final judgment was made by a truncated League board of directors. Only three men remained after Pulliman and Barney Dreyfuss, Pittsburgh's owner (who had a stake in the outcome of a dispute between the Chicago and New York teams) were disqualified. The trio agreed the game should remain a tie and be played-off at the end of the season. (Garry Herrman, owner of Cincinnati, Charley Ebbets of the Brooklyn Dodgers, and George Dovey of Boston had to, and did, reach a unanimous decision).

When New York fireman McBride fell to his death trying to keep his grip on a perch from which to see the climactic game of the 1908 season, the area around the Polo Grounds was in pandemonium. Speculators still were selling tickets to people emerging from the subway even after the ballpark had been closed by the police because the Polo Grounds had been packed beyond capacity.

With everyone inside who needed to be there, the start of the game was moved ahead from 3:00 p.m. to 2:45. More time would be needed to clear the park and empty the streets after the game than usual, so an early start would speed things up in every way. A battle royal almost broke out when the Giants' McGinnity, intent on the host team's prerogative to take infield practice when it wished, shoved Frank Chance, the Chicago manager, aside as he was hitting ground balls to his Chicago infielders. Finally the game began.

Christy Mathewson was the only man McGraw would trust for this game. He was rested. His nemesis, Mordecai "Three Fingered" Brown, had pitched in 11 of the Cubs' last 14 games, and the Cubs sent the redoubtable "Jack the Giant Killer," left-handed Pfiester to face the Giants.

To call the balls and strikes the League had assigned its best umpire, Bill Klem. Perhaps O'Day and Emslie should have been sent to work the replay of the game they had declared a tie. But, perhaps, someone remembered Hank O'Day was a Chicagoian. He had been born there, lived there, and eventually, would die there. When he was named manager of the Cubs in 1914, there were knowing winks passed by those who suspected the appointment might be a delayed reward for his fortuitous call in 1908.

Pfiester was no master of the Giants on that sunny autumn day, October 8, 1908, when the teams met in the final game of the season. His black magic didn't work, although, despite Pfiester's poor pitching, the Giants blundered away an opportunity to score heavily in the first inning by inept base-running. Still, they put the first run on the board and, with Matty on the mound, it might be enough.

However, they were to have difficulty adding to their lead, for Manager Chance waved his ace, Mordecai Brown, into the game. Once again it was a match-up between "Three Fingered" Brown and Matty, and, as usual, Brown bested the Giants' great pitcher.

Matty weakened in the third inning, although atrocious fielding by Cy Seymour really fueled the disaster. Joe Tinker, normally a weak hitting shortstop for the Cubs, hit Matty as though he had owned him during his career. Mathewson and Donlin, the captain, waved to Seymour to play deeper. They were ignored, and when a routine fly ball was lofted to left field, the reluctant Seymour back-peddled clumsily—the ball ticked off his glove for a triple. Base hits followed, and the Cubs scored four runs. Matty steadied after that, but the Giants could score only one more time and lost, 4–2. The Cubs had won the 1908 pennant.

An ugly crowd poured onto the field, angry their team had lost, enraged because they felt it was a game needlessly played to justify an overly zealous application of a rule to which no one had ever paid attention. The Chicago players, running off the hostile field, became targets for bullies. Knives and clubs were seen, but the most damage was suffered by Manager Frank Chance. He was felled from behind by a sneak attack from a bruiser who punched him in the neck.

The Cubs left the field under police protection and were taken to their train in patrol wagons. Chance recovered in time to star in the World Series against Detroit. He batted .421 as his team won easily, despite Ty Cobb's .361 effort. The Cubs won in five games—and a very hectic 1908 season was over.

This article originally appeared in the May 1988 issue of Sports History.

12

Bullet Joe Bush

Bullet Joe Bush wanted to extend his pitching career. So in 1921 he invented the fork ball, still around today.

Bullet Joe Bush was one pitch away from winning the game that would mark the New York Yankees as a dynastic super power for decades to come. Bush had the one pitch to do it with. He reared back and threw his newly discovered fork ball to the league's home run champ. Ken Williams, who had displaced Bush's teammate, Babe Ruth, for the 1922 title, popped up and the game was over.

The Yankees had overcome a two-run deficit slowly with a run in the eighth and two in the ninth. They hung on to win the final game of a crucial, end-of-the-season, three-game series. In 1922 the Yankees, who had won their first pennant ever the year before, were about to become a traditional power. They faced the St. Louis Browns, not yet sunk into perennial lethargy.

The Yankees had come into St. Louis with a slim one-game lead. Sportsmans Park was packed for games on Saturday and Sunday, and the Yankees and Browns split the pair. It made Monday's game crucial and gave the Browns the opportunity to move into a first place tie. Joe Bush, the Yankees best pitcher, would try to stop them.

The Browns were led by George Sisler, enroute to a .420 league-leading batting average. The extraordinary super star first baseman also led the league in hits and runs batted in. He was also the best base stealer, with 51.

On September 18, Sisler was a wounded warrior, with a bandaged shoulder and arm, swinging the bat one-handed. He had sat on the bench for four games until the Yankees had come to town for the crucial series. He had managed one hit in each of the first two games with New York and had brought a consecutive game hitting streak to 41. He had broken Ty Cobb's American League record, and his own would stand until 1941 when Joe DiMaggio would pass it on the way to his incredible 56-game hitting streak.

Joe Bush retired Sisler easily in four times at bat, the final time being the second out of the ninth inning. His fork ball had been dipping effectively, and the Browns had managed only five hits. Joe Bush, who customarily had trouble with his control, had walked only one and had hit a batter. When he retired Ken Williams for the final out, he registered his 25th victory of the season. He would win one more in the short time left. A peculiarity of the 1922 season was that the whole league was idle for four days late in September in order to provide a final weekend to the schedule. When the Yankees climbed onto their Pullman Monday evening, Joe Bush had pitched them into a two-game lead. They nursed it to an eventual single game margin.

Joe Bush had been in the major leagues since the tag end of the 1912 season. It was the one year Connie Mack's Philadelphia

Athletics failed to win the pennant out of five years. They had won in 1910 and 1911 and, with Joe Bush to help, won again in 1913 and 1914. A place was made for the youngster on a staff which starred Eddie Plank and Chief Bender. They would be elected to the Baseball Hall of Fame, as would Herb Pennock who was added the next year. It was a great pitching staff, and there was room for young Joe Bush. He won 30 games and lost 18 in the two years before Connie Mack broke up the team.

Then Joe Bush learned what it is to pitch for a loser. Connie Mack abruptly turned his 1914 pennant winners into tail-enders, and Joe bush won 5 and lost 15 in 1915. The next year was worse. Last again, the 1916 A's lost 109 games; and Bush was tagged for the loss in 24 of them, the most in the league. There was one bright note. On August 26, 1916, pitching the day after he had been knocked out of the box in the first inning, Joe Bush threw a no-hitter, beating Cleveland, 5–0. As a footnote to history, the final out was made on a ground ball hit to a faded Nap Lajoie. The once great second baseman was helping the A's to a patched-up lineup, taking the place of Eddie Collins. It was Lajoie's last game.

Connie Mack let Joe Bush escape the decimated Athletics; he joined another dynastic team, the Boston Red Sox, who had won pennants in 1915 and 1916 and , with Joe Bush aboard, would win their last World Series in 1918. It was Joe's third World Series appearance in six years. Then his arm went bad. Very bad.

He made only two pain-wracked starts in 1919, but finished neither. Even when the pain abated, he could no longer break off a curve ball. He tried to develop one of the trick pitches which others used. The spitball was thrown by many, but Bush tried to imitate those who scuffed the ball with emery cloth to make it take erratic patterns. But, before he could try any trick pitch, they were all outlawed before the 1920 season began.

Spitballers were allowed to continue to use saliva, but everything else was banned. Where once a ball remained in the game, darkened by grass stains, tobacco and licorice, scuffed and cut, the umpires now threw in a new ball at the first blemish. A former pitcher, Babe Ruth, had electrified baseball fans with 29 home runs in 1919, alternating between the mound and the outfield. Sold to the Yankees in 1920, he would stun the baseball world by hitting 54 home runs. He was aided by the removal of all trick pitches from the repertoire of opposing hurlers, and Joe Bush had to find another alternate to his fast ball.

Bush had large hands and long fingers. He had won 15 games in a comeback with the Red Sox in 1920, although the team, with Ruth gone and others following, dropped to second division. In 1921, Bush experimented to find a pitch that would behave like a spitter, but remain dry; one that wouldn't be spotted right away because of a defaced cover. He tried widening the gap between his forefinger and middle finger and squeezing the ball out between them. He alternated where he put his thumb under the ball and found he could make it dip sharply as it reached the plate.

As Bush threw the pitch with the same motion as his fast ball, but didn't spin it off his fingertips, the ball came to the plate slightly offspeed. Joe called his new pitch a "fork ball." Today, the same pitch travels by the trendy name, "split-finger fast ball."

Another pitcher, Eddie Rommel, also introduced a new pitch at the same time Bush was breaking in his fork ball. It was the knuckleball. Both pitches were answers to the need pitchers had for something to take the place of the banned spitter and other trick pitches.

The most successful disciple of Joe Bush didn't come along until the 1950s when Roy Face, a relief pitcher with the Pittsburgh Pirates, resurrected the fork ball. In 1959 he won 18 games, 17 of them consecutively, and lost only once.

Re-named the "split finger fast ball," the current renaissance began with another relief specialist, Bruce Sutter of the Chicago Cubs, who developed it with the guidance of pitching coach Mike Roarke in the late 1970s. Roarke, who had read the description of Bush's fork ball, agrees they are the same pitch. Soon Sutter was the top reliever in the league. He was traded to the Cardinals, his coach, Mike Roarke, going with him, and was paid a bonus of well over $1 million to sign, as a free agent, with the Atlanta Braves in 1984.

When Joe Bush discovered the fork ball, he was past the midpoint of his career and enjoyed only one super season with it. He ended up with 194 major-league wins, having had a no-decision season in 1919; otherwise he would have drawn consideration, as a 200-plus game winner, for the Baseball Hall of Fame. He had been one of the best of his time and very popular. He was often used as a pinch-hitter, played some games in the outfield and, when his major league pitching career ended, Bush went to the Pacific Coast League to play the outfield.

In later life, and retirement, Joe Bush found a new career, as a pari-mutuel clerk at Florida and New Jersey race tracks. He moved north and south, with the seasons, punching out tickets for the bettors. Race tracks boasted of days when over $1 million was wagered. Bush died in 1974, not knowing that a decade later Bruce Sutter would get that much as a bonus for throwing a modern version of the tricky fork ball.

This article first appeared in Sports History, *November 1988.*

13

Rabbit: The Human Fly

Rabbit Maranville was, or had been, the best shortstop in baseball. He was a pint sized wizard with a glove and had an impish sense of fun. His antic trail in baseball took him from Boston to Pittsburgh, from where he was shipped to the Chicago Cubs with other merrymakers, including the lefthanded banjo player, Charlie Grimm. For some unfathomable reason, Rabbit was made Chicago's manager. His pranks continued. He laughed himself out of the job. With unerring instinct, he turned up in Brooklyn. Finally, Uncle Robbie had a shortstop who could hold an infield together. However, the Rabbit only lived up to one of his reputations. It was not as a shortstop. Of course, he passed, with honors, the requirements of the "4 for 0" club, presided over by Dazzy Vance. The baseball term. "four for oh," describes a futile day at bat. For Brooklyn's band of fun seekers, a player's day at bat had no bearing on his candidacy. It was not what he did during the day that qualified him, but night time carousing.

Maranville was a member as soon as he checked into spring training in 1927. He had an extensive knowledge of speakeasies in those Prohibition years. Even more noteworthy was Rabbit's ambition to be a human fly. Hotels in the 1920s lacked air conditioning. Windows were left wide open to catch any breeze. The players' rooms were usually booked side by side along a corridor. It amused Rabbit, and scared his teammates, to climb out his window, sidle along a toe hold's width of cement, and pop in on a neighboring teammate. He would also visit when the occupants were out. He'd transfer a player's favorite razor, or a picture of a girlfriend or wife, from one player's room to another, leading to bickering accusations of petty theft among teammates.

When Brooklyn's new St. George Hotel opened in 1929 with 2,632 rooms, Rabbit Maranville unfortunately, had moved on. Mr. and Mrs. Wilbert Robinson made it their home. They occupied a suite during Uncle Robbie's final years as manager. The St. George was New York City's largest hotel, with a mirrored swimming pool in the basement and a starlight roof for dancing and dining. It would have loomed like Mount Everest for Maranville. He is better remembered not for scaling buildings but as the greatest shortstop of his era. He was to defensive play then what Ossie Smith has been in recent years. There are those who deride his presence in the Hall of Fame. They are looking only at his typical infielder's batting marks. They should check the number of times he led in fielding and defensive statistics. With a glove small enough to fit into Ossie Smith's breast pocket, playing on infields far bumpier than the carpets that gave Smith smooth bounces, the Rabbit's play awed everyone who saw him.

Excerpted from Uncle Robbie*, to be published by SABR in 1999.*

14

Hi Ladd: The Man Who Would Not Slide

Hi Ladd was an upright man of principle. One on which he would take a firm stand was his refusal to slide into a base. A towering six foot, four inches, Ladd's adamant refusal to hit the dirt confined his ball playing career to the minor leagues. In an interview for a 1915 Sunday feature article in *The Providence Journal* after he had retired from organized baseball, Ladd explained his foreboding attitude. "I would see other players slide into bases and get badly hurt. I could hear their bones crack as they broke their legs. I didn't want it to happen to me. I just couldn't abide the idea. I always went into a base standing up. I don't remember ever getting tagged out because of that."

When you consistently hit over .300 and pound the dead ball of his era with power, such an idiosyncrasy will be accepted by minor league management. Not so, in the big leagues, however, as Ladd found out with Pittsburgh in 1898. His minor league stats had caught the eye of Bill Watkins, the Pittsburgh manager, and he brought Hi Ladd to the big time. He was aghast when Ladd admitted he would never risk a slide. Hi Ladd said that he did not engage in such tactics. After one hitless, and slideless game, he was sent back to the Fall River club in the New England League.

There he had another robust season with the bat and, when the league ended its play with Labor Day games, Hi Ladd was again called to the big leagues. This time the nearby Boston team needed a player to fill a gap in the roster. Sliding Billy Hamilton, a leading base stealer, slid one time too many. As Hi Ladd could have told them, such risks often result in broken limbs. Hamilton was out for the final month of the season. His absence would not have an effect on Boston's pennant chances as they were almost 20 games ahead of the pack. They just needed someone to fill out the starting nine players for the rest of the season.

Hi Ladd lived close by in East Greenwich, Rhode Island. His season was over and he was available. He had an off season job as a house painter. When Boston contacted him, he put away his brushes and reported. He took the field in a game and knocked out his only major league hit. Manager Frank Selee, speaking encouragingly to Ladd after the game, told him that if he kept hitting, Boston would give him a contract for next season.

Hi Ladd wanted to know about this season. He was told the team would pay all his expenses but not pay him as a player. Ladd explained that he could not afford to lose the income he could earn painting houses back in Rhode Island and checked out. That was the last time anyone showed an interest in Hi Ladd as a big league player.

He became a minor league wanderer, a consistent .300 hitter. In 1899, the season after his two major league appearances, he divided his playing time between Paterson of the Atlantic League and Worcester of the Eastern League.

He opened the 1900 season with Newark of the Atlantic League and, after hitting .416 in 77 games, switched to Derby of the Connecticut League where he hit .371 to win the batting title. The next year he batted .357 for Derby and then found a long term home with Bridgeport when the Derby franchise was shifted there. His .278 average was a disappointment but it did not signal a decline in ability. Instead, he resumed a pattern of over .300 seasons until he retired in 1911. He led the league in batting with .341 in 1907.

Back home in East Greenwich, he was hailed as Hi Ladd by his neighbors. This was his baseball name. In his later years he was affectionately known as "Uncle Hiram." Early historians guessed wrongly that Hi was a short form of Hiram and he was listed that way in the early editions of MacMillan's *Baseball Encyclopedia.* He now appears as Arthur Clifford Ladd, his name when he was born in Willimantic, Connecticut on February 9, 1870. Young Arthur moved with his family to Warwick, Rhode Island, where he went to local public schools.

He was already a professional baseball player when he came to the attention of an English born baseball fan who was known as "Lord Hi, Hi." He was an extroverted enthusiast who would focus his attention on a player and banter from the grandstands with him. He called everyone "lad." "Hi, lad," he would shout. "How are you, lad?" He would keep up his chatter through the game.

When Lord Hi, Hi discovered the lad he was addressing was really named Ladd, he expanded his punning opportunities. "Hi, lad. You really are some lad, Ladd." It caught on and soon his teammates were also calling Arthur, "Hi." He not only played out his career as Hi Ladd, when his fellow townsmen met him, they'd greet him as Hi and introduce him as Hi Ladd.

He was Coach Ladd to the baseball team at East Greenwich Academy but still Hi Ladd to teammates on the town team that played as semi-pros in a weekend league. He had finally declared that his last game had been played in 1915. When the season ended he tossed his glove in the closet. The next day he dug it out again. The league standings had ended in a tie and, though East Greenwich had finished lower in the standings, the contending teams were allowed to recruit one player each from a team which had been eliminated. Arctic's team drafted Hi Ladd to play for them. In an extra inning game, Ladd came to bat with two out and a runner on first. He smashed a line drive into the outfield. The runner had not reached home plate when the ball and Ladd arrived at second base. He was safe on a stand up double and the winning run crossed the plate.

Hi Ladd never lost his love for baseball. Hoping to get an insight into Hi Ladd as a private East Greenwich resident, the writer phoned Miss Martha McPartland. She was the retired head librarian and had written the town's history. She remembered Hi Ladd very well, describing him as a courteous and polite man. Then Miss McPartland stopped: "My sister Helen, is here and I just remembered she worked for Mr. Ladd at what is now the Bostich Company, let me put her on."

Helen McPartland, a spinster like her sister, gladly reminisced. "Oh, he was such a nice man and my first boss. I had to make out payrolls from time cards and he would help me figure them out. I remember how much he loved baseball. Every spring, when the weather got nice, the men from the factory would bring their gloves to work. Afterward, they would go up to the field next to the school and play a game. Mr. Ladd would go with them, wearing his old Bridgeport uniform. He was about 60 when he finally stopped. Then he got sick and retired. Not long afterward he died of cancer at the state hospital in Cranston."

Hi Ladd died May 7, 1948. He is buried in the Washington Cemetery in Rhode Island. He rests at the center of the Ladd family plot. His headstone makes no mention of baseball or that he was the player who was called Hi Ladd. He rests with the same name with which he was born, Arthur Clifford Ladd, 78 years earlier.

15

Dixie Walker: Snubbed for Posterity by Politically Correct Media

The Boys of Summer were great, but this is the man who was "The Peepul's Cherce" in Brooklyn.

He was the most popular player in Brooklyn's history, according to Red Barber, the long-time "Voice of the Dodgers." Writing during the reign of The Boys of Summer in his 1954 book, "The Catbird Seat," Barber singled out Fred "Dixie" Walker as the all-time favorite of Dodger fans. A lifetime .306 batter over 18 major league seasons, Walker became known in the patois of Brooklyn as the "The Peepul's Cherce" for reasons that escape the pages of record books. Past injuries and the fear they would recur had made Dixie Walker an underdog. Brooklyn fans could relate to that. They lived with a perpetual inferiority complex, located on the déclassé side of the Brooklyn Bridge. On the New York side was the power of finance, the glitter of the entertainment world and the shops of Fifth Avenue. Over in "The City of Churches" were bedroom communities and the push carts loaded with merchandise on Pitkin Avenue. Dixie Walker, a discarded piece of baseball's flotsam, had bobbed into the under-achieving lives of Brooklyn Dodger fans on a waiver acquisition in 1939.

Walker had once been a rising star in the New York Yankee organization. In 1930 after hitting .401 in 73 games for Greenville in the SALLY League he moved up to Jersey City where he hit .335 in the 83 games remaining on the International League schedule. He split the 1931 season between the International League, hitting .352 in 80 games and Toledo in the American Association where he batted .303. In a full season at Newark, the top Yankee farm team in 1932, he batted .350, hit 15 home runs, knocked in 105 runs and stole 22 bases.

Advanced to the Yankees, Walker played behind Babe Ruth and Earle Combs, whose careers were waning. The stage was set for the young Georgian with the sunny disposition to claim a permanent place in the Yankee outfield. Instead, he began a string of injuries that would qualify him for a place on the All-Time Disabled List. A broken collarbone and a series of torn ligaments in his throwing shoulder, and a knee that popped in and out of its socket, benched Dixie repeatedly. His shoulder was mended by three operations, the final one drawing a transplanted tendon through a hole drilled in the bone. It worked, but was always suspect. In 1936, with the rookie Joe DiMaggio and George Selkirk already aboard and Charlie Keller and Tommy Heinrich among a stellar group of farmhands, the Yankees waived Walker to the Chicago White Sox. Despite a league leading 16 triples and a .302 average, the White Sox put him into a multi-player deal that winter with Detroit.

There, Dixie encountered unexpected fan hostility. He was "the wrong Walker." The trade between Chicago and Detroit had swapped the Tiger's own "people's choice," Gee Walker, for an impostor with the same last name. The Tiger's Walker could hit. He had batted .353 and .335 in the two seasons before he was unloaded by manager Mickey Cochrane, who took a dim view of Gee's madcap gambols on the base paths. He would blithely steal an occupied base, or nonchalantly meander away to be picked off, and he was a patsy for the hidden ball trick.

Still, the blue collar fans who could scrape up Depression-era dollars for admission to Navin Field looked upon Gee as one of their own. His foibles were tolerable. The fans forgave him everything and remembered only his accomplishments. He glowed in their eyes, not at all overshadowed by such stellar teammates as Hank Greenberg, Charlie Gehringer, Goose Goslin, and Cochrane himself. Gee's departure left an emotional vacuum Dixie Walker could not fill. Dixie was troubled by his unwarranted rejection. It pained him as badly as the way his wired-together body hurt on the baseball field. The next time Dixie Walker joined a new team he would make a conscious effort to ingratiate himself with the fans.

Dixie Walker had batted .308 for his new team in 1938 and was batting .305 when the Tigers put him—injured again—on waivers mid-way through the 1939 season. Larry MacPhail, the Dodgers General Manager, took a chance. Walker joined his new team on a western swing. Back in Brooklyn the fans listened to re-created away games which the new broadcaster, Red Barber, constructed from the bare bones of ticker taped accounts. Dixie started with a string of game-winning hits. When the Dodgers came home, the fans welcomed him much as they would adopt a tail-wagging stray puppy.

The homestand opened with a still-novel night game with the Boston Bees. Walker's sharp single to right field in his debut game at Ebbets Field broke a 10-inning tie, and the Dodgers moved ahead of the idle Giants in the standings. Right there was the key to the love affair between the Brooklyn populace and the Georgian who came to live among them. He "moidered dem Jints." In 1940, his first full season with the Dodgers, he batted .436 in games against New York.

Dixie Walker found instant rapport with the fans but his reputation for brittleness, and Larry MacPhail's intransigent preference for high-priced rookies of his own choosing, made it necessary for Walker to re-win a starting role during his first years in Brooklyn. When he finally got into the lineup in 1940 he hit .308 for the season and seemed set as the Dodger's right fielder for 1941. However, this time the veteran Paul Waner kept Dixie out of the opening day lineup. Released by the Pittsburgh Pirates, "Big Poison" had a terrific spring in Florida and came north as the starting right fielder. A telegram signed by 5,000 outraged Dodger fans demanded that Dixie Walker be returned to his rightful place in the Dodger outfield. They would concede center field to the wunderkind, Pete Reiser, but right field belonged to "The Peepul's Cherce." With Paul Waner batting only .171 after the first 11 games, Dixie Walker finally trotted out to right field. He became part of the best outfield Brooklyn would ever have. Pete Reiser was scintillating in center field. He had yet to crash into his first outfield wall. He led the league in batting, runs, doubles, triples, and slugging average. Joe Medwick, diminished somewhat by the beaning that greeted his arrival as a Dodger in 1940, still batted .318, hit 18 homers, scored 100 runs, and drove in 88.

Walker's totals were deceptive. Time and again it was Dixie who got the clutch hit, made the game-saving catch, laid down a surprise bunt, and, even though the St. Louis Cardinals were now the closest competitor, Dixie also maintained his supremacy over Bill Terry's Giants. The Dodger fans had learned that winning championships alone is not the supreme thrill. Back in 1934 Bill Terry, the sour-dispositioned Giant's manager, had taught them about gloating when he sneered, "Is Brooklyn still in the league?" Terry's sarcasm was flung back in his teeth as Brooklyn won two season-ending games from New York and allowed the St. Louis Cardinals to pass the hated Giants and snatch the 1934 pennant from the snobbish New Yorkers. The Polo Grounds had been packed with brown bagging Dodger fans gloating as their second division ragamuffins, led by a Casey Stengel who had yet to be acclaimed a managerial genius, humbled Terry's Giants.

In 1941 they were still reminding Terry that Brooklyn was still in the League—what's more, the Dodgers were leading it. Dixie Walker's popularity grew even though the Dodgers had a galaxy of stars to share the fans' adulation. "The Gold Dust Twins," the youngsters Reiser and Pee Wee Reese, veterans Medwick and Billy Herman, the smooth-fielding captain and slugger, Dolph Camilli, who would be the league's MVP, and the 22 game winners, Whit Wyatt and Kirby Higbee, were all heroes. Leo Durocher, a populist field leader, Fat Freddie Fitzsimmons, forgiven his years with the Giants, Hughie Casey converted from a so-so starter into an unhittable relief ace and Mickey Owen, who had not yet disgraced himself by demonstrating Casey could also be uncatchable, drew their share of fan support. However, the man who was best loved of all was Dixie Walker, whose .311 batting average in 1941 was his best yet. Number 11 ruled right field with the looming scoreboard and its angled cement wall, topped by a high screen, like a kingdom. He led the league's outfielders in assists.

There was more for Brooklynites to admire about Dixie Walker than his performances on the playing field. Once he had been taken to Brooklyn's bosom, he made sure he remained in the borough's embrace. He appeared at every civic and social function to which he was invited. He shared bagels and lox at B'nai B'rith get-togethers, had bacon and eggs at Holy Name Communion breakfasts, and joined the Sons of Italy for spaghetti dinners. He not only spoke humorously and graciously, he sang, too. Dixie had a sweet tenor voice and a repertoire for every occasion. He was booked as a singer with the house band at the Flatbush Theater and played to S.R.O. crowds during the off-season. Dixie and his wife and daughters remained in Brooklyn between baseball seasons. He invested in a liquor store in suburban Rockville Centre. His children went to local schools. Dixie and his family were at the Polo Grounds on December 7, 1941, when the Japanese spoiled what had been a joyous occasion by sneakily bombing Pearl Harbor. The underdog NFL Brooklyn Dodgers had beaten the top ranked New York Giants only to have that victory dwarfed by the start of World War II.

Dixie Walker had qualified for 4F draft status long before Selective Service began to convert civilians into military personnel. He was surgically patched together, and, although this did not seem to impair his baseball skills, he was thought to be an added risk to his comrades in battle. As a married man in his 30s with dependents, he could justifiably be excused from active wartime duty. Pity the Brooklyn Draft Board that might have sent Dixie Walker into military service. Once President Franklin D. Roosevelt decreed that major league baseball could continue because it was good for morale, Walker's career headed for new heights. Having Dixie in a Dodger uniform, even if surrounded by pimply faced kids and elderly rejects, was a wonderful boost for the morale of Brooklyn's civilian war effort.

To promote the sale of War Bonds, players from the Dodgers, Giants, and Yankees were auctioned off at a rally at the Waldorf Astoria in New York City in June, 1943. Business organizations bid for the right to sponsor the players. In addition, the sponsors agreed to buy additional bonds based on the player's performance. The auction yielded $123,850,000 in initial bids. Dixie Walker drew the highest bid, over 11 million dollars. After that every time he got a base hit this translated into more bond sales.

Dixie volunteered for two overseas USO trips. He went on the tough Aleutian tour and reached outposts polar explorers such as Admiral Richard Byrd had barely made. The group, which included Frank Frisch and Stan Musial, narrowly escaped being buried under an avalanche at one remote location. The next time Dixie signed up he visited the China-Burma-India theater. It was warmer but equally dangerous.

Walker took a war-time job between seasons with the Sperry Gyroscope Company, a vital military supplier. He was in charge of employee recreation programs for thousands of men and women who produced intricate instruments that kept aircraft flying. However, when the baseball season arrived, Dixie left his desk and delivered his best seasons in the big leagues. Maybe the pitching was not as tough or the fielding as sharp, but it was still the major leagues, and Dixie was the best hitter in baseball, with a .357 average in 1944. The next year he topped everyone with 124 runs batted in. He had little fear from the challenge of returning players when the war ended. However, he had another concern. Despite having settled in Brooklyn, his roots were in the south. Dixie was well named. As a transplanted southerner, Dixie Walker was in the wrong place when the time came to end baseball's segregation. General Manager Branch Rickey had decided to sign players from the Negro Leagues, Jackie Robinson foremost among them. After winning the MVP title in 1946 with Montreal of the International League, Robinson's advance to the major leagues with the Dodgers was irresistible. Yet, some players did resist.

Always an up-front man, before the 1947 season began Dixie Walker wrote to Branch Rickey and asked to be traded "for reasons I prefer not to go into." Rickey was willing to oblige Walker and let him escape the culture shock of integrated baseball. This also fit in with Rickey's established practice of trading an aging star while he still could get value for him.

Retroactive judgments are made that cast Dixie Walker as the ringleader of resistance to the breaking of the ban on black players. However, he actually preferred to give up his favored status as "The Peepul's Cherce" and simply complete the few years remaining of his major league career somewhere else. Rickey might have been willing to unload an uncomfortable Dixie Walker, but the fans still held him in high esteem.

The people of Brooklyn were divided on whether adding Jackie Robinson to their team was a baseball value that over-shadowed the social upheaval many feared integration would create. When Rickey could not make a trade that would benefit the team, he kept Walker for the pennant-winning season of 1947. Dixie hit .306 while playing 147 games, mostly in right field, and tutoring his successor, Carl Furillo. Once Dixie had an opportunity to make a personal value judgment of Robinson, he, as well as other southerners like Eddie Stanky and Pee Wee Reese, rallied to the rookie's aid. Walker gave him batting tips, and when the team arrived back in Brooklyn after winning the 1947 pennant on the road, Dixie Walker and Jackie Robinson were impromptu spokesmen for the ball club at a downtown rally.

Walker played all seven games in the 1947 World Series against the Yankees, hitting a home run in the second game. However, in December Rickey arranged one of the smartest deals he ever made when he swapped Walker to the Pittsburgh Pirates. In exchange, the shrewd Rickey got Preacher Roe, who helped pitch Brooklyn to three pennants, and Billy Cox, who became the slick fielding third baseman of the Boys of Summer.

In 1948, Dixie Walker, wearing a Pirates uniform, learned he was still "The Peepul's Cherce." Dixie and his family stood at home plate while a new car was driven through the center field gates of Ebbets Field. Gifts from merchants and from the affectionate fans were piled in a mountain of merchandise beside it.

Dixie gave his new team a final season as a full-time player, hitting .316. He was the only Pirate to top .300, helping them to move from the last place to a first division finish. Dixie Walker ended his big league playing career as a part-time player in 1949. He led the league with 13 pinch hits.

Dixie Walker continued in baseball. The integration of the national game became an accepted circumstance. Walker managed minor league teams in Atlanta, Houston, Rochester, and Toronto and coached at major league level with the Cardinals and Braves, both in Milwaukee and Atlanta. He ended back with the now transplanted Dodgers in Los Angeles from 1969 to 1976 as a batting instructor and scout.

Obviously the color of a player or a prospect no longer set off atavistic resistance with the gentlemanly Dixie Walker. Yet "pop art" anthropologists and socially sensitive baseball historians refuse to recognize that his initial resistance to integrating professional baseball was only "skin deep." A winning team, regardless of its racial makeup, does more for the cause of comradeship than politically correct rhetoric. Once Jackie Robinson and other black players backed up Leo Durocher's assessment that "these guys can win pennants and put money in our pockets," Walker as a player and later as a manager and coach readily adapted to baseball's changed racial scene.

Dixie Walker has paid an unfair price for what later day politically correct baseball historians decry as racism. If there were amends to be made, Dixie made them. Yet when the Brooklyn Dodger Hall of Fame began to select heroes of the past to honor it, it snubbed Dixie in favor of lesser icons. It would have been a great homecoming for The Peepul's Cherce. However, it wasn't until two years after his death in 1982 that Dixie was welcomed. Walker is rarely mentioned among the greats of Brooklyn's past and usually with a caveat reference to his reluctance to participate in Branch Rickey's Great Social Experiment. The ironic hard truth is that what Dixie did by initiating his own departure was exactly what much of the borough's white population was also doing. To stay or to leave became the people's choice. Most whites chose to leave...and even the franchise skipped town.

16

Quit While You're Ahead

There were no baseball worlds left for Bill Carrigan to conquer at the end of the 1916 season. His Boston Red Sox were the World's Champions. In fact, in defeating the Brooklyn Dodgers with only the loss of one game, the Red Sox had matched their 1915 World Series triumph, when they also beat the Philadelphia Phillies in five games. Back-to-back championships are a proud way to cap a career, even a short one as the 33-year-old Carrigan's managerial run had been. He took over a dissension-riddled second division Red Sox team in mid-season in 1913, brought it home second in 1914, and then led the team to pennants the next two years. Now he was leaving.

Carrigan's departure was not abrupt. He had told owner Joseph J. Lannin before the 1916 season ended that the would not return. He had spent ten years in the big leagues as Boston's catcher and as a player-manager and he was now ready to close off the athletic chapter of his life. Bill Carrigan was a natural athlete who had played two years of football at Holy Cross under the legendary Frank Cavanaugh. Later dubbed the "Iron Major" for his World War I heroics, Cavanaugh is a college football Hall of Fame member as a coach. Like Knute Rockne, he was played in a biographical movie by Pat O'Brien. In baseball, Carrigan's Holy Cross coach was Tommy McCarthy, whose 1946 election to the Baseball Hall of Fame raised eyebrows that haven't been lowered yet.

Carrigan was signed by the Red Sox after his sophomore year at Holy Cross, and after a season with Toronto in the International League, he joined Boston in 1906. He was a clever handler of pitchers, and he hit a respectable .257 for his ten-year career at a time when a catcher was not expected to hit for a high average. His final game as a player was the fourth contest of the 1916 Series. It was his only appearance against the Dodgers that fall, and he made it memorable with two hits while catching Hub Leonard's 6–2 victory.

When the Red Sox played their final regular season game, Carrigan stepped out on the field and waved a farewell to the fans. Carrigan had been born in Lewiston, Maine, and he was ready to return to his home town and start a new career. Back in Lewiston, the former Beulah Bartlett, and the family that would grow to include Bill Jr. and his two sisters, welcomed the idea of a year 'round father.

Carrigan had saved a good share of his ballplayer's salary and World Series money and was ready to invest in a business career. He went from managing a major league ballclub to managing a bank, and he also branched out as owner of a string of movie houses across the state. He had a magic touch, getting in on the growing craze for silent flickers as Chaplin, Fairbanks, and Pickford became marquee names outside his theaters. His banking career was more sedate but very successful.

Despite his success both in and out of the game, it's inevitable that Carrigan is defined for most people by his relationship with

Babe Ruth. Carrigan was the Babe's first major league manager, and much of what we know about his personality comes from the accounts of Babe Ruth's early years with Boston.

Bill Carrigan had replaced Red Sox manager Jake Stahl in 1913, after the contentious Stahl had allowed the 1912 champions to disintegrate into cantankerous factions. He was the Red Sox manager when the 19-year-old George Herman Ruth was delivered from Baltimore in mid-season. Actually, Bill Carrigan was none too pleased to have the teenage parolee from a boys training school assigned to him. Ruth, a young giant, combined the callowness of youth with an almost total lack of discipline. He needed a strong hand and steady handling. Bill Carrigan supplied it, if reluctantly. The manager was already called "Rough" by his teammates for his willingness to mix it up whenever necessary. As is usual with those who have the physique to back up a squared-jawed determination, the squat, five foot six inch, 175-pound Carrigan rarely had to lift his fists to quell a disturbance.

Ruth arrived with another outstanding pitching prospect, Ernie Shore. Of the two, Shore filled Carrigan's needs the best. Unlike Ruth, he was righthanded, and a gap in the Red Sox staff had existed since Smoky Joe Wood's strong right arm had gone lame two years before. Wood, a 34-game winner in 1912, would never regain his blazing fastball. With Carrigan's deft handling, he learned to pitch craftily and win in certain spots. But the Boston staff was led in 1914 by 20-game winner Ray Collins and Hub "Dutch" Leonard, who won 19. Both were lefties, and what Carrigan and the Sox needed was a strong young right arm.

Carrigan did put Ruth to work as soon as he had climbed off

the train from Baltimore, putting him on the mound that very afternoon and catching him himself. The Babe pitched impressively until he weakened in the seventh inning, when he left with the game tied. After Duffy Lewis drove in a go-ahead run pinch-hitting for Ruth, Leonard came in to pitch two scoreless innings of relief and preserve the Babe's first big league win. However, Carrigan rarely used the Babe at all after that, and later in the season the big kid was sent down to Providence. Years later, in an interview for Robert W. Creamer's outstanding biography, *Babe: The Legend Comes to Life,* Carrigan told the author, "I've read many times that Ruth was sent down for more seasoning, but that's not true. He was already a finished pitcher, good enough for us or anybody else. But we were out of our pennant race and Lannin [who also owned the Providence Grays of the International League] wanted to win there, too."

Ernie Shore provided a late-in-life appreciation of Bill Carrigan, telling the author and oral historian Donald Honig, "Bill Carrigan was the tops. Best manager in the world. He was close to his players, and he had their respect. I never heard a man speak ill of him."

Babe Ruth chafed at Carrigan's reluctance to use him as a rookie or give him a starting role in the 1915 World Series, but he made the most of his upgraded role in 1916. After his sensational 14-inning defeat of Brooklyn in the 1916 World Series, holding the Dodgers scoreless for the final 13 innings, the Babe shouted to Carrigan, "I told you a year ago I could take care of those National League bums and you never gave me a chance." Nonetheless, in later years, the Babe always rated Bill Carrigan as his favorite manager.

Carrigan had been faulted for not capitalizing on Ruth's hitting ability. It wasn't until after Ed Barrow had taken over the Red Sox in 1918 that the Babe began appearing in the outfield when he was not on the mound. There were sound reasons why Bill Carrigan was satisfied to let well enough alone and use Babe Ruth strictly as a pitcher. Until he was sold by the Red Sox after the 1915 season, Tris Speaker had combined with Duffy Lewis and Harry Hooper to form an outfield some historians still contend was the best of all time. Even after the great Speaker left, the pitching staff needed a full time Babe Ruth more than the team needed a new outfielder. The Babe had become the best lefthanded pitcher in the league, winning 23 games in 1916 and leading the league with a 1.24 ERA.

Although Ruth, when he connected, sent awesome drives to distant parts of ballparks, he was an inconsistent hitter and a disappointment as a pinch hitter. Carrigan sent the Babe to bat thirty times as a pinch hitter, but got only five hits for a .167 average. Overall, however, the Babe batted .286 with seven home runs while pitching for Carrigan. Nonetheless, the conservative Bill Carrigan always had the Babe bat ninth, the pitcher's traditional place in the lineup.

Carrigan contributed positively to the emerging career of the ebullient youth whose self-confidence was a danger to team harmony. The veteran players were shocked by a rookie who insisted he was entitled to a turn at bat in pre-game practice. Once they sawed the Babe's bats in half. However, Carrigan smoothed the way to acceptance and Ruth's superior skills convinced his teammates he belonged wherever he insisted he did.

The story of Bill Carrigan, the man who was smart enough to retire when he was at the top, unfortunately has a conclusion as down-sided as the triumphant 1916 departure was upbeat. Soon after Carrigan's retirement, Joseph Lannin sold the Red Sox to theatrical entrepreneur Harry Frazee. In a few years Frazee had destroyed the franchise by selling Babe Ruth to the New York Yankees in 1920. Other Red Sox stars were shipped to New York City, and Boston dropped into the cellar. They finished last—except for one heady elevator ride to seventh place—every year from 1922 to 1926.

The owner of the shattered franchise left behind by Frazee was John Quinn, who knew baseball but was broke. He appealed to Bill Carrigan to return and turn Fenway Park into Camelot once again. Still a young man in his early forties, comfortably well-off and far too idle to suit his need for challenges, Carrigan let himself be talked into a two-year contract. Alas, the magic was gone. Babe Ruth was gone. Baseball had changed. Ruth's booming bat had encouraged a new style of play, and Carrigan simply didn't have the players to meet the challenge.

It was 1927, and in New York, the Babe was the most fearsome member of the Yankees "Murderers Row." The Red Sox finished last in 1927 and 1928. Carrigan stayed for one last try in 1929, which was also a bad year for bankers. Again, the Red Sox finished in the cellar, and Bill Carrigan retired again to small town life in Lewiston. He was a popular local figure, often called upon to speak at sports gatherings. He always told them about 1916, the year he led the Red Sox to a second consecutive World Series Championship. If he had any advice, it must have been, "quit while you're ahead."

17

Joe Charboneau: Far-Out Phenom

There are phenoms, and there are phenoms. Super Joe could drink beer through his nose and open bottles with his teeth—and, for a year, hit like blazes.

When a player blazes into view with an eye-catching performance, we call him a "phenom." Great things are expected from him and, sometimes, they follow. Joe DiMaggio, Ted Williams, and Stan Musial were first hailed as "young phenoms." As playing careers lengthen and a player who debuted as a "young phenom" becomes a steady star, he ceases being "a phenom." The players we remember only as phenoms are the ones who promised stardom but faded after streaking into prominence. They are like comets.

Some disappeared because their talents were inadequate; they had a weakness others discovered. Many were tragically cut down by an injury; some even by death. Others became victims of their own weaknesses.

The best known phenoms are familiar to many baseball fans. There was Louis Sockalexis, a Penobscot Indian from Maine, who shone for only half the 1897 season with the Cleveland Spiders but left a legacy: the team was later renamed Indians in his honor. There was Harry Agganis of the 1955 Red Sox, the celebrated "Golden Greek" who died of pneumonia just as he was becoming a star first baseman. There was Bob (Hurricane) Hazle, who helped the 1957 Braves win the National League pennant, then faded fast as a squall. There was Cub second baseman Ken Hubbs, the 1962 Rookie of the Year who died in a plane crash after his second season. And there was Mark (The Bird) Fidrych, who won 19 games for the 1976 Tigers and almost single-handedly invented the curtain call, only to succumb to arm trouble.

An even more recent phenom is slipping from memory. He deserves better because his may be the weirdest phenom story of all.

"Super Joe" Charboneau was a single-season phenom who fell from grace as colorfully as he zoomed to temporary stardom with the 1980 Cleveland Indians. When a player's accomplishments are great enough to win Rookie-of-the-Year honors, and he provides writers and broadcasters volumes of bizarre publicity stunts, he becomes a gold-plated phenom.

A signal that Charboneau's off-beat antics were more than baseball management was willing to tolerate came when the Philadelphia Phillies virtually gave him away in 1978, even though he'd batted .350 in the California League.

The Indians closed their eyes to Joe's eccentricities, preferring to see in him the second coming of Rocky Colavito. And what eccentricities! Writers told about such off-field activities as pulling out his own tooth with a pair of pliers, opening beer bottles with his eye socket, and removing an unwanted tattoo with a razor blade. Not to mention winning bets by eating lighted cigarettes, swallowing eggs in their shells, and downing glasses of beer through his nose.

Having led one minor league in batting in 1978, Charboneau moved up to the Southern Association, and topped that league, too, batting .352 for Chattanooga.

His batting alone would have drawn the press. Arriving at spring training in 1980, he hit as if he were still in Chattanooga. He gave interviews, demonstrated some of his clubhouse stunts, and made the starting lineup. When the team reached Cleveland, the city was ready for him. A rock group had turned out a record, "Go, Joe Charboneau," which was played incessantly. The Cleveland Plain Dealer, dubbing him "Super Joe," made Charboneau a cover feature in their Sunday magazine. Other publications ran features about him. He hit a 500-foot shot off Tom Underwood at Yankee Stadium and seemed to bat best against the league's best pitchers. Joe's hitting feats were written up daily.

Despite a long slump, he finished with a .289 average, 23 home runs, and 87 runs batted in. These are fine marks for a first-year player only twenty-five years old. He was named American League Rookie of the Year by the Baseball Writers' Association and *The Sporting News.*

Joe Charboneau's "rookie card" in the 1981 bubble-gum sets became a gilt-edged premium, bought up by collectors and dealers sure they had gotten in on the ground floor of an investment certainty. As Charboneau marched to Cooperstown, his first baseball card would increase in value many times. However, like most "penny stocks" shoestring investors buy, the Charboneau card today isn't an investor's dream. His career bubble burst like an overchewed wad of Topps gum.

Super Joe was again the center of attention in spring training of 1981. This time it was for what he had done, not what he might do. He stopped telling about removing teeth and tattoos and consuming indigestibles. He concentrated on his batting. But he was no longer hitting.

Charboneau floundered. By mid-season he had been sent to Charleston of the International League, having hit only .210 in 48 games, with only four home runs. Disgruntled by his demotion, he hit .217 with Charleston, with no home runs in 14 games before heading home to California to ruminate on his change in fortune.

The Indians brought him to spring training again in 1982. This time the interviews focused on what went wrong and, as the 1982 season began, why they were still going wrong. Joe hit only .214 in 22 games, with a pair of home runs. He returned to Charleston and failed. Even dropped down to the scene of earlier glory, Chattanooga, Joe couldn't hit. Another season was gone.

The next season found Joe Charboneau assigned to Cleveland's Buffalo farm club, in the International League. All he got from this circumstance was an extra's role in the Robert Redford movie, "The Natural." The player who had once seemed a natural himself was suspended for a week for making obscene gestures to the Buffalo fans. They had jeered him for not running out a ground ball.

Joe could have claimed a back injury had pointed the fickle finger of fate at him. Instead, he gave the finger back to the fans and demanded to be released. Having rejected winter trade offers and an inquiry from Japan, the Indians now freed Joe to accept whatever offers came his way. None came.

Joe joined a local semi-pro team to keep in shape and played in a tournament that involved four games in a single day. His team won. When they wanted to drink a toast after the final game, no one had brought a bottle opener. Not to worry; Joe opened the beer bottles with his teeth.

Eventually, Joe got an offer. It came from the San Jose Bees, hoping a return to the California League would restore Joe to greatness. The general manager, Harry Steve, scheduled a returning-hero welcome. When the plane landed, however, no passenger named Charboneau got off. Joe had returned to his wife and two children in Santa Clara. He might not have known the way to San Jose. More likely, he wanted to recover from his back injury first.

During the winter, doctors at Duke University Hospital removed two and a half discs from Joe's back. The prognosis was that Joe would be lucky to walk, let alone run and swing a bat. Joe lost twenty-five pounds after the operation and waited for another chance. He is still waiting.

Looking back, the irrepressible Joe Charboneau pointed out how few athletes achieve as much as he did: just making the major leagues and having one starring season. "It took a good break to get here," Joe said, "and a bad break to keep me from getting back."

18

Dizzy Dean vs. Carl Hubbell

DUELS TO REMEMBER

From 1932 through 1937, the National League had two superlative pitchers, the right-handed fireballer Dizzy Dean and the left-handed master of the screwball, Carl Hubbell. Dean was the stopper for the Cardinals and Hubbell was the "Meal Ticket" of the Giants staff. They were far more than mere rivals for stardom. They were each other's nemesis, the ominous opponent to be overcome if either was to achieve his maximum individual record.

Hubbell led New York to pennants in 1933, 1936, and 1937. Dean was the 30-game winner of the St. Louis Gas House Gang champions in 1934. Both pitchers dominated NL statistics during the six seasons they were at their best. With his blinding fast ball, Dean led in strikeouts from 1932 through 1935, while Hubbell topped the league in 1937. Dean led twice in victories, 30 in 1934 and 28 in 1935. Hubbell was the league's leading winner with 23 in 1933, 26 in 1936, and 22 in 1937. In 1936 and 1937 he had the best winning percentage while Dean had led in that category in 1934.

Dizzy Dean never won an ERA title, being more inclined to

coast behind early leads, while Hubbell's 1.66, 2.30, and 2.31 marks were the best in 1933, 1934, and 1936.

A characteristic both shared was innings pitched, a harbinger of the arm problems that eventually plagued them and ended their era of league dominance. Hubbell topped 300 innings pitched from 1933 through 1936. Dean, whose 286 led the league in his rookie year of 1932, pitched more than 300 innings a season from 1934 through 1936. Dean's totals were due in large part to the ability to pitch complete games—he was the league leader in that category from 1933 through 1936. Both pitchers were used often in relief, Hubbell leading the league in saves in 1934 and Dean in 1936.

There were no Cy Young awards then, but Hubbell won the Most Valuable Player trophy in 1933 and 1936 and Dean was MVP in 1934. Clearly, Dizzy Dean and Carl Hubbell were tops in their time and a special prestige was on the line whenever they faced each other.

Hubbell was a well-established winner before baseball first heard about the pitching phenomenon the Cardinals had down in the Texas League. Hubbell had come up in 1928, had pitched a no-hitter for the Giants in 1929, and always won more than he lost, but in the early '30s, he was not yet the dominant pitcher he would become. Dean, after a spectacular 3-hit debut on the final day of the 1930 season, talked himself back to the minors for the 1931 season. He returned in 1932, still trumpeting his greatness and was now given a chance to live up to his boasts. The contrast in the two pitchers was marked by more than Hubbell being lefthanded and Dizzy throwing righty. Although his screwball was his best pitch, the quietly efficient Hubbell was not the sort of eccentric player who is dubbed a "screwball." The flamboyant Dean fitted that description and boasted of his invincibility. However, he insisted, "it ain't bragging when you can go out and do it."

Individually, Dean and Hubbell achieved great feats while establishing themselves as mound aces. Dean set a record of 17 strikeouts on July 30, 1933, and Hubbell fanned five future Hall-of-Famers in a row in the 1934 All Star Game.

The first head-to-head meeting between the two titans evoked no particular excitement. When Hubbell and Dean paired off for the first time, on August 26, 1932, both were pitching for second division teams. Each pitcher was headed for an 18-game winning season; good but not spectacular. The game at Sportsmans Park in St. Louis was not viewed as a portent of things to come, and no pennant race was at stake. Dean went the route for a 4–2 victory, with Hubbell leaving for a pinch-hitter in the eighth inning.

All of 1933 passed without a Dean-Hubbell matchup. The Giants had suddenly jelled under Bill Terry, who had succeeded the legendary John McGraw as manger the year before. Hubbell earned the nickname, "The Meal Ticket," by reliably preventing losing steaks. Dean had his first 20-game winning season but not even as wily a promoter as Branch Rickey, the St. Louis general manager, thought to rearrange the pitching rotation, to match Hubbell and Dean to fill a ball park as they would in the future.

Even in 1934 the Dean vs. Hubbell matchups were a byproduct of pitching rotation. They were not yet conceived as duels between two mound aces who were as determined to prevent the other from gaining honors as they were to win them for themselves. On May 20 the resurgent Cardinals, pennant winners in 1930 and 1931, rode into New York to challenge the Giants, 1933 champs. The Cardinals now had two Deans. Dizzy's younger brother Paul, alliteratively, but inappropriately, dubbed "Daffy" by newspaper writers, had reached the majors. Dizzy had predicted, "me and Paul will win 45 games between us." When Diz had what has proved to be the last 30-game winning season in the National League and Paul won 19, they exceeded Dizzy's boast.

With Paul on the staff, the Cardinals had traded ace pitcher, Paul Derringer, to the Cincinnati Reds for the slick-fielding Leo Durocher, the shortstop they had lacked. With Joe Medwick, Pepper Martin, and Ripper Collins, the Cardinals, led by playing manager Frank Frisch, became the tough, scrappy Gas House Gang. The troop was led by Dizzy Dean, who had more than lived up to his own extravagant expectations.

The 1934 Giants were out to repeat as World Champions, but as the season wore on, the Giants wore out. Worse, Bill Terry's gloating pre-season remark, "Is Brooklyn still in the league?" would come back to haunt him. The schedule brought the simmering second division Dodgers to the Polo Grounds. Vengeance was theirs as, led by Casey Stengel, who had yet to demonstrate his managerial genius, Brooklyn proved it was still in the league by toppling the Giants twice in the final two days.

Dizzy Dean won his only 1934 confrontation with Hubbell 9–5 in a May 20 matchup, with Hubbell leaving for a pinch-hitter in the fifth inning. When the teams met in a doubleheader in St. Louis on July 26, it was Paul Dean—who would beat the Giants four times that season—who defeated Hubbell. Big brother Diz got the victory in the nightcap game, relieving in the eighth inning. The idea of pairing the two aces in scheduled match games, strangely, did not occur until the next season. Then games between the Cards and Giants were billed as "Diz meets Hubbell."

In 1935, the Cardinals and Giants battled each other all season only to both be bowled over by the Chicago Cubs in the final weeks of the schedule. The first 1935 meeting between Dean and Hubbell was in St. Louis on July 24. Both went the distance with Hubbell a 4–2 winner. In September there were two critical meetings between the pair. The Giants came to St. Louis for a crucial series and Dizzy won the opener on September 12, beating Hubbell 5–2. Three days later the roles were reversed with the Meal Ticket halting the Giants slide, 7–3. However, while the Cardinals and Giants were see-sawing along, the Chicago Cubs went on a 21-game winning streak and passed both in the closing days of the season. The exhausted Dean brothers failed to stop the Cubs in a final five game set in St. Louis and the Cubs took the pennant.

Hubbell's year was 1936. After a slow start, the Giants—and King Carl in particular—won with amazing consistency. On July 17 Hubbell shut out Pittsburgh, 6–0. The Giants were in fifth place. From then until the end of the season, Hubbell never lost. He finished the season with 16 straight victories as the Giants coasted to the pennant.

Along the way, Dean twice tried to stop Hubbell's march. Both went the distance in New York on July 21, but Hubbell went it better, winning 2–1 in ten innings. On September 3 in St. Louis, they both tossed complete games again, with Hubbell repeating as a 2–1 winner. Their final meeting of the year was on September 14 at the Polo Grounds, but neither was a starter. Hubbell was the winner in relief of a 7–5 game. Dean had no decision.

1937 was a fateful year. It was highlighted by Hubbell extending his consecutive victories to the all-time record of 24 by winning his first eight games, while Dean twice tried his best to halt the string. On May 19 in St. Louis, Dean's frustration reached the breaking point. Angered by umpire George Barr's third balk call against him, an irate Dizzy Dean resorted to bean balls, sending Giants batters diving into the dirt. Jimmy Ripple, a Giant outfielder with less tolerance for this sort of tactic than his teammates, charged Dean on the mound. Dizzy disappeared under a pile of outraged Giants players with the Cardinals peeling off the stacked up belligerents to wage individual battles. It was one of the rare baseball free-for-alls that produced real fights, with dozens of one-on-one matchups taking place simultaneously. Dizzy was in the middle of the fracas, but Hubbell retreated and sat quietly in the dugout until the carnage subsided a half hour later. When play resumed, Hubbell methodically added another game to his winning streak.

Carl Hubbell's unbroken string was ended, not by Dizzy Dean, but by a more ancient nemesis, the Brooklyn Dodgers, on May 21 at the Polo Grounds. Dean beat Hubbell a final time on June 9, in New York, 8–1. Carl Hubbell won what was to be the last time the rivals met, June 29, winning 8 to 1 at St. Louis, just before the 1937 All Star Game. Dizzy was named to start the 1937 All Star Game. In the third inning Earl Averill smashed a line drive back at the box and the ball hit Dean's foot, fracturing a toe. When he tried to pitch again too soon, favoring the injury, he damaged his arm and the blazing fast ball was gone.

Sold during the winter to the Chicago Cubs, Dean was a lame-armed pitcher with a fading career. However, he was the decisive pitcher for the Cubs 1938 championship, with a 7–0 season, chipping in enough spot victories to put Chicago in the World Series. Here he almost slow balled his way to a win over the New York Yankees, craftily holding them to two runs until the ninth inning before the Bronx Bombers finally solved his off-speed curves. However, as his career ended, used only against second division opponents in his rare appearances, Dizzy Dean never again locked horns with King Carl Hubbell.

Hubbell completed 1937 in fine fashion, with the Giants again winning a pennant. However, in 1938 the arm miseries which beset almost all pitchers who risk the strain of pitching 300 innings too many seasons, caught up with him. He had arm surgery before the year ended. The two great pitchers faded at almost the same pace. Dean got his last decision in 1940, posting a 3–3 season and Hubbell ended with a 4–4 record in 1943. In their peak years, Hubbell won six and Dean four of their ten head-to-head battles.

19

Brits in the Baseball Hall of Fame

With traditional bulldog determination, the British have resisted all attempts to transplant the hybrid we call America's "National Pastime." They cling to the tradition of cricket. They are content to have given us the ancient game of rounders, the seedling from which our own national game has sprouted. Fans' passions are inflamed in the British Isles by bruisers in short pants. Rugby and soccer serve to rally spectator enthusiasm. However, by having brought their ancient game of rounders to export quality, and sent several of their native sons to nurture its growth, the impact of Brits on our national game has been immense. It has resulted in three sons of Britain being enshrined in the Baseball Hall of Fame in Cooperstown: Henry Chadwick, Harry Wright, and Tommy Connolly.

The irony is that baseball's Hall of Fame itself is found in Cooperstown as the result of Albert Spalding's jingoistic insistence that baseball could only have been invented by an American. The rigged Mills Report—with less substance than a Geraldo Rivera investigative TV inquiry—created a comfortable myth. The baseball establishment happily conned itself into believing a youth named Abner Doubleday scribbled the entire rule book in the dirt of a pasture in a sleepy upstate New York town to wile away a summer's afternoon in 1839. Even so, the evidence that the early English game of rounders was baseball's ancestor was so obvious that not even the creators of baseball's ultimate theme park in Cooperstown could justify the Yankee Doodle Doubleday myth. When the Baseball Museum and Hall of Fame opened in 1939, timed to a hoaxed up "Centennial" tie-in, Henry Chadwick was on an inside plaque. He is the only baseball writer ever elected to the Hall of Fame. Abner Doubleday, the local boy who grew up to be a Union General in the Civil War, was relegated to the small ballpark built in Cooperstown by the WPA to generate employment in the Depression years.

English born Chadwick, whose parents brought him to Brooklyn as a young boy, began as a newspaper stringer turning in cricket match scores to The New York Times just before the Civil War years. He created public awareness of the fledgling sport of baseball and became its arbiter of rules. A boxscore evolved largely with his input to become baseball's most treasured source of research data. Although repeatedly threatened with extinction as a newsprint feature, Henry Chadwick's boxscore will survive because baseball as a recorded historic activity cannot endure without it.

Henry Chadwick was a prolific writer and innovator of baseball guides, histories, and statistical compilations, and he contributed widely in the general press into the early years of the twentieth century. He did more than any writer to shape baseball and expand its popularity. He had a broad scope of interests, covering other sports ranging from sailing to billiards to chess. He was a musician, wrote songs, played piano, was a drama critic and—briefly—a Civil War correspondent. Henry Chadwick was a prophet unhonored in his native land but revered by those who recognize him as a true father of American baseball.

Another Englishman who crossed the Atlantic as a youth accompanying his parents was Harry Wright. His father, Sam Wright, was a professional cricketeer, whose fame had spread from the British Isles to America. In the 1840s cricket was the preferred sport of the toffs at the fashionable St. George Cricket Club on Staten Island, New York. The club imported Sam Wright to run its program. America got his oldest son as a bonus. The Wright's next two sons were born in America. They were George, who is also a member of the Baseball Hall of Fame, and Sam, Jr., who appeared only briefly in major league games.

The oldest son, Harry, and his young brothers scandalized their father by deserting the traditional British game of cricket for the emerging local game of baseball. Harry became a member of the New York Knickerbockers, a social and athletic club of young city gentlemen which had included Alexander Cartwright. Cartwright is usually credited with codifying the rules of the time and with laying out a diamond with the presciently perceived "perfect dimensions" of 90 feet equally separating four bases.

As baseball developed, Harry Wright emerged as a good player and even better organizer. When the City Fathers of Cincinnati decided a winning baseball team would create good publicity for their fast growing metropolis at the close of the Civil War, they called in Harry Wright. They gave him a free hand and an open purse to bring together the best team that money could buy. He was told to form the first openly, fully professional baseball team. It wasn't nepotism that induced Harry to sign his younger brother George, first and pay him the most. George, less single-minded about baseball than Harry, was the best player in the game. The result of Harry's recruiting was the undefeated 1869 Red Stockings. Their 56-game nationwide tour spread the popularity of the game. A full professional league was inevitable and Harry Wright went to Boston to form the team which dominated it. From 1872 to 1875 he led the Boston Red Stockings to four National Association Pennants.

Filled with a prodigal's pride in the American game of baseball, Harry Wright joined with Albert G. Spalding in 1874 to lead an All Star squad to England. The British were bored with the spectacle which resulted. Only when Harry taught a few rudiments of cricket to his teammates from the U.S.A. and beat the English at their own game were the locals impressed—but then only at the athletic ability of their visitors. The urbanity of the cricket club was undisturbed by this first in a long series of attempts to spread the American game. The new gospel of roundball failed to convert the British to baseball.

The National Association gave way to a stronger professional organization when the National League supplanted it in 1876. Harry Wright then began an 18-year NL managerial career in Boston, Providence, and Philadelphia. Wright was an early devotee of using statistics to anticipate how upcoming games would be played. He pored over newspaper accounts of every game, looking for the hot players, those whose play was off their usual standard and interpreting stats to every advantage he could gain. He kept his own boxscores, neatly transferred into leather bound notebooks in a precise copperplate hand. Harry Wright studied statistics so avidly he lost his sight for a year in 1890.

Harry Wright was a pioneer in the development of America's National Pastime. He was a key factor in the transition from a "gentleman's game" to the unabashed professional era. As a strategist, he is credited with having players back up each other on fielding plays. Henry Chadwick is entitled to be called, "The Father of Baseball" but it was Harry Wright who reared the American version of rounders well into adolescence.

Baseball was a lusty, growing sport when the Connollys crossed the Atlantic Ocean from Manchester, England, where the 13-year-old Tommy had been born to Irish parents. A scrawny five-foot-seven, the lightweight teenager conceded he lacked the size to play the new game he found when his family settled in Natick, Massachusetts in 1893. However, he took joy in the game's rules and became a sandlot umpire whose fearless impartiality caught the attention of Tim Hurst, a top National League arbiter. Hurst passed the word of his protégé on to Tim Murnane, New England's most influential baseball personality. Known as "The Silver King," Murnane had founded and ruled the New England League for 30 years. He hired young Tommy Connolly as an umpire. Murnane had been one of the players Harry Wright and Albert G. Spalding had taken to England on the 1874 visit. He became a prominent Boston sports editor as well as a ruling hand directing the development of the National Pastime in New England.

For four seasons Connolly held single-handed sway over games between New England's smoky industrial cities. Then, in 1900, to appease some team owner's wishes, the league did not back Connolly in a dispute about a player's actions. Connolly put his ball and strike indicator in his pocket and went home to Natick. The league put out the story he was ill. He did not argue. He was sick of the way umpires were treated. They were bullied, sometimes assaulted and, without the league to back them with fines and suspensions of their attackers, were left vulnerable. Connolly, who had married and was raising a brood that would total seven children, looked for a more certain kind of work.

The founding of the American League saved Tommy Connolly for a continuing baseball career and eventual election to the Baseball Hall of Fame. Ban Johnson, the American League's founder, insisted its umpires must be respected. The National League had degenerated to a level of play in which games were often decided by which team could best intimidate the umpires.

It was Connie Mack, then a tall, thin young manager whose Philadelphia Athletics would become the American League's first dynasty, who recommended Connolly. He based his endorsement on his fellow New Englander's reputation. Actually, Mack had not seen young Tommy work a game but trusted those who praised his work. When the American League began its premier season in 1901 Tommy Connolly was one of its four umpires. Only one umpire would be assigned to games among the eight teams. When three of the season's opening games were rained out, Tommy gained the unique distinction of umpiring the first American League game ever played. The sun shone in Chicago where he was the single umpire. Later in his career Tommy Connolly would also umpire the first modern World Series game, in 1903.

Despite Ban Johnson's backing and his own bantam rooster

response to the taunts of players and fans, Tommy Connolly was beleaguered. Joe McGinnity, a spitball pitcher with Baltimore, once spat in Connolly's face. Irate Red Sox fans chased Connolly into a row boat that he paddled to safety in Boston Harbor. This led to Connolly heading off arguments by quickly bouncing belligerent players and his reputation for quick-triggered response grew.

The turning point came in 1922. Babe Ruth had been suspended by Commissioner Kenesaw Mountain Landis for ignoring a ban on post season barnstorming by players who had appeared in the World Series. Ruth missed spring training and the first six weeks of the season. When he was slow to round into form, the New York fans rode him hard. The Babe did not take the insults gracefully. He tried to climb into the stands to reach a heckler only to have umpire Connolly thrust his 150 pounds in the way. Ruth allowed himself to be pushed away and led from the field.

Both men seem to have been affected by the incident. It marked a point in the careers of both. From that time on, Babe Ruth was never thrown out of a game, nor did Tommy Connolly ever banish a player. He explained his forbearance: "The fans are entitled to see the players. They didn't come out to see me dust off home plate."

Tommy Connolly continued to push this point of view through his long life in baseball. He retired as an active umpire in 1931 when he was 60. He then served as the supervisor of American League umpires until he was 83, working from an office in Chicago and constantly touring the American League ball parks. He kept his crews under a watchful eye to be sure they followed the examples he had set. He was not only the reigning authority on how an umpire should work a game, he was recognized as the preeminent authority on the rules of baseball. He even became chairman of baseball's Rules Committee.

Tommy Connolly finally announced his retirement in 1954. The year before, he and Bill Klem, his counterpart from the National League, had received the ultimate honor of election to the Baseball Hall of Fame, the first umpires to be inducted. It was an achievement for a man to contemplate during his final years. Unlike Henry Chadwick and Harry Wright, who were elected posthumously, Tommy Connolly experienced the honor in his lifetime. He lived to be 90, alert, among a large family in the house he had built in Natick, Massachusetts. It was a life whose formative years had been spent in England but was enriched by his career in baseball.

The three Brits whose plaques hang in the gallery of the Baseball Hall of Fame made unique contributions to America's "National Pastime." Perhaps now Henry Chadwick, Harry Wright, and Tommy Connolly contemplate from somewhere above with a satisfied air, as they watch the marvelous game they helped nurture from British roots transplanted in American soil—a game now poised to spread widely across the planet as the new International Pastime.

20
F. C. Lane

Baseball fans are forever advancing the cause of overlooked ball players, insisting on their worthiness of election to the Baseball Hall of Fame and enshrinement in Cooperstown. They take little interest, however, in helping the Hall of Fame bestow the honor of the J.G. Taylor Spink Award. It was a fine idea in 1962 to begin honoring those whose prose and journalism round out the total picture of baseball and elevate it above simple statistics. What the early inductees who followed the inaugural choice, Spink himself, shared was a national identity. Ring Lardner, Hugh Fullerton Jr., Grantland Rice, Red Smith, et al, had nationally known bylines. Spink himself, although not a significant writer, was the editor of the once enormously important *The Sporting News.* In later years the annual accolade has gone to writers, however worthy, who have or had regional readership. In the process, an overlooked giant from the past has been bypassed: F.C. Lane, for twenty-seven years the editor of *Baseball Magazine.*

Ferdinand Cole Lane was far more than an inkstained wretch plying an editor's trade from a Manhattan office at 70 Fifth Avenue. He was an erudite, educated man whose life in baseball was not the only noteworthy accomplishment he left behind when he died in his ninety-ninth year. *The Sporting News* and, before it expired, *The Sporting Life,* had kept a weekly eye on baseball. TSN provided boxscores and game notes, primarily. Lane, when he accepted appointment to edit *Baseball Magazine,* realized that a monthly could not compete for explicit coverage with a weekly. He focused on feature stories, mainly describing the off-field lives of players. For this insightful trait, historians and biographers are thankful.

F.C. Lane visited famous ballplayers at their homes during the off-season, writing detailed accounts of what they did far away from the ballfield. As a result, we have far richer knowledge of Honus Wagner, Walter Johnson, Grover Cleveland Alexander, and others than what we learn from memoirs and reminiscences written after their starring careers had ended. Lane would be invited to spend several days and would come away with family anecdotes and history. Visiting Coffeyville, Kansas, he learned Walter Johnson's father had once played town ball back in Ohio. A short train ride away in St. Paul, Nebraska, Lane met Grover Cleveland Alexander's father and learned what political zeal had suggested naming one of a brood of thirteen for a U.S. president. Lane, at home in any company, hunkered down with Honus Wagner and his hunting dogs and went into the fields to shoot quail with Alexander and Johnson.

His articles are richly illustrated with gravure photos, taken during visits or borrowed from family albums. A rich trove of retrievable art work, it is within the capacity of the photo section of the Baseball Hall of Fame to copy them.

The adaptable F.C. Lane was born on a wheat farm in Minnesota, on October 25, 1885. The fourth child of Alpheus Ferdinand

Lane, he toddled along as the family traversed a route back toward the east. After stops in Akron and Canton, Ohio, and a brief look around Lowell, Massachusetts, the Lanes settled in Truro on Cape Cod before finally moving to Marion.

Lane completed his secondary education at Tabor Academy and received a B.A. from Boston University in 1907. The future writer of baseball news had no known connection with the sport. As a graduate student he worked as an assistant biologist for Boston University and the Massachusetts Commission of Fisheries and Game. Visiting the Mediterranean and countries along its shores stretched his undergraduate time at Boston University to seven years. He spent six months in London, arriving with nineteen cents and scrambling to raise the fare to come home.

Troublesome lungs sequestered F.C. Lane for a while in a log cabin in Alberta, Canada, before he returned to Boston and began writing for *Baseball Magazine.* He soon was named editor and moved to New York. Ensconced in the security of his new position, Lane crossed the bridge to Brooklyn and married Emma in 1914. He was a prolific writer, turning out hundreds of articles mostly analyzing baseball's structure, its players, events, and trends. He was also a ghostwriter for inarticulate celebrities, and he produced an overlooked classic, "Batting," in 1925. It contains batting tips and observations by hundreds of early twentieth century hitters and was sold through *Baseball Magazine.*

Lane regarded Cape Cod as his home base and he returned there in the late 1930s, leaving behind volumes of work printed on now-crumbling paper. Happily for researchers, *Baseball Magazine* has been transferred to microfiche and is available from the library at the Baseball Hall of Fame. It is also available to SABR researchers at the SABR office. Credit for preserving these fragile works belongs to Mark Rucker, head of Transcendental Graphics, and Tom Heitz, former director of the National Baseball Library at the Hall of Fame.

Leaving baseball behind him, Lane was only in mid-career. From 1914 to 1943, he was chairman of the history department at Piedmont College in Demorest, Georgia. (Yes, trivia buffs, home of John Mize). He established a journalism program at the college and was awarded an honorary Doctor of Humanities degree. Lane succumbed to the wanderlust that had first struck during his college years, and became a travel writer. He circled the globe seven times with stops at both the north and south poles. Not limited to prose, Lane also published poetry. He concluded an autobiographical sketch, written in his late sixties, by saying, "My more recent writings have been largely devoted to some thirty odd articles for encyclopedias and a series of books on global geography. I have been happily married for thirty-eight years and my wife shares my many interests. Although I am losing the argument with Father Time, as the years pass too swiftly, I still find life a continuous adventure, more interesting than any of its accomplishments." Father Time granted F.C. and his wife Emma three decades more of retirement on their beloved Cape Cod. Lane died on June 30, 1984, followed ten months later by his life's companion.

A graceful writer, an erudite man, F.C. Lane was more than a contributor to the written world of baseball's past. He was an adornment. There are no more Lardners, Rices, and Red Smiths whose wide readership deserves recognition at the Hall of Fame.

Already a great many artifacts donated by the Lanes are within the walls of the Baseball Museum and Hall of Fame in Cooperstown. It is high time his name was included in the writer's wing. Fittingly, it is located in the newly rebuilt library where his considerable contributions, the editing and writing of perceptive pieces for *Baseball Magazine*, are preserved.

21

Baseball Joe Matson: The Greatest Player Who Never Was

Let others praise the literary giants who have brought their skills to baseball fiction. Wolf, Farrell, Malamud, Harris, Coover, and Kennedy deserve kudos. But I toss my cap in the air and shout, "huzzah!" for Lester Chadwick, the author who invented the exploits of the Baseball Joe series.

The canon covering Baseball Joe's career is contained in 14 novels, published by Cupples & Leon, from 1912 to 1928. These differ from other juvenile books about baseball as they trace the personal and professional history of the principal character from his early teens in *Baseball Joe of the Silver Stars*, to his ultimate major league achievement in *Baseball Joe, Pitching Wizard.*

Joe Matson is 15 years old in the first book and 34 when the series ends. He moves from town team to prep school and into Yale. Unlike Frank Merriwell who remained an undergraduate at Old Eli for dozens of dime novels, Joe Matson left after a single season of varsity pitching to enter professional baseball.

A season in the Central League and he is drafted by the St. Louis Cardinals. His potential as a rookie catches the eye of the New York Giants management and a trade is arranged which brings

Baseball Joe to the team of his role model, Christy Mathewson.

Chadwick drew extensively on the actual events of baseball to provide Baseball Joe the circumstances of the books. The series runs approximately parallel to a passing scene which saw the transition from the dead ball era to the lively ball and the advent of the home run. In the course of the 14 novels we find Joe Matson touring the world as a member of the world champion Giants, resisting the temptations of the Federal League, being shamed by the Black Sox and adapting to the lively ball.

Although the backgrounds and circumstances changed with the times, the plots did not. The books are formula-written with a villain for each, either with a conspiracy to frame Joe for a crime or to kidnap him so he will miss "the big game." Joe never failed to show up for any crucial game, often dragging a covey of villains behind him.

If you are looking for unique plotting, you'll not find it in these books. If complex personalities intrigue you, you'll be disappointed to know Baseball Joe Matson is a one-dimensional demi-god.

However, the Baseball Joe series was only intended to serve boys coming to maturity from 1912 until the eve of World War II. As the books were passed down from older brother to younger, they imparted tidbits of the actual history of the game, playing tips, strategy insights, and an understanding of the framework of organized baseball. These are peripheral values to hero-worshipping young readers. Foremost, Baseball Joe is the best of pitchers, steals bases when he wishes, and develops into a batter with the "hit 'em where they ain't" adroitness of Willie Keeler and the power to drive the ball a tad farther than Babe Ruth.

Joe combines the skills of Cobb, Speaker, Lajoie, and Wagner. About the only thing he didn't do was go behind the plate. The author was probably stumped on how to have Joe pitch to himself.

The Baseball Joe books were among the first juvenile novels we ever read, taking them in random order in the early 1930s. I doubt if all 14 trickled down from older family members whose hand-me-downs in juvenile literature kept me enthralled during my pre-teen years.

However, I recently borrowed the entire series from a friend who has collected them all. I was able to read my way from the time when young Joe Matson and his family move to Riverside, a town on a river coursing somewhere through New England, until the last book, published 16 years later. Read in maturity, these books are amazingly arcane. However, they also are tinged with a personal nostalgia for a time which was disappearing as my own adolescence began.

I am sure my own interest in baseball's past was first awakened by these books. Chadwick, a pen name borrowed knowingly from The Father of baseball writers, Henry Chadwick, injects considerable historical information into his stories. For example, while Joe is traveling by train to spring training, he meets an old man who says he played right field for the Cincinnati Red Stockings of 1869. The old-time ballplayer tells Joe about the early years of the game, adding that he was in the lineup the day Paul Hines made the first unassisted triple play.

Throughout the novels, Joe Matson experiences events which served to teach the juvenile reader the realities of life in professional baseball. Joe resents the fact that his contract can be sold without his consent, but accepts this as necessary "for the good of the game."

Joe can always see the other fellow's viewpoint, but stands with the establishment whenever a crisis occurs. A boy reading the books for excitement, for accounts of games played, for the suspense as Joe escapes one dastardly plot after another, unconsciously absorbs a great deal of baseball background.

Chadwick blended fact and fiction. He barely hid the actual identity of real life players: Hornsby was Mormsby; Ruth was Roth ("look out for his beanball") as a pitcher and Kid Rose, later, as a slugger. Joe's idol and mentor on the Giants was Hughson, famous for his fadeaway. McRae is the bellicose Giant's manager.

Baseball Joe Matson began playing in New England, as a boy, on a town team, after his family had moved to Riverside. The Matson family consisted of the father, an inventor and early century wimp. He is constantly being swindled by evil partners whose ill intent is always apparent to his son. Mother Matson, who hopes young Joe will enter the ministry, flutters from crisis to crisis, and presumably found Joe, and his sister, Clara, a year younger, under a leaf in the cabbage patch.

The family is 110 percent four square in every virtue but Joe is the first to recognize he has been living in the twentieth century for a decade. Even so, Joe's boyhood transportation is by bike, with an oil lamp on the handlebars, or by hiring a livery rig from the town stable to chase fleeing villains.

Joe's athletic skills are utilized from time to time by the author to resolve a crisis. Joe enables a man to escape a burning building by hurling up a ball of yarn and attaching a stout rope to it so the man can slide down to safety.

In another situation, Joe first meets Mabel Varley, the romance of his life, when she caroms past him, helpless in a carriage lurching behind a runaway horse. Joe stops the animal in its tracks by throwing a stone and hitting the horse in the head, knocking it unconscious.

This first meeting with Mabel begins a succession of appearances in subsequent books which even the most juvenile of readers realized must someday lead Baseball Joe to the altar. Actually, Joe's courtship of Mabel extends from *Baseball Joe in the Central League,* through four intervening books, until Joe and Mabel finally tie the knot in *Baseball Joe, Home Run King.*

There was a break in the series after 1918, due, most likely, to the First World War and the scarcity of paper for juvenile books. Although the books parallel the real events in baseball, the author seems to have overlooked World War I. Unlike Matty, the obvious counterpart for the fictionalized Matson, Baseball Joe not only doesn't go to war, he is oblivious of it.

It is quite likely that the Edward Stratemeyer "fiction mill" changed horses behind the pseudonym, Lester Chadwick, at this point. To give this project a literary mystique it doesn't deserve—after all, we're not going to divide into camps over authorship, (no Baconians need apply)—it can be observed that the books from 1912 to 1918 contain vastly more baseball historical references. Also, the dialogue is characteristically dotted with what I will suggest is "the Stratemeyer stammer."

This is a dialogue device, in which the personal pronoun is repeated to connote stress and determination: "I—I'd rather fight than give in."

But more significant in the books from 1922 on, is that Joe's upward mobility, having been attained on the Giants, no longer serves as the book's achievement pinnacle. Where Joe had been able to end each book looking forward to a coming season played on a higher level—sandlot, to prep, to college, to minors, to majors, to the Giants—once with New York, each successive season has to top the last. This was to lead to problems for the author, whoever wielded the pen behind the pen name.

Eventually, Baseball Joe had done it all. He rarely won a crucial game without pitching a no-hitter. When a base hit would do, he customarily belted the ball out of sight. He had been carried off the field in triumph by his teammates so often they were becoming stoop-shouldered by the task.

Whether it was ordained that *Baseball Joe, Pitching Wizard,* was to be Joe Matson's swan song, instead of another of a continuing series of extraordinary accomplishments, is left to conjecture by those familiar with the publishing world. I think it was.

There had been a lapse of three years since Baseball Joe had left his readers agape in wonderment. In 1925's Baseball Joe, Champion of the League, the Giants win more games than any team ever had. Joe, of course, pitches the final victory and, for a variation on the theme of personal contribution, doesn't hit a home run. Instead, he scores from first base on a single.

This caps a season in which Joe Matson leads the leagues in niceness, decency, and celibacy; and incidentally, batting average, home runs, stolen bases, and, when pitching, strikeouts and earned run average. It didn't seem possible for Joe to exceed the excess of success in the future.

Sensibly, the author behind the series—let's credit Edward Stratemeyer with blocking out these books, if not providing the final manuscript—tried to phase Joe out. Missing from the list of Baseball Joe books in the Grobani bibliography is the 1926 *Baseball Joe, Club Owner.*

Joe leaves the major leagues with a sore arm, the consequence of evil doings by the villains in the prior volume. This plot seems to be an effort to close the circle of novels at twelve. When the publisher agreed to permit Joe to leave the big leagues, there was a tacit awareness this would deprive the books of the most attractive element for juvenile readers. We—for I was among them—wanted Joe to conquer more baseball worlds, not settle down in a front office job in a minor league city.

Joe is back in his boyhood hometown, Riverside, now strangely relocated in the Midwest. It might be that a new hand has taken up the pen behind the pseudonym and didn't remember Riverside was in New England, or the marketing people at Cupples & Leon may have thought it better for circulation to locate in mid-America.

Joe buys the franchise and finds three of his old Silver Star teammates still in the lineup. He encounters a new set of blackguards and reveals himself a closet bigot. At one point he explains, about Moe Russnak, the book's bad guy, "He's a Jew that lives in Pentolia (rival city). Not that I have anything against him because of his race. Our shortstop, Levy, is a Jew and he's as fine a fellow as there is on the team."

Having delivered himself of the classic brotherhood bromide, but not introduced Levy to his sister, Clara, who will wed Joe's best friend, another WASP, Joe manages the team, in a non-playing role, to the pennant. He then gives the franchise to his dependent father, whose patents have been stolen again and again during the series, and his brother-in-law, Mabel's brother, Reggie Varley.

The series might have ended at that point, but someone decided, in 1928, to bring Joe back to the major leagues, his arm restored. One can sense Lester Chadwick chafing at having to find more worlds—and World Series—for his protagonist to conquer. Possibly it crossed the author's mind to have Baseball Joe tumble off Coogan's Bluff, locked in combat with the book's villain, as Conan Doyle, bored by the exploits of Sherlock Holmes, had sent him over Reichenbach Falls in the clutches of Professor Moriarity.

In the end, Chadwick used a more appropriate means and more diabolical. He gave the plot a final twist by writing finis to a series with a climax that could never be exceeded in a subsequent book.

Joe had purged baseball of two teammates who had accepted bribes from gamblers. Despite having to replace them with two untested rookies, the Giants win yet another pennant and provide Joe with an obligatory encore in the subsequent World Series. Baseball Joe's readers know their hero will win: we read only to learn how he will do it this time.

Joe is concerned about the two rookies who have replaced the crooked veterans. He worries how they will stand up to the pressure of championship games and fears they will embarrass themselves by making crucial errors on balls hit to them. Joe has the solution. He avoids the risk of shaky-handed fielders by not allowing the ball to be batted to them. His solution? *He methodically strikes out all 27 batters as they come to the plate.*

If there's to be a plaque honoring Baseball Joe Matson erected in the Baseball Hall of Fiction Fame, let it be noted that Joseph Matson, born in 1894, died of over-achievement in 1928. The series ended at that point. The books remained in circulation for a decade or more longer and still appear in secondhand bookstores. They are fun to read, loaded with historic detail, and, if they were part of your own boyhood, leave you awash in nostalgia.

22

Larrupin' Lou Bids the Fans Adieu

There was no bounce in Lou Gehrig's step as he walked into the depot dining room of Union Station in Kansas City. His roommate, Bill Dickey, carried two equipment bags, his and Lou's. The World Champion New York Yankees were in town to play an exhibition game with their AAA farm team, the Kansas City Blues of the American Association. Back east, the new Baseball Hall of Fame was being dedicated in Cooperstown, New York. It was June 11, 1939.

During the night a westbound Union Pacific train had dropped the two Pullmans used by the Yankees on a siding. The team, sleepy-eyed and wearing rumpled suits (their manager insisted they must), would have breakfast in the depot dining room before riding cabs over to the ball park for the sold out game. When the game was over, only Lou Gehrig would check into a hotel after his teammates left. The next day Gehrig would take a train to Rochester, Minnesota, and visit the Mayo Clinic. Someone there might be able to tell him why, at 36, he felt like a man in his sixties.

The Yankees owners, taking advantage of an off day on the major league schedules for the Hall of Fame ceremony, had added this stop to their western swing. The day before they had brushed aside the last place Browns twice before a sprinkling of depression era fans in St. Louis. Today would be different. Over 20,000 tickets had been sold to fans eager to see the famous Yankees. The new star, Joe DiMaggio, would face off against his older brother, Vince, a center fielder, like Joe. Vince was leading the American Association in batting and home runs. Local enthusiasts argued Vince was the best of the ball playing DiMaggio brothers.

The newspapers had warned that Lou Gehrig would not play. He had been missing from the Yankees lineup since May 2, when his consecutive game string had ended at 2,130 straight games. As the team's captain, he traveled with the team, carrying the lineup cards to the umpires before each game, then returning to the dugout to puzzle over his lost strength and coordination.

Later that day, Lou Gehrig would explain to reporters, "I guess everybody wonders why I'm going to the Mayo Clinic. But I can't believe there's something wrong with me. It's not conceivable that I could go to pieces so suddenly. I feel fine, feel strong, and have the urge to play, but without warning this year I've apparently collapsed. I'd like to play some more and I want somebody to tell me what's wrong. Usually a fellow slows up gradually."

When Gehrig handed the starting lineup card to the home-plate umpire, surprisingly his name was on it. His replacement in the Yankee lineup, Babe Dahlgren, had been crossed out and Gehrig would bat eighth. He explained that as long as so many people had come to see him, he would try to play a few innings for them. He handled four putouts at first base and it was the third inning before Gehrig came to bat.

The wide stance in the lefthanded batter's box was familiar.

Gehrig squared off the way he always had. The bat was held the same way. But the menace was gone. He made contact and the box score tells us that he grounded out, second to first. When the Yankees took the field again, Dahlgren was at first base. Larrupin' Lou Gehrig had batted for the last time as a New York Yankee. He would never play a game of baseball again.

The fans got their money's worth. The Yankees, winning 4–1, kept their stars, Gordon, Keller, Rolfe, Henrich, and Crosetti, on the field for six innings. Joe DiMaggio, with a bandaged right wrist, was hitless in three times at bat. His brother, Vince, singled in his three times up. Neither hit a home run. A brisk wind was blowing in on an otherwise ideal sunny June afternoon.

After the game the police had to rescue the Yankees from crowds of autograph seekers. Inside the clubhouse, the Blues youngest player, the future Yankee shortstop, Phil Rizzuto, was a happy youngster gathering autographs for himself.

On July 4, after he had learned his fate from the Mayo Clinic, Lou Gehrig would make his formal farewell to the fans in special ceremonies at Yankee Stadium. The scene is familiar, both from newsreels which show a tearful Gehrig saying, "Today, I'm the luckiest man on the face of the earth," or actor Gary Cooper recreating the scene in the movie, "The Pride of the Yankees."

However, it was to a typical Midwestern baseball crowd, few of whom had ever seen him play before, that the once indestructible Iron Horse said his last goodbye as a player. The slugger called "Larrupin' Lou" for the velocity of base hits crashing off his bat, had made one final, awkward appearance. The time left to Larrupin' Lou was short. He died on June 2, 1941, not quite two years after his last ball field appearance, playing first base in the uniform of the Yankees in Kansas City far from New York City and the Yankee Stadium.

23

My Three Great World Series

It has been this writer's good fortune to turn out three full-length biographies: Wilbert Robinson; Walter Johnson; and Grover Cleveland Alexander. Each includes a World Series which is made memorable by the achievements of The Big Train, Ol' Pete, and the misfortunes of Uncle Robbie.

They are extracted for this collection by agreement with the publishers of the Johnson and Alexander biographies, Diamond Communications, Inc. "Uncle Robbie," co-authored with Norman Macht, will be published in 1999 for distribution to SABR's membership as well as bookstores.

1920: The Most Eventful World Series Ever Played

Brooklyn was slightly favored to win the 1920 World Series by the baseball press, but the fans' sympathy was with the Cleveland Indians. Since Ray Chapman's fatal beaning by Carl Mays in August, fans everywhere had rooted for the Indians. The success of his rookie replacement, Joe Sewell, renewed their expectations. Playing manager Tris Speaker, was still a super star. The lineup that would face Brooklyn was potent. "The Gray Eagle" would flank himself according to who pitched for the other team. Charley Jamieson or Steve Evans would be in left field and in right field he platooned Elmer Smith, Jack Graney, and the former pitching ace of the Red Sox, Joe Wood. "Smokey Joe" could barely throw the ball back to the infield, but his bat was potent.

Jimmy Johnston's brother, Doc Johnston, shared first base duties with George "Tioga" Burns. The Johnston brothers made a new World Series record by being the first brothers to face each other in the championship series. A player whose last name, Wambsgannss, would be immortalized in trivia questions forever, appeared in boxscores as "Wamby." He was a fine fielder and fair batsman. The rookie, Joe Sewell, was now playing an inspired game at shortstop. The fans and players had not forgotten Ray Chapman, of course, and the Indians wore a black mourning band in his memory on the left sleeves of their uniforms. At third base was a Brooklyn nemesis. In the 1916 World Series, playing for the Red Sox, Larry Gardner hit two home runs and led all players with six runs batted in. Steve O'Neil and Les Nunmaker shared the catching. The staff could not match Brooklyn in depth. They had only three double figure winners, but all had 20 or more victories. Jim Bagby led all with 31 wins. Spitballer Stan Coveleski had won 24 and Ray Caldwell 20. There had been no fourth starter on the staff until the late season addition of Duster Mails in August. Uncle Robbie remembered Mails who had dubbed himself "The Great" when he joined Brooklyn in 1915. He would call himself "The Great Mails" during a long and mostly PCL career. However, it was his high inside pitch that caused batters to call him "Duster." He had been an unused pitcher on Brooklyn's roster for the 1916 World Series. In 1917 he went to Pittsburgh on waivers but never pitched for them. Instead, he was sent to Sacramento, possibly to mature. He did as a pitcher but continued to act up to his juvenile reputation.

In 1916 the Dodgers/Robins, the nicknames were interchangeable depending on which paper you read, had set off bravely for Boston only to lose as soon as they got there. In 1920 they would start the Series at home. They celebrated by introducing new cream colored uniforms with dark pin stripes. Pin stripes are supposed to make the wearer appear slimmer. This sartorial tip did not benefit the rotund Uncle Robbie, however.

The World Series opened with a full metropolitan flare. New York Mayor John Hylan entered Ebbets Field waving a Brooklyn pennant (the former city was now part of his political domain.) The trumpets of the Police Department band blew a fanfare as the mayor bowed to the chilled crowd. Tuesday, October 5, was a raw day. The Mayor, in public view, had to keep warm as best he could.

Up in the press box each writer was slipped a half pint of whiskey with the compliments of owner Charles H. Ebbets. They sipped gratefully throughout the game. One writer was so appreciative that he stated his approval of Charley's kindness in his story of the game. Charley's gesture might have been gracious, but it was also illegal. The next day the Federal Government raided Ebbets Field. Prohibition agents, blue noses sniffing suspiciously, searched the press area and even ransacked Ebbets' private office. Charley, of course, had been tipped off to the raid and had moved the whiskey to safety.

Although Burleigh Grimes had won 21 games and his .676 winning percentage edged out Grover Alexander, Robbie gave the opening assignment to the World Series experienced Rube Marquard. Tris Speaker responded by withholding his league leading pitcher, 31 game winner, Jim Bagby. Instead, spitballer Stan Coveleski went to the mound.

Ivy Olson lost little time in providing a bone headed play and Cleveland capitalized on it. When George Burns' wind blown pop fly fell beyond the reach of the lumbering Ed Konetchy, Ivy watched in bemusement. The first baseman rifled a throw to second base to stop Burns from advancing. Alas, Ivy Olson had not covered the bag. Burns scored as the errant throw ended up in the left field corner. As he often did, next Olson turned in a dazzling play to get the first out of the inning. However, Joe Wood was walked and young Joe Sewell rifled a single which moved Wood to third base. Steve O'Neil doubled to left and Wood scored with Sewell stopping at third. Coveleski grounded to first baseman Ed Konetchy who stepped on the base and threw to the plate. Sewell stopped and tried to get back to third base but was tagged out in a rundown. Coveleski had the Dodgers swinging feebly at his swerving spitballs. Cleveland added a third run in the fourth inning on a pair of doubles by Wood and O'Neil (his second). Zack Wheat scored Brooklyn's only run in the seventh. After doubling to lead off, he moved to third on an infield out and scored on another.

Down a game in a best of nine series, wasn't too severe a handicap, the Dodgers fans assured themselves. "Boily'll get 'em tomorrow," they promised each other. Uncle Robbie sent his ace, Burleigh Grimes ("Boily" in the patois of Flatbush) to the mound in Game Two. Jim Bagby held Brooklyn to three runs. But Grimes was more effective in the clutches and shutout the Indians on seven hits.

Sherry Smith, whom Uncle Robbie favored in a must win situation, again rose to the occasion and won a tough game, 2–1. Brooklyn's pair of runs came in the first inning off Ray Caldwell. Duster Mails came in to relieve and stopped the Robins cold. He turned them back inning after inning while Sherry Smith did the same. The Indians threatened in the fifth when Sewell walked and O'Neil singled with one out. Mails, insisting he was as good a hitter as a pitcher, hit the ball sharply only to have Ivy Olson turn it into a spectacular double play.

Cleveland threatened again in the eighth inning. With one out, O'Neil got his second single. Mails was due up but this time Speaker sent in a pinch hitter, Les Nunmaker. However, he, too, hit into a clutch double play, ending the inning. Cleveland went out in order in the ninth and the Dodger fans exhaled in relief. Sherry Smith had scraped through with a three hit shut out. The Dodgers led the World Series, two games to one.

Now came what only a few understand to be the turning point of the World Series. The greedy owners had decided a best of nine series could bring in more money at the box office than the standard best of seven games. This meant that, although they led by a 2–1 margin, there would now be four straight games in Cleveland. The confident Robins did not fear the prospects of losing all four games to the Indians and losing the Series. "Wait for us here," Eddie Bennett, the mascot, was told. "We'll be back to wrap up the Series, if we don't win it in Cleveland." Eddie Bennett's dark visaged face grew darker. The hunchback had expected, as a reward for the good luck he had brought the team, for the thousands of back rubs he had endured, that he would travel to Cleveland with the team. Betrayed, he was devastated and angry. If many people can believe in a "Curse of the Bambino," why not "The Curse of the Mascot?" Eddie Bennett's fury was that of jilted demon from hell.

"A coise on yez," Bennett swore, in Brooklynese. He left the bats and equipment for someone else to pack and ship to Cleveland. He was finished with the ungrateful Dodgers. No one ever accepted the blame for the costly blunder of snubbing the team's good luck charm. The public couldn't believe it of the beloved Uncle Robbie. They assumed he just hadn't thought about the mascot, being too busy working on his pitching rotation for the rest of the Series. They could believe it of Charley Ebbets. One of the pleasures of going to the ball park was to heckle Ebbets about his tight-fistedness. He would shout back at his tormentors, "How come I'm the only big league owner without a car? I have to ride the trolley to the games."

We don't know how Eddie Bennet spent his time after the World Series. How he survived the winter, we can only guess. However, the baseball world knows that the next season he persuaded the 1921 New York Yankees that, indeed, he had the power to bring good luck, or if he was crossed, bad luck. He only had to point out that, once he had jinxed his former employers, the Brooklyn Dodgers, they went to Cleveland without him and lost four straight games and the World Series. They only came back to Brooklyn to clean out their lockers. Eddie Bennett was not there to help them. With the Yankees, Eddie Bennett became the best known mascot of all time. They didn't object to paying his travel expenses to the next three World Series. In 1921–23, their opponents were the New York Giants and subway fare to the Polo Grounds was only a nickel.

The "Curse of the Mascot" took effect even before the first game was played in Cleveland. The first headline of the afternoon papers announced: "Marquard Arrested As Ticket Scalper." That morning the police claimed they heard Rube Marquard try to sell eight box seats for $350. They had been bought for $52.80. Rube, protesting that a mistake had been made, was released on his own cognizance pending a hearing on Monday. The Rube, who was far from a bucolic hayseed, having become a New Yorker with a Broadway taste, went to the ball park and even pitched three scoreless relief innings. It was in a losing cause as Stan Coveleski again beat Brooklyn, 5–1. The series was even and Eddie Bennett's hex was working.

In Game Five, a chilly breeze blew off Lake Erie like Eddie Bennett's icy wrath. Three unusual first time events happened, one of which has never been repeated. Surely three staggering misfortunes in one game weren't happenstance.

The pride of Uncle Robbie's staff, Burleigh Grimes, who had pitched a shut out in the second game might have needed more rest between starts. It seemed to be a bad choice by the manager. The first two batters singled and then, on a sacrifice bunt by Tris Speaker, Grimes fell down in pursuit of the ball and the bases were full. Then Elmer Smith hit the first ever grand slam home run in a World Series game. In the fourth inning pitcher Jim Bagby came to bat. There were temporary stands in center field which were open ended. Bagby's drive found an opening in the jerry-built structure and he became the first pitcher to hit a home run in a World Series.

Now trailing in the game, 7–0, the Dodgers showed signs of life in the fifth inning. They opened with a pair of singles. Clarence Mitchell, who had relieved Grimes an inning earlier, came to bat. No need for a pinch-hitter, reasoned Uncle Robbie. Mitchell was a fine hitter, sometimes playing first base and often a pinch-hitter himself. Sensing the turning point of the game was at hand, even if seven runs behind, Robbie called for a hit and run play. The base runners, Kilduff and Miller, broke with the pitch and Mitchell swung. He hit a scorching line drive over second base. Bill Wambsganss, dashing over to cover second on the play, leaped and made a one-hand catch of Mitchell's line drive. He came down almost on second base, kicked the sack to retire Kilduff for out number two, and turned to find Otto Miller standing dumbfounded a few feet away. Wamby reached out and touched the Dodger baserunner to complete an unassisted triple play. It was not only a first time event, it has never been repeated in World Series play and only rarely in regular season play.

Disgusted, the Dodger fans wanted to blame somebody, even if it had to be Uncle Robbie, for ordering a risky play when so far behind. Robbie's explanation was that he thought he could get back into contention. It wouldn't have mattered. Given the reprieve, Jim Bagby completed the shutout and Indians led the Series three games to two.

In a 1935 column, sports writer Frank Menke recalled an event that followed the game. Uncle Robbie, simmering over the way his team had lost the critical game that afternoon returned to his hotel. A sympathetic bell captain provided the bourbon and ice Robbie needed to cool his anger. He sprawled in a chair to console himself with a pitcher of icy libation. However, the more he drank the madder he got. When Menke arrived at the Robinson suite, intending to get Robbie's views for the bylined column Menke was ghosting for the Brooklyn manager, he had to bang on the door before Uncle Robbie answered.

"What the hell do you want?" demanded the Dodger boss, blocking the doorway. Menke's reason did not impress Uncle Robbie. He glared at the inquiring reporter and began to swish the icy contents of his glass. Robbie flung the bourbon highball at the reporter, who ducked as the drink went over his head. At that moment two strangers were passing in the hallway. One of them caught the full effect as Uncle Robbie's drink splashed down his suit.

"Who done that?" the outraged hotel guest demanded. Robbie had gone back inside and only Menke was standing outside the door. He thought quickly: "The guy who threw the drink is inside, but you don't want to disturb him. He's been drinking and gotten nasty. He happens to be Jack Dempsey," Menke improvised. At the thought of the Manassa Mauler, the heavy weight champ, charging at them, the men hurried down the stairs. They didn't wait for the elevator, but descended six steps at a time.

The next day the Dodgers ran into Duster Mails again. Although Sherry Smith limited the Indians to only two runs, Mails pitched a three hit shutout. In a best of seven series, it would have been all over. However, Cleveland still needed another victory.

Before the Dodgers went to the ball park that afternoon, Rube Marquard had his day in court. A Cleveland municipal judge listened while the pitcher explained he was trying to dispose of one ticket, at face value, for a friend. Cleveland had the home court advantage and the Rube was found guilty of scalping and fined $25. A few hours later, his teammates plodded through nine more consecutive scoreless innings. Stan Coveleski won his third game and closed out the Series.

Charley Ebbets had always been careful to leave team discipline to Uncle Robbie. The Marquard scalping incident, however, outraged him. He had warned his Brooklyn patrons to identify themselves and get World Series tickets at regular box office prices. He hadn't anticipated chicanery in Cleveland. Certainly not by one of his own players. A self-made man who lived on the earnings of his ball club, he savored the company of the wealthy men who owned the other teams. Marquard had embarrassed Ebbets where it hurt the most.

Just before Christmas, Ebbets gave himself a present. Once he'd swapped Casey Stengel to the Cincinnati Reds to rid himself of a player who embarrassed him. Now he disposed of Marquard the same way. However, as he had in getting Tommy Griffith for

Casey, he got value for Marquard from Cincinnati. Dutch Ruether had led the Reds to the pennant in 1919 with 19 wins and six losses. In 1920 he was 16–12. Perhaps the Reds thought he was slipping. He was a 21 game winner for Uncle Robbie in 1922 and, after being traded, helped pitch the Washington Senators to the 1925 pennant with an 18–7 record. He finished his career, going 13–6 with the great 1927 New York Yankees.

"The Curse of the Mascot" which had doomed the Dodgers, had long lasting results. 1920 was the last pennant won by a Brooklyn team until 1941. There were near misses when Robbie came heartbreakingly close to a championship before his time in Brooklyn ended. A World Championship flag would not fly over Ebbets Field until 1957. By then the Boys of Summer, idols of the youth of Brooklyn, had blotted out the memory of earlier heroes. The youngsters of the post-World War II era are now grown men. They have no tribal memories of earlier times at Ebbets Field.

If it happened before Sandy Koufax, before Jackie, The Duke, Hodges, Furillo, Campy, Newk, and Oisk, it probably never happened. If it did, they didn't care. Many of them never even mourned the move of the Dodgers from Brooklyn to Los Angeles, probably the final blow delivered by Eddie Bennett's "Curse of the Mascot."

1924: Walter Johnson's Greatest Moment

Even before the Senators finally clinched the pennant, Walter Johnson sent a two-word telegram from Boston to Coffeyville. "Come on!" he wired Hazel on Sunday, and she packed up the two youngest children, Bobby and Carolyn, and with Minnie Johnson at her side, headed for Washington. Walter Jr. and Eddie wailed at being left behind with Aunt Effie.

It had taken 18 years for Walter Johnson to reach the World Series, and 10 for Hazel to see her husband achieve his goal. With the pennant won, on the eve of the World Series, Walter Johnson announced he planned to retire. The wire services carried his statement:

"I realize that I cannot go much further. My arm is still good but I know I haven't the stuff I used to have. When the season started I had fully made up my mind to retire at the end of this year. Now it all depends on what comes up this winter.

If I can get located in baseball somewhere in the West, that would suit me perfectly. I want to get settled. I have four little children and I want to get out of baseball before I get useless. If I can help Washington to win a world pennant this fall, that certainly would be the time for me to quit."

A vanguard of Senators reached Washington from Boston early Tuesday morning. Walter Johnson, Clark Griffith, Bucky Harris, and Sam Rice arrived on the 7:30 a.m. Federal Express. The others remained behind to play Tuesday's now meaningless final game with the Red Sox.

On Wednesday afternoon all the players, riding in open touring cars, were led down Pennsylvania Avenue by a mounted United States cavalry band. The boulevard, where Washington paraded its presidents to their inaugurations and welcomed its military heroes back from wars, was lined 10-deep with cheering, laughing, and excited citizens.

The elite red-jacketed Washington Riding and Hunt Club cantered by, their mounts prancing to the band's music. They were followed by limousines carrying politicians and business leaders. Then came the players, riding three to an open car. Bucky Harris was in the lead car, but the cheers were loudest when Walter Johnson, in the next car, waved to the crowds. The route ended at the Ellipse, where President Coolidge, accompanied by every officeholder who could find space on the reviewing stand, welcomed the team. Seats had been found for Hazel Johnson and Minnie Johnson, and they watched as the president presented a trophy to Bucky Harris. Clark Griffith and Harris thanked the president: they thanked the fans, they thanked the players, and, most of all, they thanked God for Walter Johnson.

Radio broadcasting and baseball were forming a symbiotic relationship in 1924. During the season WCAP kept listeners pressed against their earphones or loudspeakers to hear Stuart Hayes give the scores and highlights of Washington's games. The day after the welcoming parade, Hayes broadcast studio interviews with Walter Johnson, Clark Griffith, Bucky Harris, and Nick Altrock. Sales of radios boomed with the word that Graham McNamee would broadcast the World Series games live from the Polo Grounds and Griffith Stadium. Station WEAF in New York and WCAP would combine their fledgling facilities. McNamee, who would become the first "big name" sports broadcaster, despite a flimsy knowledge of games, had become famous for broadcasting the 1924 Democratic and Republican national conventions.

Walter Johnson was busy rounding up opening game tickets for visitors from Coffeyville. He had promised his neighbors, "If we win and you get here, I'll make sure you get to see the game." He worried more about this obligation, perhaps, than pitching the opening game. The commissioner's office had control of tickets and a familiar pattern emerged. Staunch fans of the home team, those who had supported them through the dark years, discovered large blocks of tickets had been set aside for out-of-towners. The best seats were assigned to the "connected"—in politics, business, or sports.

When he was not distracted trying to round up tickets, Walter Johnson was variously reported to be relaxed and confident or nervously worrying he might let his supporters down. Friendly legend has it that he was cool and unconcerned. Joe Engel, a neighbor of Johnson's, who was a former pitcher and was a scout for the Senators in 1924, recalled that they had played cassino in the clubhouse until it was time for his friend Barney to go out and pitch the opening game. "We talked about everything 'cept baseball," Engel said. "He asked me if I thought 'Bob,' one of the hunting hounds out at his farm, would 'run tonight.' We were intending to work the dogs after the game."

Engel became a minor league equivalent of Bill Veeck, featuring bizarre promotions as owner of the Chattanooga Lookouts. Perhaps the account of Art Nehf, the New York Giants starting pitcher, is more reliable. In a February 1947 *Baseball Magazine* story, Frank Graham reported Nehf telling him, "The photographers got Walter and me together to take our pictures shaking hands and I could see what a strain he was under. Here he was, about to start his first World Series game after all the years of waiting and he knew what was expected of him. He also must have known that, all over the country, literally millions of people were hoping, wishing, even praying for him to win. He was so nervous that his hand trembled as I grasped it and I felt very sorry for him. But I didn't feel sorry for him when the game began. Much as I admired him, I never really knew what a really great pitcher he was until that day."

Take your choice as to how Walter Johnson felt. The record shows how he pitched. The pregame ceremonies began with the presentation of a dark green Lincoln limousine, valued at $8,000, to Walter Johnson, bought by donations from the fans. It did not matter that winning the Most Valuable Player title no longer brought a Chalmers car with it; Johnson's admirers topped it with a superior one. A silver plate mounted on the hood proclaimed the love and admiration of the thousands of donors who had chipped in to buy him the Lincoln limo. The Automobile Club of American had given Johnson a lifetime membership, Metropolitan Life insured the car for as long as it ran, and the District of Columbia issued a special license plate, number 100,000.

Proudest of all were Hazel and Minnie Johnson, the wife and mother of the man at the emotional center of attention. It was the first baseball game Walter's mother had ever seen. She knew nothing of the game's rules but took a mother's pride in the obvious high regard in which everyone held her son. The ladies were escorted by Rev. Brewster Adams, the pastor of the Baptist Church in Reno; Hazel's father could not attend, his mayoral duties keeping him in Reno, Nevada. The pastor was a hearty, athletic "man's man" who was close to the Roberts and Johnson families. He was the perfect escort and had been sent as Reno's emissary.

The Senators were truly called "America's Team," particularly outside of New York City. Walter Johnson was America's most heroic figure. The country had rooted for Washington over the New York Yankees and now wanted them to defeat the New York Giants. Most people across the country did not care much for New Yorkers, their city, or their baseball teams. The Yankees and Giants had monopolized the World Series since 1921, reducing the games to intramural contests played at the Polo Grounds, until the previous year when Yankee Stadium became an even bigger Gotham showcase.

John McGraw's Giants were slightly favored by the oddsmakers when the World Series started on Saturday. The same smart money that had backed the Yankees to win and Washington to fold, was now wagered on the National League Champions. It was the Giants fourth appearance in a row. After meeting Babe Ruth and the Yankees for the past three years, Bucky Harris's Senators looked easy. Walter Johnson might win a game, even two, reckoned McGraw, but he believed he had an even better staff. Yes, Washington had a smooth infield, but he had a better one which hit with more power. The Giants had George Kelly at first when he wasn't playing second base or the outfield, Frankie Frisch and Travis Jackson in the middle, and a teenager, Freddie Lindstrom, at third base. Heinie Groh, the regular at third, was out of the series with a damaged knee.

Lindstrom was an impressive recruit, headed, as were the others, for the Baseball Hall of Fame. An undue influence later on the selections of the Veterans Committee by the persuasive Frank Frisch might have had more to do with so many of the 1924 Giants ending up in Cooperstown than their records supported, but Frisch swung the portal for his infield mates and Ross Youngs, too. Hack Wilson and Bill Terry, prominent alternates on the team, made the Hall of Fame without a push from Frisch.

The Giants' pitching was formidable, although lacking in immortals. Art Nehf, at his best in World Series competition, led the staff. Virgil Barnes, Jack Bentley, and Hugh McQuillan were the other starters. McGraw had spent $50,000 to bring McQuillan from the Braves and twice that, it was reported, to pry Bentley loose from Baltimore. The International League could withhold its players from the majors and Jack Dunn built a dynasty on the Chesapeake as a result. Bentley had been a protégé of Johnson's when he was a young pitcher on the Washington staff. McGraw was never sure whether he should pitch him or get his bat in the lineup as a regular. Such ambivalence, plus spending his best career years as a minor league superstar, kept Bentley from gaining the honors he should have achieved. McQuillan, called "Handsome Hugh," was a puzzle of unrealized promise, too. Both pitchers figured significantly later in Johnson's career.

Before the curtain could rise on the 1924 World Series, another scandal broke. The New York Giants had barely struggled to a fourth pennant. The National League race was even more tightly contested than the battle the Yankees and Senators had waged. There were three teams switching first place among themselves until the final days. Brooklyn and Pittsburgh were in contention until the Giants managed to win by a game and a half over the Dodgers and were three ahead of the Pirates at the end. The specter of New York gamblers, who had bet the Giants would win the pennant by at least two games, arose to haunt organized baseball and its czar, Judge Landis.

Heinie Sand, a player for the futile Phillies, the Giant's final opponent, was approached with a bribe offered by Jimmy O'Connell, a young New York outfielder. The two knew each other from the Pacific Coast League, and McGraw's coach, Cozy Dolan, suggested to O'Connell that he try to get the Philadelphia team to ease up in the game of September 27. Sand turned in his supposed buddy, reporting the bribe offer of $500 to Art Fletcher, his manager, who called Landis. Alerted on the eve of the World Series, the commissioner held a hearing with National League president John Heydler sitting in. O'Connell did not deny he had made an offer, but claimed he was used by Dolan, with the knowledge of Giant stars Frisch, Kelly, and Youngs. Landis dismissed O'Connell's charge against his teammates, except for Dolan. On October 1, on the eve of the World Series, Commissioner Landis announced that Jimmy O'Connell and Cozy Dolan were forever banished from baseball.

Ban Johnson, believing he should have shared in the hearings with Landis and Heydler as a third member of the ruling triumvirate, was outraged. He argued that the whole World Series should be called off, lest any remaining suspicion of crookedness carry over. His protests were ignored, and he refused to attend the games.

Judge Landis was concerned about the image of baseball. The Black Sox scandal still stained the game. To add to his concerns, the umpires were talking of striking to get better terms for working the World Series. The honor was not enough, said veteran arbiters Bill Klem and Tommy Connolly. Bill Dinneen and Ernie Quigley concurred. The umpires shook hands in agreement among themselves that unless the World Series paid the men who ran the game shares of the gate receipts equivalent to that paid to the players, they would strike before the next year's event. However, the discontent and betrayals that had surfaced were matters of off-field administration. What the fans cared about would take place in the ballpark.

The presidential party arrived only five minutes before the 2:00 p.m. start. Babe Ruth brushed past the Secret Service men and shook the president's hand. The players formed in ranks before the first base dugout, and a military band from nearby Fort Myer broke into the first strains of "The Star Spangled Banner." The crowd stood with bared heads while the flag rose to the top of the flagpole behind the center-field bleachers. It waved in the gentle breeze of the Indian summer afternoon.

President Coolidge was photographed throwing out the first ball. Umpire Connolly waited to make the catch, but the high arcing toss which cleared the cameramen in front of the presidential box was far off the mark. Coolidge was trying for distance, not accuracy. However, Tommy Connolly sprinted after it and made a leaping, one-handed catch, saving Coolidge an error and making one of the best plays of the day. Having the World Series open in Washington was a wonderful theater for a man running to be elected president. Calvin Coolidge was finishing out Harding's term and wanted to be elected to one of his own. A few days before the World Series, it was announced that Walter Johnson would vote for

Coolidge. This did not surprise anyone as Johnson's conservatism was well known. Future "politically correct" adherents might be startled to learn that "Mother" Jones, famed labor agitator, visited the White House and was photographed assuring Calvin Coolidge of her vote. To present an image of impartiality, Coolidge kept his cool during the early innings, only gradually thawing until he became as involved a home team partisan as his wife Grace, the First Lady of Fans.

There was no public-address system but the one-arm megaphone announcer. E. Lawrence Phillips, after receiving the information from umpire Tommy Connolly, hollered to the crowd and the press, "The batteries for New York, Nehf and Gowdy; for Washington, Johnson and Ruel." Connolly had umpired the first game played in the American League in 1901 and the first World Series in 1903. He never hesitated to name the 1924 championship series as the best he ever worked. Sports historians broaden this to identify the 1924 meeting between the Senators and the Giants as the most emotionally intense World Series ever played.

The stage was set. President and Mrs. Coolidge watched from their field box. Grantland Rice, covering for the New York Herald, and Bill Corum, writing for the New York Times, whose views would be syndicated nationally, were at their typewriters in the press box, as were ghostwriters for Babe Ruth, Ty Cobb, and George Sisler. Behind home plate, holding a hand mike and peering through chicken-wire screening, Graham McNamee cleared his throat. Then Tommy Connolly yelled, "Play Ball," and Freddie Lindstrom, an 18-year-old boy, stepped into the batter's box. On the mound, a 36-year-old veteran didn't wait for Muddy Ruel's sign. Lindstrom knew what was coming. Everyone in the ballpark knew Walter Johnson's first pitch would be a fastball, as hard as he could still throw it. The most thrilling World Series ever played had begun.

JOHNSON FAILS IN SERIES OPENER

Umpire Connolly watched Walter Johnson's first pitch closely. It thudded into Muddy Ruel's mitt. A bit outside, he decided. Ball one. On a two and one count, Freddie Lindstrom lifted a soft fly ball to center field. Frankie Frisch attempted to bunt for a single, but Ossie Bluege's one-handed pickup and throw nailed the Fordham Flash at first. Johnson brought the count to three and two on Ross Youngs, and got the call for his first strikeout. Youngs argued and threw his bat away in protest.

Washington went out in order and quickly the Giants were at bat again. Long George Kelly lifted a lazy fly ball to left field. Goose Goslin drifted back and tumbled over the low railing fronting the temporary bleachers. Goslin fell into the first row of spectators. Several rows farther back someone in the jerry-built seats caught Kelly's home run. The Giants had scored their first run. Artie Nehf continued to cut the Washington batters down. He gave up two walks but pitched hitless ball until the fourth inning. In the top of the fourth, Johnson fanned the side but not in order. After two were out, Bill Terry hit an off-field home run into those temporary stands in left field. The extra seats they provided put more money in the till, but so far, only the Giants had put baseballs in the seats. In the bottom half of the fourth, Joe Judge broke the ice with a sharp single, but there were two out and Bluege made the third.

Walter Johnson picked up where he left off, striking out Travis

Jackson. Gowdy singled, was forced at second, and a fly out ended the inning. The Senators went out quickly in the fifth, as did the Giants in the top of the sixth. Only the two cheap home runs kept the game from being a scoreless duel. Then Washington got its first run. McNeely doubled down the left-field foul line and scored on two ground outs. Goslin beat out an infield single that Nehf deflected to Frisch, hurting his pitching hand. After a delay, Goslin tried to steal second but was cut down.

The Giants threatened in the seventh inning. Hack Wilson singled, but Washington's lightning-fast double play—Bluege to Harris to Judge—cleared the bases. Gowdy claimed a Johnson pitch nicked his finger, but Umpire Connolly disagreed. Gowdy still got to first base on a walk. Artie Nehf singled Gowdy to second, and both advanced on a Walter Johnson wild pitch. Lindstrom grounded to Peckinpaugh for the third out.

President Coolidge abandoned impartiality in the home half of the seventh. He stood up with Grace and the hometown fans. "Silent Cal" nodded his approval when, with two out, Peckinpaugh singled and stole second. Muddy Ruel drew a pass, and it was up to Walter Johnson to even the score. He hit a line drive over second that Frankie Frisch snared with a leaping catch. The Giant captain happily loped off the field, tossing the ball in the air.

It was getting late. The Giants threatened again in the eighth but, on a double steal attempt, Ruel faked a throw to second and nailed Ross Youngs at third. In the bottom of the eighth Nehf set the Senators down in order. It was getting later.

The Giants almost scored again in the ninth. Hack Wilson led off with a single and Travis Jackson sacrificed him to second.

Johnson bore down and fanned Hank Gowdy with a wide curve that he missed by a foot. Artie Nehf, a good hitting pitcher who had hit five home runs in 1924, singled sharply to right field, but the squat Wilson, chugging around third, was out at the plate on Rice's rifle-sharp throw to Ruel. It was still a 2–1 game, and Washington had one last chance.

It started badly: Judge was called out on strikes. Then Bluege singled off the tip of Jackson's glove. When Roger Peckinpaugh drove a double off the left-field wall, Bluege scored the tying run and the crowd went wild. All kinds of wearing apparel and disposable debris came from the stands. Gloves, hats, programs, seat cushions, a tardy straw boater, were flung in abandon. The police had to rush to right field to keep the spectators from jumping down to the field. Pandemonium reigned, then subsided. Washington had only tied the score. The excitement built again when Ruel grounded out to Jackson and Peckinpaugh moved to third base. We'll never know what excesses of emotion waited in check. With the winning run 90 feet from home plate, the game was in Walter Johnson's hands. Alas, he hit a high fly to George Kelly in center field, and the crowd settled down for extra innings. The Secret Service men whispered about leaving, but Mrs. Coolidge told the president that if he left now, he would go home without her.

Walter Johnson started into overtime as though the game had just begun. He struck out Lindstrom, his tenth victim. Frisch singled and, after another out, stole second with one of his head-first dives. Johnson then poured in fastballs to fan the dangerous George Kelly.

Tommy Connolly, an American League umpire, kept a wary eye on Artie Nehf, who was known to doctor a ball. With one out in the bottom of the tenth, the arbiter took a discolored ball away from the Giant's crafty southpaw and gave him a nice clean one in its place. Bucky Harris knocked it past Lindstrom. Sam Rice singled Harris to second and Washington's fans rose in mass anticipation. Goslin just missed a game-winning hit when his drive down the right-field foul stripe was inches on the wrong side of the line. He then flew out. It was Joe Judge's turn to be frustrated next as his long drive into the right-field stands curved foul at the last moment. Then he drove the ball to Ross Youngs in deep right-center to make the third out.

McNeely, far from a sure-handed outfielder, was also not very sure footed, slipping while chasing Terry's fly ball to open the eleventh. But, he turned it into a circus catch. Walter Johnson, pitching with his seemingly tireless sidearm motion, made Wilson his twelfth strikeout victim, and Jackson grounded out.

Once more President Coolidge stood up with the crowd and clapped his hands to urge the Senators to rally. Again, Connolly warned Nehf, who had discolored another ball: the sun was setting and the shadows made a darkened ball harder to see. Washington went out in order. The game moved into the twelfth inning.

Would Johnson tire at last? He seemed to weaken when he hit Hank Gowdy with a pitch that would have been ball four. Then Artie Nehf got his third hit of the game and the Senators unraveled. McNeely threw wildly to second trying to force the slow-footed Gowdy on Nehf's hit, but the ball went wide and ended up bouncing against the stands behind first base. Muddy Ruel chased it down, but Gowdy was on third and Nehf on second with no one out. Jack Bentley pinch-hit and Johnson, working around him, loaded the bases. Billy Southworth ran for Bentley. Frisch hit a ground ball to Harris, who forced Gowdy at the plate. Then on a short fly to center, Earl McNeely pulled up and the ball fell in for a Texas League single. It was a ball McNeely should have caught, or missed only after diving for it. Nehf scored the go-ahead run. Then Kelly scored Southworth with a deep fly. Terry loaded the bases again with a single, but Goslin tracked down Wilson's fly ball in left field. The Giants led by two runs. Could the Senators rally?

The Giants rearranged their defense. Kelly moved to second base, Frisch to third, and Southworth to center. Walter Johnson was due to lead off, but Harris sent the left-handed Mule Shirley in to pinch-hit. Whether it was bad strategy to replace the right-handed hitting Johnson against lefty-throwing Art Nehf did not matter. Shirley's high fly was dropped by Jackson for a two-base error. McNeely flied to Southworth, then Bucky Harris singled to score Shirley and close to within one run of a tie. Sam Rice singled to center, sending Harris to third, but was out trying to stretch his hit into a double. On the next play the versatile Kelly, now at second base, made a great barehanded play on Goslin's slow roller and caught him by a step at first for the third and final out.

Walter Johnson had come close to victory, but the day belonged to Artie Nehf and the Giants. The fans slowly filed out of the ballpark. A flying squadron of Secret Service agents bundled the presidential party into cars pulled up in front of their box seats. President Coolidge murmured his condolences to several Washington players and promised he would be back and see them win. The presidential party drove to the Potomac Basin where the presidential yacht, The Mayflower, waited to take them on an evening cruise.

The press crowded into the clubhouses for assessments by the rival managers. John J. McGraw was gracious in victory, but condescending in judgment. "We got a break in the twelfth inning," he acknowledged, "by Rice trying to stretch his single into two bases. If he had stayed on first there would have been only one out when Goslin hit to Kelly and Harris would have scored the tying run. As it was, Goslin's tap made the third out and gave us the game."

That was not the way Bucky Harris saw it. "We might have played it safe in the twelfth and earned a tie, but we were willing to take the chance of winning when Rice tried to reach second on his single. If he was safe we would have tied the score anyway when Goslin bounced to Kelly, and we would have had a man in scoring position. It was the right play to make and I'm not blaming Rice or Altrock, who was coaching at first base, for telling him to go on."

McGraw's praise was mostly for his own pitcher, Art Nehf. He pitched a wonderful game, boasted the Giants manager, adding, "As did Walter Johnson."

Bucky Harris poured out his admiration for his veteran: "Johnson pitched a wonderful game. With men on bases he was almost invincible and those home runs would have been caught on a larger field."

In a corner of the clubhouse sat Walter Johnson. He had labored so long and so energetically through 12 innings that he drooped with fatigue. His eyes glistened and his voice trembled as he said, "It was hard to lose. I would have given anything to have won that game for Washington and the people who have expected so much of me. But I gave them everything I had and it wasn't good enough. I'm tired—you bet I'm tired—but I'll be all right again and I'm ready to go back in there anytime Bucky wants me."

Forty thousand people had watched the titanic struggle inside Griffith Stadium. Hundreds of thousands more had followed the game away from the ballpark. In Washington and New York City huge throngs gathered wherever the game was reported on scoreboards. They clustered on sidewalks outside radio stores or anywhere Graham McNamee's voice could be heard. It was estimated that 100,000 people in the metropolitan area had listened to the game being "radiated," as broadcasting was called. As many as a million listeners were estimated in the full coverage range of the improvised network. The next day the broadcast pattern would be repeated, except that, since it was Sunday, WEAF would be replaced by WNYC. Graham McNamee's station had religious programs scheduled but allowed him to work on the Sabbath for the other station.

Before going into the locker room, Walter Johnson had signaled the Reverend Adams to get the ladies to the safety of the corridor under the stands leading to the clubhouse. Hazel was saddened, and Minnie was puzzled but aware that something unwanted had happened to her son. Eventually, they all got back to the shelter and gloom of the Johnson's house. Walter had fallen short of his goal and his fans' expectations. He had carried the quest 12 innings. There would be another game, maybe two, he assured the others. The house was filled with flowers, plants, and gift baskets which well-wishers had sent. Now, instead of a joyful display, the tokens seemed funereal. In the morning, Walter solved that problem. He and the Reverend loaded everything into the new Lincoln limo and, with Hazel and Minnie, drove to Walter Reed Army Hospital, where the Big Train found time to visit with the military patients.

1924: BASEBALL'S MOST DRAMATIC WORLD SERIES ROLLS ALONG

Jonathan Thompson Walton Zachary, called "Tom" for brevity, was Bucky Harris' choice for the second game of the 1924 World Series. A rangy lefthander from the mountains of North Carolina, Zachary was seasoned and had been sharp in his late-season assignments. All games are crucial in a seven-game series, but the second game, when you have lost the first and must play the next three in the other team's park, is doubly critical. Another 40,000 people packed Griffith Stadium, knowing that unless the Senators won that day, it would likely be the last baseball game they would see that year. Missing were the political figures and men of position. These dignitaries are always on hand for festive openings, but they never come to the second game. Mrs. Coolidge would have to settle for listening to Graham McNamee's account on radio aboard The Mayflower. The presidential yacht went for a Sunday sail on Chesepeake Bay and off the breezy Virginia capes. Coolidge was running for election, and there were blocks of southern Baptist voters and strongholds where Puritan values held that playing baseball on the Lord's Day was sinful. Walter Johnson had taken his family to an early church service, then hurried to the ball park. He could help in some way, he hoped, although he would not pitch again until the series shifted to New York.

The fans, some of whom had paid ticket speculators as much as $75, found their seats, consoling each other, "We'll never see another game like the one Walter lost yesterday." They almost did. In a short series every break, bobble, and blunder is decisive. Game Two had them all.

The Giants started fast on successive singles by Lindstrom and Frisch. Ross Youngs popped up his sacrifice bunt try to Zachary. Then Bucky Harris, who missed a base-line tag of Frisch after scooping up Kelly's grounder, threw high to Peckinpaugh trying for a force-out, and the bases were full. An early rout? No. The slick Senators infield reeled off a Bluege-to-Harris-to-Judge double play and the home team fans breathed easy.

They let out a sudden roar in the bottom of the inning when, after two were out, Rice singled and Goose Goslin, after Rice had stolen second, lined a line drive into the temporary bleachers. Ross Youngs fell into the stands trying to reach the ball, as Goslin himself had done the day before. However, tables turn, and the Goose was on his way to a Ruthian World Series. He had led the league in RBIs but, in the unusually spacious Griffith Stadium, had been limited to 16 home runs, tops on the team. Judge beat out a slow roller down the first base line, but Bluege hit into a force play. The Senators had an early lead, and the teams settled down into a tense series of scoreless innings.

Neither team threatened until the bottom of the fifth, when Bucky Harris lashed a line drive into the inviting left-field bleachers to give Tom Zachary a three-run lead with the game more than half over. Washington's relief specialist, Allan Russell, was available, and the super-stopper, Fred Marberry, was also sitting in the bull pen. Harris wanted to save him to start the third game, and it wasn't until the seventh inning anyone had to warm up. Even so, although the Giants scored a run after two singles, another lightning-fast twin killing, from Bluege to Harris to Judge, snuffed out the threat. A run scored, but the third out came on a fly ball and the pitchers in the bull pen sat down. Both teams were hitless in the eighth and, with a 3–1 lead, many fans began to edge toward the exits. Sunday dinner waited at home. However, the exodus stopped short when the Giants came to life in the top of the ninth.

Zachary, who had been pitching like a machine, walked Frisch on four straight balls. Ross Youngs, after just missing a game-tying homer on a long foul ball down the right-field line, popped up to Peckinpaugh. After a disputed call on a pitch Ruel and Zachary thought was a third strike, Kelly singled to right, and Frisch, running as though he was the tying run, scored on a very close play at the plate. This time Klem stirred the Washington bench and fans with a call that seemed to them to be motivated by his National League allegiance. From the stands Frisch looked to have been tagged out, but Klem, closer up, decided his feet touched the plate before Ruel touched him. Despite the play at the plate, Kelly remained at first. He moved to second when Bucky Harris made a sensational, glove-hand pickup of a hard ground ball and threw out Irish Meusel. Washington was one out away from the win that would tie the series. It was a long time coming. Hack Wilson singled and Kelly scored in a tangle of bodies. Rice's throw bounced low, and when Ruel dug it out of the dirt, Long George Kelly dove over the catcher to reach home plate. Ruel lost the ball and Wilson moved to second as the go-ahead run. It was time to stop the Giants rally. Bucky Harris thanked Tom Zachary for a job well done and beckoned big Fred Marberry in from the bull pen. He could not have been more efficient. He blew three straight strikes past Travis Jackson.

Would the teams play another extra-inning game? Would Marberry be used up stemming Giant rallies inning after inning and not be able to pitch the opening game in New York? It did not take long to find out. Judge walked and Bluege sacrificed the winning run to second. Too bad, thought the Senators, that first base was open with the hot-hitting Roger Peckinpaugh coming to bat. Surely the Giants would walk him; his run did not count, anyway. The logical choice was to try for a double play with the slow-running catcher Muddy Ruel due up. Surely a manager as smart and experienced as John J. McGraw would order an intentional walk. He did not. Instead, he instructed Jack Bentley to pitch to Peckinpaugh. The count went to two and one and then Peckinpaugh smashed a double past Lindstrom and Judge raced home with the winning run. It did not quite equal the dramatic finish of the previous day's 12-inning game, but it had the greater benefit of evening the World Series as the teams moved to the Polo Grounds for the third game.

Game Three had the same crowd-involving dramatics as the first two games, but was viewed disdainfully by those who expect higher standards in World Series play. The 6–4 Giants win was viewed as a downright shoddy contest, except for Frankie Frisch's heroics. He flashed all over the ballpark to snare looping fly balls and snap up sizzling grounders. Both teams used four pitchers, with only the Giants veteran Mule Watson earning press-box approval for his game-saving relief stint.

Roger Peckinpaugh, the hero of Game Two, had strained a tendon running out his ninth-inning, game-winning hit. He packed his leg in ice for hours before the game and limped to his shortstop position. He could only hurt the team, Harris decided, and shifted Bluege to short and put Ralph Miller at third base.

Fred Marberry was ineffective as a starter, not the sharp ace he had been in relief the day before. By the fourth inning he was gone with Washington trailing, 4–2. The Giant's starter, Hugh McQuillan, also failed to last the fourth inning. Rosy Ryan replaced him and not only held the Senators in check but became the first National League pitcher to homer in World Series play. The Giants widened the lead to 5–2 with a run in the sixth. Washington got it back in the eighth, but New York scored again in their half of the inning and took a three-run lead into the final frame. With a surprising number of the Polo Ground patrons loudly rooting for a Washington rally, the gods of mischance stirred themselves once more.

Bucky Harris blooped a ball safely into center field but Rice popped up to third. Goslin—whose Texas Leaguer bids earlier in the game provided the tough chances that Frisch, running out from under his hat, had grabbed—crossed up everyone by bunting. Ryan fielded the ball but could make no play. Harris went to second. Then Joe Judge lined a single to right field and the bases were loaded.

Claude Jonnard, McGraw's first call out of the bull pen in tight situations, replaced Ryan. For added security, Billy Southworth took over center field from Long George Kelly. Ossie Bluege drew a walk, forcing in Harris. McGraw made another change. In strolled Mule Watson, ambling slowly to let the pressure build up. With the bases loaded and the game on the line, Watson reckoned the more he fussed before throwing the ball, the more it would string out Ralph Miller, the batter. He was right. Miller fouled to Lindstrom. When Muddy Ruel's ground ball to third base was gobbled up by young Freddie Lindstrom, the teenager who made all the put-outs in the inning, Lindstrom stepped on third base, and the Giants were the winners.

Game Four became Goose Goslin's game. He had four hits and knocked in five runs. His hard hitting, including a three-run homer in the third inning, opened up such a lead on the Giants that George Mogridge had little difficulty in keeping the Giants at bay. Bucky Harris turned in two more scintillating plays to cut off New York rallies. When New York loaded the bases in the ninth inning, trailing 7–4 with George Kelly, the potential tying run, at bat, Fred Marberry responded as he had in the second game. Kelly, whose 21 home runs helped him to win the National League RBI title, had the power to tie the game. Marberry struck him out on three straight pitches.

Game Five was supposed to be Walter Johnson's revenge. Maybe Harris asked too much of a 36-year-old veteran who had worked 12 very hard innings and was pitching on three days' rest. With the series tied again at two apiece, Harris did not want to risk falling behind. With a Johnson victory at the Polo Grounds, the Senators would need to win only one of two remaining games, both possibly at home. The site of a seventh game was not decided until after the fifth game's outcome raised the possibility that it would be needed. Then a toss of the coin would determine whether the final game would require a return to the Polo Grounds or if the teams would stay in Washington and play it there. Anyway, Walter Johnson was a legend. He had pitched three shutouts in four days in New York City once before. But that had been in 1908, when Johnson was 20 years old. However, optimism was high as the Senators took early practice.

Walter Johnson was such a nice man that he kept signing autographs and posing for snapshots near the stands when he should have been loosening his pitching arm. The *New York Times* observed he had signed 66 programs and posed for a half-dozen photographs, including one photo with a very elderly man who had to be half-supported by the pitcher while a friend snapped the picture. In a modern era, when even the World Series is reported with 30-second soundbite journalism, it is surprising to review the coverage given by the *Times.* Granted, the New York Giants were a local team, but still, every game, home and away, was reported with a front-page story which was continued to the sports section for extended coverage. More viewpoints and sidebar pieces half filled the next page.

From the pregame observations we know that a weakened Christy Mathewson, bundled in an overcoat, watched from an upper-tier seat. Babe Ruth and Ty Cobb sat side by side signing programs and ticket stubs next to the Senators' dugout for a half-hour before the game. Casey Stengel was there, reliving the two home runs he had hit for the Giants the previous fall before being traded away.

There was comment that the Giants' brand-new World Series uniforms were already showing wear from the headlong dives of Frankie Frisch and sliding catches of Ross Youngs.

It was apparent from the start that Walter Johnson was not the pitcher of yore. In fact, he wasn't even half the pitcher he had been in Game One. A bare report of the game, inning by inning, makes it appear that Johnson was hooked up in a pitcher's duel with the Giants' starter, Jack Bentley. Walter Johnson received a great hand from the crowd when he walked to the mound to start the game. Lindstrom immediately singled. Frisch hit a high foul pop-up caught near the Washington dugout, and Youngs hit a deep fly ball which Earl McNeely raced back and caught in center field. Lindstrom ended the inning by trying to steal second base. It went that way throughout the opening innings. Seasoned observers kept expecting the Giants to overcome their eagerness to take a cut at a fastball that was no longer traveling at express speed. The Big Train was lumbering like a freight train on an upgrade. The Giants did more to put themselves out than Johnson did.

Walter Johnson's aged arm might be tired, but his bat was still quick. He slammed a drive off the left-field wall. However, he rounded first base too far, stumbled trying to get back, and was tagged out by Bill Terry when Hack Wilson's throw beat him back to the bag. Nick Altrock, the first base coach, was at fault, Harris decided, and replaced him with Nemo Leibold. McNeely beat out a bunt to third base and Harris got an infield hit. The bases should have been loaded. Instead, Bentley got out of the inning on a pop-up and ground out.

In the third inning, Jackson beat out a slow roller to short, and Johnson got his first strikeout with Hank Gowdy looking at a 3–2 pitch. Jack Bentley did not wait. He singled on the first pitch and Jackson went to third. He scored when Lindstrom out-legged another slow roller. Frisch grounded to Bluege, playing shortstop in place of the still sidelined Roger Peckinpaugh. Bluege threw to third baseman Miller, who missed the tag on Lindstrom. The bases were filled. Next, Ross Youngs hit a line drive to Sam Rice. Bentley got confused. He had to go back and tag up, and Rice's throw, relayed by Johnson, nailed him at the plate. Johnson had escaped, trailing only 1–0.

Washington tied the game in the fourth on Judge's leadoff single, a sacrifice, an infield out, and a single by Miller. He tried to stretch this to a double but Ross Youngs threw him out. A run scored but another opportunity was wasted.

Johnson again evaded trouble in the Giants' fourth. He got another 3–2 third-strike call, this time George Kelly watched the pitch go by. Then Bill Terry hit a monstrously high drive into right-center and reached third. Only Sam Rice's great throw pinned him there. When Hack Wilson lined the ball back to the box, Johnson's glove saved him. He speared the ball and trapped Terry off third. Jackson hit a high fly ball back to Bucky Harris. Walter Johnson was getting by, but on luck, the Giants overeagerness, and his innate, all-around ability.

The Senators went out one, two, three to start the fifth inning, and Johnson was back at work with hardly time to catch his breath. Gowdy greeted him with a single to right, and Jack Bentley showed why McGraw was torn between using him as a hitter or as a pitcher. He hit a towering drive into the upper right-field grandstand. Lindstrom popped up and Frisch had a wind-blown double fall out of McNeely's reach. A low pitch caught Ross Youngs on the ankle and he limped to first base. On the brink of absolute ruin, the inner defense pulled off an inning-ending double play, Bluege to Harris to Judge. It could have been worse. It would be. The sixth and seventh innings were scoreless. The Giants helped Johnson survive with dumb base running.

In the eighth the Senators closed to within a run of the lead. Goslin hit a line drive to the upper tier of the right-field grandstand. His third homer of the series tied Babe Ruth's record set the year before, and once again a series game seemed headed for a final-inning showdown.

Bucky Harris was determined to go all the way with Walter Johnson. In retrospect, Johnson had not done too badly. The Giants had six hits and three runs. Hindsight, and the absence of sentimentality, says it was the spot for Fred Marberry or Allan Russell. They were not even warming up.

Kelly opened up with a sharp single and Terry walked. Hack Wilson bunted the ball, and Walter Johnson, who had not made an error all season, booted the ball. Everyone was safe, the bases were loaded, and no one was out. In the old days, Walter Johnson might have hitched up his belt and fanned the side. These were not the old days—only Walter Johnson was old. Jackson's long fly to Rice scored Kelly. Gowdy's ground ball was too slow to turn into a double play and Terry moved to third base. Hugh McQuillan, who had replaced Bentley in the top of the inning, stayed in to hit for himself. Even he was fearless against Johnson's diminished fastball. A weak batter, he bailed out, taking a wide sweeping cut at the ball. It looped into short left field for a single that scored Terry. It was not over yet. Freddie Lindstrom stroked his fourth hit of the game and Gowdy scored the third run of the inning. Before Frankie Frisch hit into a force play to end the inning, a fight nearly started in the press box. Some cynic shouted at the battered Johnson, "Take him out." This enraged Billy Evans, Johnson's admirer, who was covering the game as a reporter. He climbed over two rows of seats and typewriters to get at the loudmouth. He explained later, after being subdued, "It hurt to have someone shout that old line at a great player like Walter Johnson. I realize it was unprofessional of me to step out and assert myself, but it seemed a shame to razz a man like Walter who was in there giving all he had."

Trailing 6–2, the Senators went out meekly. Yet, even as they trooped into the clubhouse, a spirit of almost unjustified optimism began to be felt. Everyone was saddened that Barney had not pitched the way America had hoped and prayed he would. But the Senators, down three games to two, insisted the glass was really half full. When Bucky Harris brought the news that Clark Griffith had won the toss to decide where the seventh game would be played, they assumed that a seventh game would be necessary. The Senators took it almost for granted that Tom Zachary would win the sixth game. Once they were at home, the team believed they were better than the Giants. And, Bucky Harris was already plotting a strategy to pull on McGraw in Game Seven. When the team boarded the early evening train for Washington at Pennsylvania Station it was hard to tell who were the winners. In Washington, 5,000 die-hard fans waited for the team to arrive. Walter Johnson, carrying his youngest son on his shoulder, cleared the way for Hazel, who was carrying Carolyn, and his mother. He heard shouts of sympathy, but the loudest voices insisted the Senators were far from beaten.

JOHNSON'S GREATEST TRIUMPH

Griffith Stadium was again packed to its newly expanded capacity. The Senators believed this would be the penultimate game of the 1924 World Series. A team of destiny, which is how Bucky Harris viewed his crew, fulfills its mission in whatever way it must. If the scenario lacked victories pitched by Walter Johnson, a team triumph would be all the more impressive. Tom Zachary, George Mogridge, and Fred Marberry had pitched well. Now it was up to Zachary to pitch even better than he had in his first start. He would be up against the Giants' ace, Artie Nehf, winner over Walter Johnson in the opening game, in a duel of lefthanders.

President Coolidge surprised people by accompanying Mrs. Coolidge to the game. She, the die-hard fan, had been expected: he had not. Their party arrived only a few minutes before game time. As they began to descend the steps behind home plate toward their box seats, the army band began playing "The Star Spangled Banner" too soon. The crowd arose and the president removed his hat and stood at attention in the aisle. There was no throwing out a first ball or extra formalities. The Coolidges, like thousands of other couples and fans, were there to see a ball game.

Roger Peckinpaugh was back at shortstop. His movements were tentative as though he dared not risk sudden starts and stops. With the left-handed Zachary on the mound, John McGraw started his right-handed lineup. Mostly this meant George Kelly would open at first base and the dangerous young Bill Terry would wait on the bench. The versatile Kelly could play the outfield or second base whenever Terry played against a right-handed starter. Artie Nehf's left hand had healed since he injured it in the opening game, and he was well rested. The rotation of the four umpires put the National League's Bill Klem behind the plate.

Freddie Lindstrom pushed a bunt toward Ossie Bluege, back at third base, and was out by a half-step. Frankie Frisch doubled down the right-field foul line, but when Ross Youngs hit back to Zachary, Frisch was caught off second base and tagged out in a rundown. A former broken field runner at Fordham, Frisch jockeyed on the base path long enough for Youngs to move to second base. The first run scored on Kelly's single. Zachary survived a shaky start when Sam Rice chased down a long fly by Irish Meusal. From then on Zachary was in full control of the Giants batters. The opening inning run was all he had yielded through the rest of the game. Except for one lapse, Artie Nehf matched Zachary's string of runless innings with a row of zeroes of his own. He faltered only in the fifth inning.

The inspired Roger Peckinpaugh lashed a clean single into left field, and Muddy Ruel moved him into scoring position with a sacrifice bunt. Zachary's roller to Kelly got Peckinpaugh to third base, but now there were two out. Nehf walked McNeely on four straight pitches. McNeely then stole second base with the gimpy-legged Peckinpaugh only feinting a double-steal break to the plate. McGraw had to choose. He could pass Bucky Harris, his rival manager who was a hot batter, and have Nehf pitch to the left-handed hitting Sam Rice, the Senators' best batter. The righthanders Rosy Ryan and Mule Watson were working in the bull pen, but first McGraw had to choose whether to pitch to Harris. He made the wrong choice.

With a full count, Harris hit an outside pitch into right field and both runners scored. Youngs' throw was too late to catch the sliding Earl McNeely. Washington was ahead and the crowd went wild. Harris had moved to second on the play at the plate, but Rice was called out on strikes and Tom Zachary was asked to maintain the slim, one-run lead. It was a razor-thin margin on which to rest a season's hopes, but it held up due as much to splendid fielding as to Zachary's finesse and control. Except for a single when Rice just failed to make a shoestring catch on a Wilson short fly, no Giant reached base. Not until the ninth inning.

After Ross Youngs popped up to Bluege, George Kelly singled to right field and Billy Southworth ran for him. Irish Meusal, after first hitting a long foul ball over the top of the left-field stands, hit a ground ball over second base. Peckinpaugh barely got to the ball. He tried to stop and had to flip the ball backhanded to Harris, who grabbed it barehanded for the force play on Southworth. Peckinpaugh's leg buckled again and he crumbled to the ground. Once more, Peckingpaugh had to be helped from the field. The standing fans cheered him as, refusing to be carried, he hopped to the bench, with his arms around the shoulders of two teammates. Bluege again moved to shortstop and Tommy Taylor took over at third base. Tom Zachary then ended the game by striking out Hack Wilson.

There was a degree of restraint in the postgame celebration. There had been drama but no surprise. It was as though the sixth game was played—its outcome a foregone conclusion—only to make the seventh and final game possible. The teams had played each other to a standstill, but tomorrow, one would have to give way.

Thousands of fans left the ballpark and got on line to buy tickets for the next day's game, willing to wait through the night until the box-office windows opened at 10:00 a.m. Due to planning a schedule and ticket distribution for six games instead of the potential of seven, the arrangements provided only a coupon to be exchanged for admission if a seventh game became necessary. Because the home-team choice was left for a coin toss after the fifth game, seventh-game tickets were difficult to obtain. Although the bleacher seats and general-admission stands filled early, stretches of seats went unoccupied, and scalpers had to take face value for most of their ducats.

The game to decide the World Championship became one of the most written about in baseball history. Bill Corum's account, written without a byline for the *New York Times*, is among the selections in Charles Einstein's The Fireside Book of Baseball Stories, and Grantland Rice was given an award by the Baseball Writer's Association for the best news account of the year for his coverage in the *New York Herald Tribune.* Rice's lead was: "Destiny, waiting for the final curtain, stepped from the wings today and handed the king his crown."

In preparing for the game, Bucky Harris had one strategy move to make. He wanted to nullify the left-handed hitting Bill Terry. The ploy was an old one: pretend you are going to start a righthander and then switch to a lefty once you have Terry in the starting lineup. That would force McGraw to replace him with a right-handed batter by moving George Kelly to first base and using one of his right-handed hitting outfielders, Hack Wilson or Irish Meusal. Ross Youngs was a fixture regardless of who pitched. The Senators showcased Curly Ogden, right-handed and a spot starter during the season. However, to keep McGraw guessing, George

Mogridge, the lefty, and Firpo Marberry, the righty, warmed up down in the bull pen. Zachary was finished and there were no plans for Walter Johnson.

McGraw took the bait. He guessed that Ogden was a ruse and named Bill Terry as his first baseman. Youngs, Kelly, and Meusal formed the outfield. Heinie Groh was still unable to play, so Freddie Lindstrom, who had been a rookie revelation at third, again started in his place. Once again, Hank Gowdy was behind the bat. Now in his fourteenth season, having missed 1918 for World War I service, he had caught less than half of the Giants' games. Pancho Synder, who caught more often, was among McGraw's "walking wounded" and able only to pinch-hit.

McGraw gave the starting assignment to Virgil Barnes even though he had not been effective in the third game. He had everyone else ready to help out, even Artie Nehf, the previous day's tough-luck starter.

Curly Ogden was supposed to face one batter as he was required to do when he had been announced. But when he blew Freddie Lindstrom away on three pitches, Harris let him continue. Then when Frankie Frisch walked, Harris summoned his left-hander, George Mogridge. He kept Marberry in readiness. Mogridge fanned Ross Youngs and got Kelly on an easy ground out.

Barnes set the Senators down in order, and the game moved through its opening innings quickly and without either team threatening. Bill Terry was easy for Mogridge, grounding out and striking out. The ice-breaker came in the fourth inning when Bucky Harris drove a ball over the left-field wall. Hack Wilson ran back as far as the temporary bleachers and fell over the low railing.

However, the ball carried out of the ballpark, a full-size homer at any time.

New York took the lead at the top of the sixth inning. Ross Youngs walked and raced to third on Kelly's single past short. Now McGraw replaced Terry, sending Meusal in to bat for him. And Harris countered by bringing in Firpo Marberry. Meusal's sacrifice fly to right brought home Youngs with the tying run. Then Washington's defense cracked. After Wilson singled, sending Kelly to third, Joe Judge fumbled a ground ball. Kelly scored and Wilson reached third on the error. Next Gowdy hit a double-play ball to Bluege, but it went through him for another error and Wilson scored. Marberry got the pitcher, Barnes, on a short fly to right and struck out Lindstrom. The Giants had a 3–1 lead. Maybe they would have had more had McGraw pinch-hit for Barnes or squeezed Jackson home. However, except for the Harris homer, Barnes had pitched a great game. He continued his mastery for another inning, but in the eighth he weakened and McGraw was slow to relieve him.

With one out, veteran Nemo Leibold pinch-hit a double and Muddy Ruel got his first hit of the series, a hard drive off George Kelly's first baseman's mitt. Bennie Tate, a rookie backup catcher, who had a .500 average as a pinch hitter during the season, hit for Marberry and walked to load the bases. Mule Shirley ran for Tate, but all the runners held their bases when McNeely's fly was too short for Leibold to risk trying to score. It left matters to manager Bucky Harris. Two out, bases loaded, an inning to play: a perfect scenario for the Boy Wonder, and he played his role with a lot of help from fate. Harris hit a ground ball to third base, which took a high bound over Lindstrom's head for a two-base hit, and Leibold and Ruel came thundering home. The score was tied and the fans went into a frenzy. McGraw lifted Barnes and called on Artie Nehf to pitch to Sam Rice. All he wanted from Nehf was one-third of an inning, and he got it. Rice grounded out to first base.

The fans were on their feet in anticipation of Bucky Harris' next move. There was only one pitcher warming up in the bull pen. He had been throwing since Tate batted for Marberry. It was Walter Johnson. Harris pointed to him and Bill Klem summoned him. The waves of applause, the shouts of encouragement, echoed through Griffith Stadium. Walter Johnson seemed to shed the years as he walked with his unmistakable ploughboy stride to the pitcher's mound. He was back again to claim his title, King of the Hill. His warm-up pitches whistled to the plate. Ruel asked to see the curve and it broke sharply, dropping to an outside corner. Walter Johnson was ready to hold the Giants at bay until the Senators could score again.

Today he was not an old-timer trying to get by on the memory of a fastball. People who could compare the warrior on the mound to the one of legend swore he was the Johnson of old. He faced a Herculean challenge and would be tested inning by inning until he completed his tasks or was defeated by them. No one was warming up to come to Johnson's rescue. Bucky Harris explained later, "You go with your best."

Lindstrom popped to third, but Frankie Frisch boomed a triple to deep center field. There was task number one: keep the Fordham Flash at third base. Harris and Johnson had sized up Ross Youngs and George Kelly. Of the two, Johnson was confident he had Kelly's number. An intentional walk to Youngs put Johnson's judgment on the line. He struck out George Kelly on three pitches. On the third strike Ross Youngs stole second, Ruel not wanting to risk a throw with Frisch on third. Irish Meusel grounded to third base, where Miller was now playing, and was thrown out at first.

It seemed the fates favored the Senators when with one out Joe Judge singled to center. Bluege hit to Kelly but Travis Jackson dropped the ball trying for a double play. Judge went to third base on the error. The Washington fans smelled victory. However, McGraw brought in Hugh McQuillan to pitch to Ralph Miller. A .133 hitter in only nine regular-season games, Miller was overmatched. However, with Peckinpaugh injured and Taylor out of the game, Harris hoped for the best. He got the worst: a 6–4–3 double play, and Walter Johnson went back to work to hold New York for another inning.

Wilson walked, but Travis Jackson was called out on strikes and Hank Gowdy hit the ball back to Johnson, who whirled and pegged it to Bluege, who relayed it to Judge for an inning-ending double play.

It appeared for a moment that the scenario would call for Johnson himself to provide the ultimate highlight, a game-winning homerun. He drove a fly to deep left-center field, but Hack Wilson had enough room to haul it in just short of the fence. After McNeely struck out, Johnson had to take the mound for his eleventh-inning challenge.

McGraw sent Heinie Groh, out of the series with a leg injury, to pinch-hit for McQuillan, and he used his famous "bottle-bat" to poke a single into right field. He gave way to a pinch runner, Billy

Southworth. Lindstrom sacrificed and the dangerous Frankie Frisch stepped into the batter's box. Last time up against Johnson, Frisch had boomed a triple. This time he went down swinging. Would it be Ross Youngs or George Kelly for the third out? For the fourth time in the game, Youngs was walked. Kelly again proved easy for Johnson, who struck him out, leaving the runner stranded.

Jack Bentley took up McGraw's cause from the mound in the eleventh inning. He had lost Game Two and won Game Five. Washington threatened when, with two out, Goslin dropped a Texas League double into left-center. McGraw's managerial wheels were spinning. He walked Joe Judge to set up a force play at second. In the event of a single to the outfield, he wanted the best throwing arm where the ball was most likely to go. Youngs, the better thrower, moved to left and Meusal to right field. Bluege hit a ground ball to Jackson, who flipped it to Frisch for the force-out.

Hercules had been confronted with twelve difficult labors; Johnson faced his fourth inning's challenge determined to perform as many tasks as it took until his team could score. He would outdo Hercules if he had to. Irish Meusal singled to left, but Wilson fanned. It was Johnson's fifth strikeout. Jackson forced Meusel at second and Gowdy flied to left.

The afternoon sun was dropping fast toward the horizon. Hercules had no time limit set on performing his labors; Johnson had to finish his tasks before darkness came and forced another game to be played. It was time for other gods to stir themselves.

Youngs and Meusal returned to their original outfield posts. After Miller grounded out, Muddy Ruel lifted a pop foul behind the plate. Veteran Hank Gowdy had caught a thousand of these.

But he had never tried it with his mask tangled around his foot. As he pivoted to line up the ball, Gowdy stepped on the mask he had dropped near the plate. He tried to kick it loose, stumbled, and dropped the ball. An error. The gods watching from afar howled in glee. Given another chance, Ruel hit a double. Now came Walter Johnson. A solid single should win the game. Again, the gods snickered. A mere mortal, Johnson hit a ground ball to shortstop. The ball was fumbled by Travis Jackson; Ruel held second while Johnson hurried to first base. Another error. Fate had one last trick up its sleeve. Remember the ground ball Harris had hit in the eighth inning? The one that took a high hop over Lindstrom's head? It was deja vu time. Earl McNeely's routine ground ball skidded along the ground toward Freddie Lindstrom. It, too, hit a pebble—or something—that caused it to leap high over the third baseman while the runners raced around the bases. Muddy Ruel, running on any batted ball, rounded third base while the ball bounded toward left fielder Meusel. Ruel was slow. A hard charge on the ball and a strong throw might have cut down the winning run. Meusel reached the ball, looked at the distance Ruel still had to cover, and decided the throw would be wasted. He stuck the ball in his pocket and raced for the safety of the clubhouse.

Down on the field thousands of delirious fans erupted from the stands. They pummeled McNeely almost senseless in a frenzy of joy. The players who had been on the field, Johnson in particular, needed to be rescued. Police pushed, players pulled, and Johnson inched his way to the dugout. He kept gasping out his happiness, a wondrous acceptance of the way fate had finally broken for him.

If he had looked toward the presidential box, he would have seen a rare sight. Calvin Coolidge was publicly performing like an average fan. Ford Frick, who would one day be commissioner of baseball, was a reporter covering the game. He wrote in his autobiography that Coolidge had danced on the dugout roof. More believably, it was Grace Coolidge, disheveled and ecstatic, who reportedly hopped onto the dugout roof. Maybe the Coolidges did the Charleston. Everyone was going mad. A celebration broke out across the District of Columbia, and the partying went on endlessly. A wall of noise began inside Griffith Stadium and traveled like a sonic boom across the city. Guns were fired, whistles blown, horns tooted, voices were made hoarse with endless shouts. No baseball celebration since has equaled it. The fans had it their way. No mounted police had galloped onto the field to stem a tide of enthusiasts. No public-address system appealed to an assumption of good sportsmanship among the masses asking that they please refrain from entering the playing area. No warnings of impending arrests were made. The police focused on getting the players and officials to safe havens. The fans in their wild demonstrations did not set fire to cars, burn buildings, or loot stores. By today's standards, it might seem tame. At the time, it was enough to hit an emotional high and sustain it by exclaiming over the wonderful luck to live in the same city as Walter Johnson.

Clark Griffith summarized the outcome, saying, "That mask up and bit Gowdy. He was going to catch that pop foul and it grabbed him away from it. Had to be that God was on our side today. Else, how did those pebbles get in front of Lindstrom not once but twice?"

The clangor and joyful noisemaking was long in dying down. Fred Lieb, in his wonderful baseball memoir, *Baseball As I Have Known It,* tells how the victory celebration affected Judge Landis. He explains he was alone with the commissioner on a little balcony outside his room in the Raleigh Hotel. Below, along Pennsylvania Avenue, snake-danced a joy-maddened crowd. They beat drums, some beat washtubs with large spoons, some blew horns. Anything that could make a noise was used in this joyous paean of victory.

Lieb concluded, "Landis put his hand on my shoulder and looked directly in my eyes as he said, 'Freddy, what we are looking at now—could this be the highest point of what we affectionately call our national sport? Greece had its sports and its Olympics; they must have reached a zenith and then waned. The same for the sports of ancient Rome: there must have been a year at which they were at their peak. I repeat, Freddy, are we looking at the zenith of baseball?'"

Looking back, Lieb concluded that Washington's affection for its 1924 team was baseball's finest moment up to that point. Then he added that even Landis had lived to see other demonstrations as big and delirious. In one sense, Landis' perception that he was witnessing a zenith was correct. The moment of triumph had lifted Walter Johnson to the peak of achievement. He had fulfilled himself, with his wife and mother watching. No husband or son could offer more to those he loved most.

Everything that followed would be anticlimactic. Eventually, his time as the supreme idol of the fans would pass. There are many people who boast of themselves as great baseball fans, who have never heard his name, let alone know of his feats. In his remaining lifetime, great tragedy lay ahead. Disappointments and failures, too. It is good that he savored the moment and sensed it was time to step down from the pedestal. Remember, even before the dramatic World Series and his eventual triumph, he had told reporters of his wish to end his big league career at that point. With the World Series behind him, Walter Johnson set out to find a new destiny.

1926: Alexander the Great's Greatest Triumph

A sentimentalist might look at the result of the 1926 pennant race and the World Series and say, Grover Cleveland Alexander's greatest triumph was over his own weakness. He staggered to his feet after drinking himself off the Chicago Cubs and stayed sober enough for half a season to pitch the Cardinals to the first pennant they had ever won. His ultimate success in the World Series found him accused of winning despite his weakness. A realist would size up Grover Cleveland Alexander as a man too proud of his pitching ability and too committed to friendship, loyalty, and a supportive woman to let them down.

A baseball purist would compare Alexander's 1926 World Series pitching feats to those of Mathewson or Johnson and place him at the top with them. Johnson and Alexander reached the pinnacle as relievers in a final seventh game. Matty's three shutouts in a five-game Series in 1905 were the epitome of dominance.

The 1926 triumph of the Cardinals, a team of country boys, took place in New York City, the center of sports sophistication. The pennant was clinched in the Polo Grounds, and the climactic game of the World Series played at Yankee Stadium. Babe Ruth and the sluggers of Murderer's Row were expected to defeat St. Louis as easily as the Boston Red Sox had wiped out Alexander's Philadelphia Phillies in 1915. Maybe the old guy could win one game again, but the relentless power of the Yankees would roll over the Cardinals. Even their superstar, Rogers Hornsby, was 15 pounds underweight and, at .316, 41 points below his .358 lifetime average. From a league-leading 39 home runs in 1925 he had wilted to 11. To make his situation worse, his mother in Texas, after a year's illness, had died on the eve of the Series opener. He elected to remain with his team, and the family postponed the burial until he could get there.

Manager Hornsby had his staff ready. Even Alex was rested enough, but he decided to finesse the Yankees. Miller Huggins, who had once managed the Cardinals and had brought Hornsby to the major leagues, elected to open with the stylish southpaw, Herb Pennock. Hornsby countered with the equally stylish lefty, "Wee Willie" Sherdel. All successful lefthanders who throw curveballs are called, "stylish." Only strikeout lefties, like Grove and Koufax, are identified otherwise. Sherdel's size made him a David compared to the Goliaths in the Yankee lineup. Babe Ruth, Lou Gehrig, and Bob Meusel towered over six feet and swung heavy bats. The rookie slugger, Tony Lazzeri, lacked a half inch of the six-foot mark.

Game One opened with 61,658 people filling Yankee Stadium, and St. Louis jumped into a lead on a double by Taylor Douthit and a single by Sunny Jim Bottomley. That was the last hit off Pennock until Bottomley's second single, in the ninth inning. Meanwhile, Sherdel exhibited the other expected characteristic of a lefthander. He was wild. He walked Combs, Ruth, and Meusel and gave up a first-inning run on Gehrig's infield out. The only other run in the 2–1 duel came in the sixth inning when, after Ruth walked and was moved up to second on Meusel's bunt, Gehrig singled him home. That was it. Murderer's Row had been muted but, behind Pennock's brilliant pitching, the favored Yankees were off to a winning start.

Game Two demanded that Hornsby pitch his very best man. He gave the ball to Alexander and let the 39-year-old veteran pitch his ballgame. Alex did not begin auspiciously. The Yankees scored first, getting two runs on singles by Meusel, Lazzeri, and Dugan. Alexander's wild throw attempting to stop a double steal indicated the Broadway wise guys were right, that he was too old to tame the Yankees and probably not in shape, either. But, after Earle Combs led off the third inning with a single, Ol' Pete settled down. He retired the next 21 Yankee batters, no one reaching base, and he ambled off the field a 6–2 winner. Alex had struck out 10 batters and allowed four singles. Billy Southworth and weak-hitting Tommy Thevenow homered while the Yankees' big bats were silenced. The teams piled onto westward bound trains for the next three games to be played in St. Louis.

The next day, Monday, an off-day in Series play, the Cardinal's victory train pulled into the Washington Avenue Station in St. Louis. It was a city holiday, and the streets were jammed from curb to store fronts with fans waiting for the cavalcade to go by. The throngs overflowed the sidewalks and clogged the streets. Mayor Victor Miller and owner Sam Breadon rode in the lead car but the fans craned their necks to look down the line for the cars where Alex and Amy and Rogers and Jeanette Hornsby were surging against a tide of humanity. There was danger in the fans' exuberance, and the white-faced wives were happy to reach the protection of the reviewing stand in Market Square. After speeches and cheers, the players slipped away to go to their homes and get ready to resume the Series the next day at Sportsman's Park.

The Cardinals sent their ace knuckleballer, Jesse Haines, to tame the Yankees, and he slammed the door on the cage. Haines fluttered the ball past the vicious swings of Ruth, Gehrig, and company, sprinkling five singles across nine shutout innings. To cap his performance, Jesse hit a two-run homer in the 4–0 win. Cardinal fans could hardly believe their team was disposing of the American League champions so easily.

In Game Four, Babe Ruth erupted. The first time he came to bat, he hit the first pitch over the right-field bleachers and out of the ballpark. Next time he hammered a drive over the right-center-field bleachers. After a fifth-inning walk, he delivered the coup de grace, a drive which landed where no ball ever had before, deep in the dead-center-field bleachers. It was the first time anyone had ever belted three four-baggers in one World Series game. The Series was now tied at two wins apiece. The Yankees had feasted on Flint Rhem's fastball after having been teased by Sherdel, Alex, and Haines.

Strategy and the rotation called for Wee Willie Sherdel to duel again with Herb Pennock in Game Five. And, once more the two stylish lefties kept scoring at a minimum. The game reached the tenth inning, tied at a run apiece. Then Lazzeri's sacrifice fly scored a run and Pennock closed out his masterfully pitched game, 2–1. The Yankees had taken the lead and were headed back to New York where they expected to finish off the persistent Cardinals.

Alexander was not about to let the Yankees win the World Series. He was even better than he had been in Game Two. Bob Shawkey was the Yankees' starter. Heck, Alex had beaten him back in Attleboro, Massachusetts when they pitched for local teams after the 1920 season. Today it was even easier. Alex coasted to a 10–2 victory. He told manager Hornsby he would be ready if needed the next day. To a questioning look, Alex replied, "If it makes you feel better, I'll ride back to the hotel in the cab with you and ride out here tomorrow for the game."

Myth, with a cynical edge of the know-it-all's cheap wisdom, has distorted what happened to Alex between the final out of Game Six and his entry into Game Seven. Did he celebrate the way Ol' Pete was expected to relax? A report that placed him at Billy LaHiffe's midtown speakeasy, where the press and celebrities drank, was rampant. Alex had closed the place, the wise guys snickered. Assumptions that Alex had turned up at Yankee Stadium, hung over and bleary eyed, are based on this unsubstantiated report. Everyone who has bought into the story in the years that follow accepted it, not because it was witnessed by anyone but because its easy assumption made a good story.

Alcoholism was not understood to be a disease in 1926 and Alcoholics Anonymous was still a gleam in the bloodshot eyes of the afflicted. It was expected that you made fun of a staggering drunk. Jokes about morning afters were a trademark of the Prohibition era. Alexander's reputation made him a convenient target for claims that he had fallen into the gutter the night after bringing the World Series to a final game.

Allowing for bias, here's what Amy told *Los Angeles Times* reporter Frank Finch. "After Alex won the sixth game Hornsby said to him, 'Now don't celebrate too much, I may need you tomorrow.' Well Alex celebrated, and so did most of the other players, but he definitely was not drunk during the seventh game. Hornsby told me years later, '*The biggest mistake we made, Amy, was in not denying the story from the start. At the time it made good reading, so we let it go.*' "

In another recollection, Amy Alexander said she and her husband had gone upstairs to their room early. She mixed them each a highball and they went to bed. Recently, A.D. Suehsdorf, an honored baseball biographer and historian, wrote a profile of Bob Meusel. He discovered Meusel's widow still lived in Los Angeles and talked with her. Spurred by a historian's curiosity, he asked Mrs. Meusel, "Did you see anything of Grover Cleveland Alexander before the final game?"

"Oh, yes," she responded, "I saw the Alexanders in the lobby of the hotel and he looked perfectly fine."

Did Alex wait until Amy was asleep and then slip off into the night and grab a cab to LaHiffe's? We doubt it.

The day of the fateful Game Seven was rainy and cold. The fans, being fair- weather Yankee followers, were already discouraged. Only 38,093 bought tickets, only slightly more than half filling the huge stadium. As game time neared, the rain stopped and, although the day remained overcast and threatening, the game began. Waite Hoyt, winner of Game Four, was the Yankees' starter and Jess Haines went to work for the Cardinals.

Where was Alexander? He had been sent to the bull pen to be in charge of the relief corps. Hornsby had told him, "Keep your eye on Sherdel and Bell. Keep them warmed up and if I need help I'll depend on you to tell me which looks best." Hi Bell was the team's right-handed reliever and Sherdel, the clever lefty. Hornsby wanted to be prepared however the batter swung if a crisis arose.

In 1945 A.S. Barnes & Company, Inc. published John P. Carmichael's *My Greatest Days in Baseball.* The leadoff article, written by the nationally famous sports magazine writer, Francis Powers, was a first-person account by Alex of the final game of the 1926 World Series. He had told the story a thousand times, never once varying his account of whether he was sober or not. He had the scene fixed forever in his mind. Included is a description of the circumstances of the bullpens at Yankee Stadium. From the accounts which followed, the Cards might have been under binocular surveillance from the press box. Here's what Alex recalled, "The bullpen in the Yankee Stadium is under the bleachers and when you're down there you can't tell what's going on out on the field only for the yells of the fans overhead. When the bench wants to get in touch with the bullpen there's a telephone. It's the only real fancy, modern bullpen in baseball. Well, I was sitting around down there, not doing very much throwing, when the phone rang and an excited voice said, 'Send in Alexander.'"

Rogers Hornsby doesn't remember a telephone being used, but certainly cellular phones did not exist and he was at second base when the Jesse Haines' crisis was reached.

"Knuckleball" no longer describes a pitch held by the knuckles. The method now is to use the tips of the fingers to prevent the ball from spinning as it leaves the pitcher's hand. Haines used all his knuckles and, by the seventh inning, they had been scraped raw and were bleeding. The Cardinal's lead, the result of three unearned runs, was about to melt. There were two out, but the Yankees, trailing by a run, had loaded the bases on three walks. Coming to the plate was the feared rookie, Tony Lazzeri. During his first season, he had hit more home runs and driven in more runners than Lou Gehrig. He had also led the league in strikeouts with 90. Ruth fanned only 76 times that season. However, Lazzeri had developed a reputation for clutch performances. He was called "Poosh 'Em Up Tony," with an innocent ethnic exuberance of the time, because of this dependability. If not Babe Ruth, then Lazzeri was the batter the fans wanted at the plate in the clutch.

There are many eyewitness accounts of Alex's long stroll in from the bullpen. Babe Ruth would later write, "Just to see old Pete out there on the mound, with that cocky little undersize cap pulled down over one ear, chewing away at his tobacco and pitching baseballs as easy as pitching hay is enough to take the heart out of a fellow."

Before Alexander took his very slow walk toward immortality, he had to get his bearings. "I take a few hurried throws and then start for the box," he told Powers. "There's been a lot of stories about how long it took me to walk from the bull pen to the mound and how I looked, and all that. Well, as I said, I didn't know what had happened when I was called.

"So when I come out from under the bleachers I see the bases filled and Lazzeri standing in the box. Tony is up there all alone, with everyone in that Sunday crowd watching him. So I just said to myself, 'Take your time. Lazzeri isn't feeling any too good up there and let him stew.'"

The sequence of pitches that Alex threw to Lazzeri has been charted. He had handled Lazzeri with curves the day before and started out with one for a quick strike. He tried another, off the plate this time, and Lazzeri checked his swing. Catcher Bob O'Farrell suggested they cross up Lazzeri, who would be expecting another curve. Alex agreed and put the ball tight on the inside. Crack! Lazzeri nailed it, but Alex had kept it inside enough so that it landed in the left-field bleachers safely foul. A few feet to the right and Alex would have been the goat, having given up a grand slam home run. Instead, he needed only one more strike. Once again he broke off his famous curve. It had caused batters to curse him as "Old Down and Away." Newsreel clips and photos show Lazzeri, awkwardly off-balance, trying to reach the ball as it swept past for strike three.

In some accounts the game ended there. It would have made for superior theater, but there were two innings more to play and the Yankees were still only one run behind, 3–2. Alex planned ahead. The batter he feared most was Babe Ruth. If he came up with a runner on base, he could end the game with a home run. Alex avoided that possibility by retiring the Yankees in order in the eighth and getting the first two batters in the ninth. Now Babe Ruth stepped up to the plate. A home run could tie the game, but Alex had no intention of letting the Babe hit one. He worked the corners and brought the count to three and two. Then came a pitch everyone but umpire George Hildebrand thought was strike three. The ump did not call it.

Alex never claimed the quote, but it has been widely reported he walked in toward the plate. "Where was the pitch?" he asked. Hildebrand held his palms inches apart. "It missed by that much." "For that much you might have given an old guy a break," Alex is supposed to have said.

However, before any damage could be done, Babe Ruth settled the game another way. On Alex's first pitch he bolted for second base. There was no steal sign, no hit and run, just Babe Ruth thundering toward the next base. Bob O'Farrell's throw whistled past

Alex and drilled into Hornsby's glove. The Cardinal manager's moment of triumph came as Babe Ruth slid futilely into his tag. The Cardinals leaped onto each other, pounding Ol' Pete with congratulations. It was the supreme moment of his career.

Like Walter Johnson, when he won the deciding game of the 1924 World Series in extra innings, this moment was destined to be the absolute apex of Alexander's life. Other successes would follow. He would top 20 wins again and pitch in another World Series. He would break Matty's record for total victories. Yet, like Johnson, everything after the supreme triumph would be anti-climactic. The road would run downhill, slightly at first, then, for Grover Cleveland Alexander, drop away to oblivion.

24

The Fly Paper Caper

Appalled!

That's what Thelma Zanderzeal was!

The editor of the Ulsterville Weekly Advocate knew the next pejorative word in Thelma's letter would be "outraged."

Thelma was a mainstay among those who wrote Letters to the Editor. She had negative opinions about a wide range of topics and was willing to share them with the readers of the county's weekly.

This letter's target was the soggy section of the community called Pig Hollow. A century and a half ago a farmer, tired of breaking his plough in the rocky soil, had turned his hand to raising pigs. Back then Ulsterville was a busy port on the Delaware & Hudson Canal. The farmer, Ezra Spivey, shipped his pork, in barrels, up and down the canal. He exported, in hams and sausages, everything his pig farm raised except its stench. That stayed behind.

To get upwind from the pig sties down in the hollow, the merchant class of the thriving town moved up on the hills which rose above the valley floor.

Thelma Zanderzeal's ancestors had been among those who

edged farther and farther up the hillside as Ezra Spivey enlarged his holdings down in the hollow.

The first of an unbroken line of Revered Zanderzeals had built a chapel at the very top of the mountain where the parishioners could be closer to God and more distant from Spivey's pig farm. Here the first Reverend Zanderzeal had poured forth fire and brimstone sermons.

Thelma's brother, Henry, was the incumbent reverend. The flock had diminished in recent years to a handful of faithful whose youthful sins had long been expiated. Now, white haired and bent, they sat in pews each Sunday reminiscing while the Reverend Zanderzeal prodded them to recall the sinful days they had once enjoyed.

Thelma's letter writing campaigns had been aimed at local targets, mostly arising from environmental causes. Her brother, Rev. Henry Zanderzeal, had ranged farther afield. In the 1960s, when a clergyman in the forefront of protesters could claim a TV camera's attention, he had linked arms with proponents of a wide range of social issues.

He had adopted the dramatic technique of chaining himself with handcuffs to strategically placed gates, fences, and pillars. Most of his colleagues of the turbulent sixties were now church going Yuppies, favoring faiths more establishment oriented than Reverend Zanderzeal's brand of updated Dutch Reform dogma. He continued to make the rounds of demonstrations, handcuffs ready. He had been manacled in public view more times than Harry Houdini.

A few months earlier Reverend Zanderzeal had returned from Florida where he had almost drowned welcoming a group of bedraggled Haitian refugees who had arrived in a water-logged boat. He had pushed his way past the immigration authorities and, with a flourish, chained himself to the tilted mast, minutes before the boat sank.

With a snarl of exasperation, an immigration official had leaped aboard the sinking boat. He frisked the Reverend and found the keys to the cuffs. The two men were waist-deep in water when the rescuer finally freed the clergyman. He had been tempted to drop the key in the water.

Reverend Zanderzeal's spirits, too, seemed dampened after this experience. The authorities had pretended to mistake him for one of the refugees and interned him for two weeks, a white face peering out of the compound.

At first he had attempted to provide religious solace for the internees but had been shunted aside by their voodoo priest. He had tried to understand the strange rites and adapt himself to their rituals but had failed. Drained and disillusioned, he had accepted his release from detention. He had withdrawn to the parsonage, his spear bent hopelessly out of shape, his last quixotic cause abandoned. His last act of brotherhood was to allow the Haitians' spiritual leader to prick both of their thumbs and press them together.

Thelma, alone among the crusading Zanderzeals, kept the family flame of indignation lit. She had now taken aim against the present-day Spiveys, the Pig Hollow family which could trace its roots to the original smoke house in the region. Her environmentalist's instincts were aroused by the Spivey's malodorous enterprise.

The present-day Spiveys no longer slaughtered their own hogs. They just raised them and shipped them over to a packing plant in

Saugerties. The one thing they demanded back were barrels of pigs feet.

Pickled pigs feet were a family delicacy and Betsy Spivey, the youngest daughter on the place, used an old family recipe to put them up in Mason jars. There were Spiveys in every glen, up and down the Catskills, and Betsey was hard pressed to keep up with the insatiable cravings of her clansmen. She did set aside a few jars of pickled pigs feet for a select few people outside the Spivey clan. One of these was her minister.

Revered Zanderzeal had one passion other than correcting social evils. He loved pickled pigs feet. As a boy, the incumbent pastor had learned, at church suppers, the special appeal of pickled pigs feet and craved them ever since.

When he had come back from the debacle in Florida, Thelma had tried to nurse her brother back to health in ways approved by contemporary nutritionists. Health foods and environmental issues seem to attract the same followers.

The Reverend tried. He nibbled at carrot sticks and permitted Thelma to sprinkle wheat germ over everything on his plate. It was counter productive. A lean, angular man to begin with, he lost weight instead of regaining it. Nothing in Thelma's guides to good nutrition aimed at putting on pounds, only at taking them off.

Each Sunday the pastor would drag himself out of bed and struggle into the chapel. After several weeks the effort to mount the pulpit became too great. He would lean against it and exhort against sin, and man's inhumanity to man, in a feeble voice. The fires of his sermons were banked, the brimstone was put on simmer.

What seemed to keep him going was the expectation that, after services, one of the Spiveys would leave a week's supply of pigs feet on the parsonage steps. The Reverend would wave farewell to his dwindling flock and ask Thelma to carry the cardboard carton of Mason jars into the house. Thelma did it, twitching with disapproval.

As she watched her brother waste away, despite the good, wholesome food she forced him to eat, she concluded it must be the one thing he ate which was undoing all the benefits of good nutrition. It was the pig's feet.

Thelma was fair minded enough to accept that, no matter how unenticing their source, pigs feet had been eaten by generations of her own family. The long line of Zanderzeals stretched back along a parallel track with generations of pig raising Spiveys. The first chapel and the original smokehouse had been raised the same year, back when DeWitt Clinton was the governor.

None of her forebears had shown ill effects from eating pigs feet. Therefore, Thelma deduced, the present supply must be contaminated. Her mind jumped to PCBs. They must abound in a place where pigs are raised, she assumed. What was more likely to be a source of soil contamination than the muddy pens in which pigs wallow? Her mind ran rampant. Even the swill on which they were fattened was probably impure.

In her letter Thelma elevated her suspicions to sure fact, as she saw it. Her charges against the Spiveys raised a problem for the local editor. He weighed his options. He could simply not print the letter. After a week went by, Thelma Zanderzeal would phone. If she was unsatisfied she would march on the newspaper office. Worse, she might picket. Once, over some feminist issue, she wanted the woman who took classified ads over the phone to get equal pay with the pressmen, she drew TV coverage from all over.

The editor shuddered in recollection. Thelma Zanderzeal was as formidable on the picket line as her brother was chaining himself to public buildings. She was a world class picketer.

Of course, the letter could simply be printed. The Spiveys, he knew, were touchy about their pig farm. A letter claiming their land was contaminated, without proof to back it up, would bring a law suit. the *Ulsterville Weekly Advocate* was not the *New York Times* or the Columbia Broadcasting System. The paper not only couldn't afford to lose a libel suit, it couldn't pay lawyers to defend them in court.

For almost 200 years the town had tried to shut down the pig farm, but always for reasons which were unenforceable. The Spiveys, old land grants in hand, would go to court and get justice. No matter how often the town got its wind up, the Spiveys continued their malodorous ways, generation after generation.

This left a third alternate, to give viability to Thelma's hunch about the PCBs. The paper couldn't get involved. Investigative journalism's time had not yet come to the county weekly level. If there was to be any investigation, Thelma Zanderzeal would have to do it. The editor phoned her.

"Hello, Miss Thelma, this is Barney Friel, at the paper. We've got this letter of yours here and, to be honest about it, we can't print it, much as we'd like to."

Barney Friel, who had been editor when Thelma was born, waited while she repeated her charges.

"I know. Sure seems like it would be true, but we can't run the letter without proof. That's what I'm calling you about."

The editor went on, conspiratorially, pointing out that Thelma had connections among environmentalists. Heck, she was one of them. It seemed to him it would be a simple matter for Thelma to sneak into the pig farm some night and get a sample of the soil and send it up to Albany to be tested.

Thelma realized the editor was right. No one, in the past, had been able to close down the Spivey's pig farm. Now, where good taste had failed, good regulations could be enforced. Let the Spiveys argue the right of their pigs to wallow where they saw fit, Thelma would march on their place with an injunction once she had the positive evidence to bring to a judge. The editor was relieved that Thelma had accepted his suggestion. Now he could put the matter aside until he heard from her again. If she turned up hard evidence the soil was contaminated with PCBs, it would rate more than a letter to the editor. It would be a front page story!

Thelma Zanderzeal had two worries. Her concern for her brother's rapidly deteriorating health came first. But, she knew, his insistence on eating the pickled pigs feet from the Spivey's farm was the cause of his wasted condition. Stop the pigs feet, Thelma rationalized, and she could nurse him back to health.

Thelma had not been able to persuade her brother to let her call in Dr. Briggs, the town's general practitioner. Stubbornly, the Reverend Zanderzeal insisted there was nothing wrong and, if there was, God would attend to it in His own way and in His own time.

Thelma had to concede a minister should have the right to believe in divine intercession, particularly when he was devoutly insistent that others also believe in the power of prayer. She settled for letting her brother follow his path while she took one that led directly to the Spivey pig farm.

Thelma decided she would act on the newspaper editor's suggestion that very night. It would be dark and moonless, she knew from the calendar on the kitchen wall. She found an emptied Mason jar to take with her. She rinsed it thoroughly to remove any traces of the pigs feet it had contained. She would be fair. When she filled it with soil taken from the Spivey place she wanted her sample to stand on its own merit.

Thelma remembered a lecture she had attended on tactics peace-loving anti-nuke demonstrators used to infiltrate nuclear power plants they wanted to blow up. Dark clothing. When it came time to go she pulled on black leotards and slipped into an extra large black cardigan sweater from her brother's clerical wardrobe. It came to her knees, but with the sleeves rolled up, it would be suitable.

She looked in on her brother before she left. He was asleep. He now made his bed in the study, unable to climb to his upstairs bedroom. He took up only a sliver of space on the horsehide sofa. His wasted body was cocooned in comforters and down- filled pillows cushioned his sagging head. Even without Dr. Brigg's consultation, Thelma suspected her brother's condition might not last long enough for God to notice it. With tonight's mission behind her, she could not wait for the official verdict to come back from the laboratory in Albany. She would summon Dr. Briggs, first thing in the morning, despite her brother's protests.

Thelma Zanderzeal drove down the mountain, rushing at first, then more slowly as she came closer to Pig Hollow. She parked as close as she thought was safe. She sniffed the night air and knew she was near her goal.

She had a small flashlight in her sweater pocket but did not want to use it unless absolutely necessary. In the faint starlight she saw the rickety rail fence that marked the border of the Spivey property. She stopped to listen.

Not far off she heard the nocturnal grunting that told of pigs still awake. Sound carried on the dank, damp night air. She would have to be stealthy. If she could hear the pigs they could hear her. For all she knew they might be better at protecting a farm from marauders than Dobermans.

She went on as silently as she could, using the shadows of old outbuildings, sagging in disuse. In the dark, Thelma repeatedly stepped in something that was either muck or dung, she was not sure which. She worked her way toward the one building in which there was a lighted window. Before she scooped up the sample of soil she had come for, she would peek inside to see what deeds a still awake Spivey might be up to. She edged up to the lighted window and peered in.

Thelma Zanderzeal hadn't seen Betsy Spivey in years. They were the same age and had grown up in Ulsterville. However, Thelma had gone away to school and Betsy had hardly gone at all. Thelma had no difficulty in recognizing Betsy. She had the Spivey nose, more than rubicund, it was definitely porcine.

The shed was apparently used for the preparation of pickled pigs feet. At one end sat the barrels, brim full of brine, in which the feet of slaughtered pigs bobbed like apples in a tub on Halloween night. Betsy stood at a stove, an old wood burning one on which a large black pot boiled like a witch's cauldron. She was tossing something into it. Not pigs feet.

Thelma strained to see what Betsy was cooking. She did not understand. On a table close to the stove were cartons from which Betsy would take small, cylindrical packages. She opened each in turn and pulled out a long, ribbon-like roll of yellow, shiny paper. She clipped off each roll and dropped it into the cauldron. She had to shake most of them loose from her fingers.

Whatever it was she saw through the window, this was not what Thelma had expected to see. Confused, her courage began to desert her. She picked her way back to the fence, sniffing hopefully for clearer air. She walked back to where she had parked her car, in the dark, out of sight, if not smell, of the pig farm.

Only then did she realize she had not taken a sample of the soil she was sure contained Poly Chlorinated Biphenols. An empty Mason jar mocked her forgetfulness. She could not bring herself to go back. Confused, she wanted to think more about what she had seen, about the strange ritual Betsy Spivey had been performing.

Thelma Zanderzeal drove back up the mountain to the parsonage. She looked in on her brother, unstirring in a dim night light. Deep in troubled thought she went upstairs to her bedroom. She wanted a hot shower to wash away the smell she thought still clung to her. When the water was as hot as she could stand it, she let it pour over her. It cleansed her body but could not wash away the sight of Betsy Spivey bending over the cauldron on the stove. She imagined she heard Betsy Spivey cackling.

Thelma dried herself, pulled on a clean, cotton nightgown, and went to bed. She couldn't sleep. The mystery of the pig farm nagged at her mind. What was indigenous to pig farms? What did they have, other than their smell? Flies!

Thelma sat bolt upright. Of course, flies! What Betsy Spivey had been dropping into the kettle was flypaper, unrolled to expose the sticky surface. Why in the world would anyone boil fly paper? The gummy strips would be reduced to pulp. If you let it boil long enough all you would have would be a residue. Of what?

Thelma thought hard. Somewhere in her environmental reading, or perhaps at a lecture she attended, she had learned something of chemicals used to kill flies. No, not a spray. She tried to remember how fly paper had worked when she had seen it in use, years ago when she and her brother, Henry, were children.

The idea, of course, was to have a fly light on it and be unable to get free. She remembered them buzzing. Her brother, before he grew up to be a clergyman, used to laugh at the sight. He'd make her shriek the way he would take a pair of tweezers and remove the fly's wings before they had stopped whirring. It upset him if the fly died first.

Whether out of mercy or not, the people who made fly paper had coated the surface, not only with a sticky substance, but with a chemical treatment to provide a swift end for the flies imprisoned there. Thelma searched her memory. Someone had told her what was used. She had it! Arsenic!

Thelma lay awake through the few hours that remained until dawn, agonizing over her suspicions. She writhed in recrimination, an environmentalist betrayed. The effect on her brother, that she had so righteously blamed on PCBs, was a tawdry matter of old-fashioned arsenic poisoning.

Why her brother? He had done no harm to the Spiveys. He had

sailed right past them to wider horizons which beckoned him to assail wrongs far from his own home. To Betsy? Thelma remembered there had been whispering and giggling when they were growing up. Her brother Henry and Betsy had strayed into the woods one time when the young people had gone on a picnic.

No, Thelma shrugged that thought away. There had been nothing to it. Henry had both God and cleanliness on his side. He had gone off to the seminary where all Zanderzeals went to be ordained. No. If Betsy was reacting to some fancied betrayal, too many years had passed for it to aggravate her now into sending a former swain poisoned pigs feet.

If it was anyone in the Zanderzeal family for whom Betsy who might have a grudge, it had to be Thelma herself. Had someone at the *Ulsterville Weekly Advocate* leaked her letter to the editor? Before she could rush downstairs to consult with her brother about possible violation of her First Amendment rights—he'd know, of course—she remembered the poisoning had started long before she had penned her letter.

It was already dawn and birds, indifferent to the turmoil which wracked Thelma's mind, were chirping away. She got out of bed knowing what she had to do.

First, she must see to her brother's comfort, then phone the doctor. No matter if Henry continued to protest his clergyman's right to refuse medical attention, there was a difference between someone being destroyed out of ignorance of PCBs and being deliberately poisoned with arsenic. Betsy Spivey had crossed that line and Thelma Zanderzeal would both thwart her intentions and see she was punished.

A cold shower set the tone for Thelma's expected day. She would make her rounds briskly. Her brother, first. Make him comfy. Then, from where he couldn't hear, phone Dr. Briggs and, guardedly, tell him matters were worse to a point she must now intervene to protect her brother. She would leave the door unlocked so that the doctor could come to see her brother while she took her evidence to Albany.

Thelma went downstairs and checked in the pantry. As she had expected, several jars chock full of pigs feet, pickled in both brine and, now she knew, arsenic, were on the shelf. Her brother was no longer able to eat anything. She would put two or three of the pigs feet on a plate and set it beside his bed. It comforted him to gaze on them, she assumed.

She hoped to find her brother awake and lucid enough to understand she would be absent for part of the day. She could be back shortly, after lunch, if she hurried. She knew her mission would impel her with its urgency. She would assure her brother someone would stop in during the morning. She wouldn't tell him it would be Dr. Briggs.

Thelma didn't find the Reverend Zanderzeal awake. She found him dead. Sometime during the night he had silently slipped away, gone to handcuff himself to the Pearly Gates.

She was shocked by her discovery, of course, but not unprepared for it. She took strength from having it confirmed that her brother had, indeed, been poisoned. She pulled the eiderdown comforter up to cover his gaunt face, whose skin was stretched tautly, just barely able to cover the skull.

Thelma went into the alcove where the phone was kept on a

desk, beside the typewriter. Her's now. She looked covetously at it. She could write letters to her heart's content, no longer constrained to wait until her brother had pecked out a Sunday sermon.

She phoned Dr. Briggs. It was too early for him to be in his office. A recorded voice answered, suggesting the caller take two aspirin and leave a message. When she heard the signal to proceed, she began, "this is Thelma Zanderzeal, doctor. You had better come up to the parsonage as soon as you can. It's my brother."

At this point her self-control broke and she sobbed until, recovering her composure, she was ready to talk further. Too late. The next cycle had begun on the recorder and when the pre-recorded voice of Dr. Briggs began to recommend two aspirin, she sobbed and hung up. The doctor had been summoned, that's what was important. She was anxious to get on to Albany.

She wrapped the Mason jar in a kitchen towel. Not only was it loaded with poisoned pigs feet, the jar was probably covered in Betsy Spivey's fingerprints. She carried it to her car and set off down the mountain road.

It was nine o'clock when she found the laboratory building in Albany and nine thirty by the time she had located Dr. Bernard Segal's office inside it. She knew the chemist from shared environmental projects. They had served on committees together. As a state employee he was constrained from joining Thelma on a picket line, but he had once winked at her when duty required he cross one.

She went briskly into Dr. Segal's office but the chemist had not yet donned his white smock for the day's work. Thelma stood uncertainly, holding her towel-wrapped Mason jar in front of her.

"Just leave it here, dearie," a puffy faced receptionist wheezed. "Write him a note, what it's all about. He'll be in sometime soon, I'm sure."

Thelma accepted the pad and pencil the receptionist offered and jotted a short note to the chemist, telling him she wanted his opinion about the contents of the jar she had brought.

"Why don't you run along to the cafeteria, dearie," suggested the asthmatic receptionist. "Have a cup of coffee or some breakfast and come back later."

Thelma realized, to her surprise, she was hungry. In her haste to have her friend, Dr. Segal, assure her that her brother had been poisoned, she had rushed off to the hospital without even a cup of herbal tea to warm her.

She had found her way to the cafeteria simply by following the lines of state employees headed to the first of the morning coffee breaks their union insisted they take. It took longer than Thelma had expected to get a cup of tea and a piece of toast to nibble with it and she got lost several times trying to find the right corridor to take back to Dr. Segal's office. The state employee traffic was mostly one way, moving toward the cafeteria. Finally, she saw the door with the familiar department name on it.

"Dr. Segal's in now, dearie," the receptionist greeted her. "He says you can go right in."

Thelma went toward the closed inner door and, expectantly, with excitement rising, flung the door open and screamed!

Dr. Segal, sitting on the edge of his desk, looked up startled. He almost dropped the fork with which he was eating a pigs foot. A half emptied jar sat on the desk beside him.

"Your note said you wanted my opinion. All right, Thelma, they're delicious. You put them up?"

"They're poisoned. They've got arsenic in them!"

"Nonsense. You've no reason to poison me," Dr. Segal replied, logically. "Anyway, I'd be dead by now. I'm afraid I made something of a pig of myself, if you'll pardon the expression."

"You shouldn't have eaten them. They're evidence."

"O.K., I shouldn't have eaten them. What's the difference, I'm not Orthodox."

Thelma did not want to let go of her hope her brother had been poisoned. Something had to explain his death, the way his body had wasted away. Surely, death by slow poisoning fit the bill. Perhaps the doses were small and only the cumulative effect was lethal. Maybe Dr. Segal would become ill later. She insisted he test the remaining contents of the jar for arsenic.

"It's a simple test," he told her, "and simply a waste of time and excellent pigs feet. But, I'll do it."

He led her into his laboratory and allowed her to watch, telling her what would signal the presence of the poison. To her disappointment, she saw nothing.

"Can I finish these later, with my lunch?" asked the chemist, putting his hand on the still half-full Mason jar.

Resignedly, Thelma nodded, not even caring anymore that Dr. Segal's meaty hand was smearing Betsy Spivey's telltale fingerprints on the Mason jar. Confused, dejected, and bereaved, Thelma drove back to Ulsterville. When she arrived at the parsonage she found the police waiting with Dr. Briggs. They waited outside the house.

An ambulance from the county emergency service also waited, its flasher lights revolving indignantly. Two white coated attendants were arguing with the doctor.

"Not me, doc. I ain't touching him. We're not supposed to pick up stiffs anyway, only people who are sick or hurt. Not that I think you're gonna get no undertaker to handle him either. Embalm him? No way!"

The doctor, noticing Thelma's arrival, shushed the attendants to silence and they sauntered off, each assuring the other of the correctness of their position.

"What's the matter, doctor? Hasn't my brother's body been removed yet?"

"Well, Miss Thelma, we seem to have a problem here. You got any idea what your brother died from?"

Thelma, her hopes dashed that he had been poisoned, shook her head. Some other explanation would have to be found. The doctor, she assumed, would find it.

The doctor led Thelma away from the house, away from where others could hear.

"Now, Miss Thelma, I'm a doctor. You can tell me things you might not want other people to know about. Your brother, he never married, right?"

Puzzled, Thelma confirmed her brother's batchelorhood.

"And," the doctor pressed on, "I don't seem to remember him dating any girls, when we were growing up. In fact," he went on, "that Betsy Spivey used to hint there was something wrong with a boy who'd take a girl into the woods and spout the Bible to her. On the other hand," the doctor conceded. "I can't say I recall the

Reverend being particularly partial toward any of his fellow men. Do you follow me?"

She did. She was truly appalled and her rage at the doctor's presumptions grew.

"Let's say that, for whatever cause, your brother has died from something that scares the people who have to handle it from here on. Best we can hope for is a quick cremation. You got any religious scruples against that? Be done in good taste, of course."

Thelma stared at the doctor. She was dimly aware of the terrible thing that had been happening to sexual deviates and drug users. Her brother was neither. Before his health had deteriorated, her brother had fulminated against both from his pulpit. He called their fatal illness God's vengeance. The only thing he couldn't understand about this demonstration of God's wrath was what He had against Haitians.

The thought stopped the fury which was mounting against Dr. Brigg's presumption. She recalled her brother's last valiant act of friendship to strangers, his support of the Haitian boat people. When the Reverend came home he never talked much about the weeks he had been interned with the Haitians he had gone to succor.

Thelma had pieced together enough to understand that the immigration authorities, tired of do-gooders, had pretended to believe the Reverend Zanderzeal was an illegal alien, shipped over with the other Haitians. His identification papers had gone down with the ship in the trousers pulled from him by the angry immigration man looking for the key to the handcuffs.

It had taken weeks to get the Reverend out of the compound. Thelma remembered when he had come home. He would sit for hours, staring into space, a look of horror and revulsion fixed on his face. And, on his arms, where the veins showed the most, were the healing scars of some beastly ceremony, concelebrated with a voodoo priest.

Numbly, Thelma gave her consent to have her brother's body removed and cremated as soon as possible. Hours later an undertaker, either ignorant of the situation or bribed by inducements to accept the assignment, came over from Kingston and hurriedly loaded the late Reverend Zanderzeal, wrapped in plastic sheeting, into his hearse.

When the next week's issue of the *Ulsterville Weekly Advocate* came out, Thelma's letter was not among the ones printed by the editor.

A respectful obituary for the late Rev. Henry Zanderzeal ran on an inside page. The editor glossed over the cause of death. Dr. Briggs had filed an innocuous death certificate and the police, if they suspected anything at all, looked the other way. There was gossip, of course, spread by the two attendants from the emergency ambulance, but nothing appeared in the paper.

The Spivey pig farm soon was in the news again. Whether Thelma's visit to Albany had provoked it or not was uncertain, but a team of health inspectors had gone over the place. Found poison. Arsenic.

Betsy Spivey explained it was for the rats. She went on to admit she got it from boiling old fly paper, hated to waste it. No point in going to some drug store, she said. The Spiveys were against signing their name to anything, and the druggist insisted they sign the poison book before he'd sell them any arsenic.

One of the Spiveys had remembered there used to be arsenic in fly paper, and, sure enough, out in one of the sheds they found cartons of old rolls, still sticky and containing the poison the government wouldn't let fly paper manufacturers use any more. Boil it down and you had a nice effective rat poison. Nothing wrong with cutting costs of running a pig farm, was there?

Nothing wrong, the inspectors had to concede.

Before We Go

Writers need readers. A certain bonding takes place when an author connects with the reader. I will presume you found the material in this collection humorous when it was intended to be, poignant when appropriate, and carefully researched. I delayed a writing career until retirement made it affordable. It took time to realize the validity of the advice, "write what you know about." A lifelong interest in sports, baseball in particular, ordained that I would find such success as I have had in writing baseball history. There's one more book to come. In 1999, The Society of American Baseball Research will publish *Uncle Robbie.* It was co-written with a fine historian and writer, Norman Macht, a colleague in SABR. I had been building a file of material about Wilbert Robinson for ten or more years. By the time I had demonstrated I could craft a biography, I experienced the sort of physical signs that caution you to limit your expectations. I invited Norman to divide the book. It was a logical division as half of Robinson's career, both playing and later years, happened in Baltimore and that's where Norman lived. I had grown up in Brooklyn and Uncle Robbie was the first manager of our team I knew. With Uncle Robbie accepted for 1999 publication, I wrote a number of new pieces and with some retrieved material, discovered I had a collection that would support a final book. At least, one about sports.

From now on, however long that might be, I will write fiction. I am virtually housebound and cannot get around to doing the kind of research necessary for baseball writing. I put one non-baseball story, "The Fly Paper Caper," in this collection.

I feel a bit like Paul Gallico, who withdrew from sports writing to take on general fiction. He bowed out with a bang with "A Farewell to Sports." He gave up his post as sports editor and columnist of the *New York Daily News* to take on the precarious role of writer of fiction. Gallico was in his late 30s when he switched and wrote fiction until he died in 1978. I'm doing the same thing…but I'm starting when I'm 78. The sands of time are trickling through my life's hourglass, but I know neither how many grains remain or at what rate they are passing.

However, I have had a wonderful retirement, saddened by the loss of my darling wife, Sally. I have a daughter who has begun a career in museum management in New York City. Beth and Jerry's five children are progressing in fine style. Looking back is an historian's joy. Looking forward allows me to say, "you don't have to be a millionaire to live like one."

Jack Kavanagh
Greenville, R.I.

Index

D

E

F

G

H

J

K

L

M

N

O

P

Q

R

S

T

U

V

W

Y

Z

About the Author

Jack Kavanagh is, like Red Smith, Jimmy Breslin, John McNulty, Jimmy Cannon and John Kiernan, a second generation Irishman. We suspect all are descended from the *seanchais*, traditional Gaelic storytellers, and were destined to write with easy wit and imagination.

Jack Kavanagh delayed risking the perils of self-supporting freelance work until he retired. Then, in 15 productive years, he published four full-length baseball books, one non-sport biography, a dozen "Juvvies" including Alexander, Johnson, Wagner, Hornsby, Dean and Joe Jackson, in Baseball, and Byrd, Montana, Ewing and Barry Sanders. Dozens of individual articles in national publications have carried his byline. Widowed after 50 years of marriage, he has a daughter, Beth, and her five children, and a son, Brian. He lives now, still a working writer, in a comfortable retirement residence in Greenville, Rhode Island.

Other Diamond Communications books by Jack Kavanagh:

Walter Johnson: A Life
Available in hardcover and trade paperback. The Macmillan-SABR award-winning biography of baseball's "Big Train."

Ol' Pete: The Grover Cleveland Alexander Story
Available in hardcover. Kavanagh's stirring look at a pitching legend.

A Mother's Mission: The Sue Molhan Story
Available in hardcover. A mother fights for victims' rights and mediation after her son is murdered.